"Aided by her formidable intelligence and willingness to try any-thing, she spent a year road-testing every theory about happiness she could get her hands on, using her own life as the road."

—*Time*

"Before I even finished the book, I had already preordered multiple copies of Gretchen Rubin's latest title, *The Happiness Project*. Which means if you're looking for an enlightening, laugh-aloud read, get the book and forget the rest of this review."

—*Christian Science Monitor*

"Rubin writes with keen senses of self and narrative, balancing the personal and the universal with a light touch. Rubin's project makes curiously compulsive reading, which is enough to make any reader happy."   —*Publishers Weekly* (starred review)

"Well-researched and sharply written, she sprinkles her text with observations on happiness from Aristotle and Plutarch, Samuel Johnson and Martin Seligman, the Dalai Lama and Oprah."

—*Cleveland Plain Dealer*

"Rubin masterfully interweaves touching and often funny personal anecdotes into the analysis of her progress, resulting in a friendly, approachable, and compulsively readable narrative that will not only make you want to start your own Happiness Project, but will also make you want to invite Rubin out for a cup of coffee."

—*San Diego Union-Tribune*

"Without any cutesy gimmicks or made-for-the-movies twists. . . . Rubin's methods are contagious. . . . [She] wins readers with her honest, straightforward style."

—*Miami Herald*

"Happiness is contagious. And so is *The Happiness Project*. Once you've read Gretchen Rubin's tale of a year searching for satisfaction, you'll want to start your own happiness project and get your friends and family to join you. This is the rare book that will make you both smile and think—often on the same page."

—Daniel H. Pink, author of *A Whole New Mind*

"Packed with fascinating facts about the science of happiness and rich examples of how she improves her life through changes small and big, *The Happiness Project* made me happier by just reading it."

—*BookPage*

"This book made me happy in the first five pages. And the more I read it, the happier I got. It's filled with great insights that have changed every part of my life, from love to money, from work to play, from writing to Diet Coke."

—A. J. Jacobs, author of *The Year of Living Biblically: One Man's Humble Quest to Follow the Bible as Literally as Possible*

"*The Happiness Project* is a wonderful book. Gretchen Rubin shows how you can be happier, starting right now, with small, actionable steps accessible to everyone. Among her many attainable strategies, her discovery of the connection between inner happiness and outer order is spot-on!"

—Julie Morgenstern, author of *SHED Your Stuff, Change Your Life*

"A cross between the Dalai Lama's *The Art of Happiness* and Elizabeth Gilbert's *Eat, Pray, Love*, and seamlessly buttressed by insights from sources as diverse as psychological scientists, novelists, poets, and philosophers, Gretchen Rubin has written a book that readers will revisit again and again as they seek to fulfill their own dreams for happiness."

—Sonya Lyubomirsky, author of *The How of Happiness: A New Approach to Getting the Life You Want*

"Gretchen Rubin's superpower is curiosity."

—Brené Brown, author of *Daring Greatly*

About the Author

GRETCHEN RUBIN writes about happiness, habits, and human nature, and her books include the blockbuster bestsellers *The Happiness Project, Better Than Before, The Four Tendencies,* and *Happier at Home.* She has an enormous following, in print and online, and her books have sold three million copies worldwide, in more than thirty languages. On her popular podcast *Happier with Gretchen Rubin,* she discusses happiness and good habits with her sister Elizabeth Craft, and on her site gretchenrubin .com she regularly reports on her adventures in pursuit of happiness. A graduate of Yale and Yale Law School, Gretchen Rubin was clerking for Supreme Court Justice Sandra Day O'Connor when she realized she wanted to be a writer. She lives in New York City with her husband and two daughters.

THE HAPPINESS PROJECT

THE

HAPPINESS

PROJECT

TENTH ANNIVERSARY EDITION

*Or, Why I Spent a Year Trying to Sing in the Morning,
Clean My Closets, Fight Right, Read Aristotle, and
Generally Have More Fun*

Gretchen Rubin

HARPER

NEW YORK · LONDON · TORONTO · SYDNEY

HARPER

The names and identifying details of certain individuals have been changed to protect their privacy.

A hardcover edition of this book was published in 2009 by HarperCollins Publishers.

HarperCollins books may be purchased for educational, business, or sales promotional use. For information, please e-mail the Special Markets Department at SPsales@harpercollins.com.

FIRST HARPER PAPERBACKS EDITION PUBLISHED 2011.

Designed by Ellen Cipriano

The Library of Congress has catalogued the hardcover edition as follows:
Rubin, Gretchen Craft.
The happiness project / by Gretchen Rubin. — 1st ed.
p.   cm.
ISBN 978-0-06-158325-4
1. Happiness. 2. Self-actualization (Psychology) I. Title.
BF575.H27R83 2009
158—dc22   2009001412

ISBN 978-0-06-288874-7 (tenth anniversary edition.)

19   20   21   22   LSC   10   9   8   7   6   5

FOR MY FAMILY

SAMUEL JOHNSON: "As the Spanish proverb says, 'He, who would bring home the wealth of the Indies, must carry the wealth of the Indies with him.'"

—JAMES BOSWELL, *THE LIFE OF SAMUEL JOHNSON*

There is no duty we so much underrate as the duty of being happy.

—ROBERT LOUIS STEVENSON

CONTENTS

A NOTE TO THE READER

A "happiness project" is an approach to changing your life. First is the preparation stage, when you identify what brings you joy, satisfaction, and engagement, and also what brings you guilt, anger, boredom, and remorse. Second is the making of resolutions, when you identify the concrete actions that will boost your happiness. Then comes the interesting part: keeping your resolutions.

This book is the story of my happiness project—what I tried, what I learned. Your project would look different from mine, but it's the rare person who can't benefit from a happiness project. To help you think about your own happiness project, I regularly post suggestions on my blog and I discuss happiness and much more on my weekly podcast, *Happier with Gretchen Rubin*.

But I hope that the most compelling inspiration for your happiness project is the book you hold in your hands. Of course, because it's the story of *my* happiness project, it reflects my particular situation, values, and interests. "Well," you might think, "if everyone's happiness project is unique, why should I bother to read about her project?"

During my study of happiness, I noticed something that surprised me: I often learn more from one person's highly idiosyncratic experiences than I do from sources that detail universal principles or cite up-to-date studies. I find greater value in what specific individuals tell me worked for them than in any other kind of argument—and that's true even when we seem to have nothing in common. In my case, for example, I would never have supposed that a witty lexicographer with Tourette's syndrome, a twentysomething tubercular saint, a hypocritical Russian novelist, and one of the Founding Fathers would be my most helpful guides—but so it happened.

I hope that reading the account of my happiness project will encourage you to start your own. Whenever you read this, and wherever you are, you are in the right place to begin.

THE HAPPINESS PROJECT

GETTING STARTED

I'd always vaguely expected to outgrow my limitations.

One day, I'd stop twisting my hair, and wearing running shoes all the time, and eating exactly the same food every day. I'd remember my friends' birthdays, I'd learn Photoshop, I wouldn't let my daughter watch TV during breakfast. I'd read Shakespeare. I'd spend more time laughing and having fun, I'd be more polite, I'd visit museums more often, I wouldn't be scared to drive.

One April day, on a morning just like every other morning, I had a sudden realization: I was in danger of wasting my life. As I stared out the rain-spattered window of a city bus, I saw that the years were slipping by. "What do I want from life, anyway?" I asked myself. "Well . . . I want to be *happy*." But I had never thought about what made me happy or how I might be happier.

I had much to be happy about. I was married to Jamie, the tall, dark, and handsome love of my life; we had two delightful young daughters, seven-year-old Eliza and one-year-old Eleanor; I was a writer, after having started out as a lawyer; I was living in my favorite city, New York; I had close relationships with my parents, sister, and in-laws; I had friends; I had my health; I didn't have to color my hair. But too often I sniped at my husband or the cable guy. I felt dejected after even a minor professional setback. I drifted out of touch with old friends, I lost my temper easily, I suffered bouts of melancholy, insecurity, listlessness, and free-floating guilt.

As I looked out the blurry bus window, I saw two figures cross the street—a woman about my age trying simultaneously to balance an umbrella, look at her cell phone, and push a stroller carrying a yellow-slickered child. The sight gave me a jolt of recognition: *that's me,* I thought, there I am. I have a stroller, a cell phone, an alarm clock, an apartment, a neighborhood. Right now, I'm riding the same crosstown bus that I take across the park, back and forth. This is my life—but I never give any thought to it.

I wasn't depressed and I wasn't having a midlife crisis, but I was suffering from midlife malaise—a recurrent sense of discontent and almost a feeling of disbelief. "Can this be me?" I'd wonder as I picked up the morning newspapers or sat down to read my e-mail. "Can this be me?" My friends and I joked about the "beautiful house" feeling, when, as in the David Byrne song "Once in a Lifetime," we'd periodically experience the shock of thinking "This is not my beautiful house."

"Is this really *it*?" I found myself wondering, and answering, "Yep, this is it."

But though at times I felt dissatisfied, that something was missing, I also never forgot how fortunate I was. When I woke up in the middle of the night, as I often did, I'd walk from one room to another to gaze at my sleeping husband tangled in the sheets and my daughters surrounded by their stuffed animals, all safe. I had everything I could possibly want—yet I was failing to appreciate it. Bogged down in petty complaints and passing crises, weary of struggling with my own nature, I too often failed to comprehend the splendor of what I had. I didn't want to keep taking these days for granted. The words of the writer Colette had haunted me for years: "What a wonderful life I've had! I only wish I'd realized it sooner." I didn't want to look back, at the end of my life or after some great catastrophe, and think, "How happy I used to be *then,* if only I'd realized it."

I needed to think about this. How could I discipline myself to feel grateful for my ordinary day? How could I set a higher standard for myself as a wife, a mother, a writer, a friend? How could I let go of everyday annoyances to keep a larger, more transcendent perspective? I could barely remember to stop at the drugstore to buy toothpaste—it didn't seem realistic to think that I could incorporate these high aims into my everyday routine.

The bus was hardly moving, but I could hardly keep pace with my own thoughts. "I've got to tackle this," I told myself. "As soon as I have some free time, I should start a happiness project." But I never had any free time. When life was taking its ordinary course, it was hard to remember what really mattered; if I wanted a happiness project, I'd have to *make* the time. I had a brief vision of myself living for a month on a picturesque, windswept island, where each day I would gather seashells, read Aristotle, and write in an elegant parchment journal. Nope, I admitted, that's not going to happen. I needed to find a way to do it *here* and *now*. I needed to change the lens through which I viewed everything familiar.

All these thoughts flooded through my mind, and as I sat on that crowded bus, I grasped two things: I wasn't as happy as I could be, and my life wasn't going to change unless I made it change. In that single moment, with that realization, I decided to dedicate a year to trying to be happier.

I made up my mind on a Tuesday morning, and by Wednesday afternoon, I had a stack of library books teetering on the edge of my desk. I could hardly find room for them; my tiny office, perched on the roof of our apartment building, was already too crowded with reference materials for the Kennedy biography I was writing, mixed with notices from my daughter Eliza's first-grade teacher about class trips, strep throat, and a food drive.

I couldn't just jump into this happiness project. I had a lot to learn before I was ready for my year to begin. After my first few weeks of heavy reading, as I toyed with different ideas about how to set up my experiment, I called my younger sister, Elizabeth.

After listening to a twenty-minute disquisition on my initial thoughts on happiness, my sister said, "I don't think you realize just how weird you are—but," she added hastily, "in a *good* way."

"Everyone is weird. That's why everyone's happiness project would be different. We're all idiosyncratic."

"Maybe, but I just don't think you realize how funny it is to hear you talk about it."

"Why is it funny?"

"It's just that you're approaching the question of happiness in such a dogged, systematic way."

I didn't understand what she meant. "You mean how I'm trying to turn goals like 'Contemplate death' or 'Embrace now' into action items?"

"Exactly," she answered. "I don't even know what an 'action item' *is*."

"That's business school jargon."

"Okay, whatever. All I'm saying is, your happiness project reveals more about you than you realize."

Of course she was right. They say that people teach what they need to learn. By adopting the role of happiness teacher, if only for myself, I was trying to find the method to conquer my particular faults and limitations.

It was time to expect more of myself. Yet as I thought about happiness, I kept running up against paradoxes. I wanted to change myself but accept myself. I wanted to take myself less seriously—and also more seriously. I wanted to use my time well, but I also wanted to wander, to play, to read at whim. I wanted to think about myself so I could forget myself. I was always on the edge of agitation; I wanted to let go of envy and anxiety about the future, yet keep my energy and ambition. Elizabeth's observation made me wonder about my motivations. Was I searching for spiritual growth and a life more dedicated to transcendent principles—or was my happiness project just an attempt to extend my driven, perfectionist ways to every aspect of my life?

My happiness project was both. I wanted to perfect my character, but, given my nature, that would probably involve charts, deliverables, to-do lists, new vocabulary terms, and compulsive note taking.

Many of the greatest minds have tackled the question of happiness, so as I started my research, I plunged into Plato, Boethius, Montaigne, Bertrand Russell, Thoreau, and Schopenhauer. The world's great religions explain the nature of happiness, so I explored a wide range of traditions, from the familiar to the esoteric. Scientific interest in positive psychology has exploded in the last few decades, and I read Martin Seligman, Daniel Kahneman, Daniel Gilbert, Barry Schwartz, Ed Diener, Mihaly Csikszentmihalyi, and Sonja Lyubomirsky. Popular culture, too, is bursting with happiness experts, so I consulted everyone from Oprah to Julie Morgenstern to David Allen. Some of the most interesting insights on happiness came from my favorite novelists, such as Leo Tolstoy, Virginia Woolf, and Marilynne Robinson—in fact, some novels, such as Michael Frayn's *A Landing on the Sun*, Ann Patchett's *Bel Canto*, and Ian McEwan's *Saturday*, seemed to be the careful working out of theories of happiness.

One minute I was reading philosophy and biography; the next, *Psychology Today*. The pile of books next to my bed included Malcolm Gladwell's *Blink*, Adam Smith's *The Theory of Moral Sentiments*, Elizabeth von Arnim's *Elizabeth and Her German Garden*, the Dalai Lama's *The Art of Happiness*, and "FlyLady" Marla Cilley's *Sink Reflections*. At dinner with friends, I found wisdom in a fortune cookie: "Look for happiness under your own roof."

My reading showed me that I had to answer two crucial questions before I went any further. First, did I believe it was *possible* to make myself happier? After all, the "set-point" theory holds that a person's basic level of happiness doesn't fluctuate much, except briefly.

My conclusion: yes, it is possible.

According to current research, in the determination of a person's level of happiness, genetics accounts for about 50 percent; life circumstances, such as age, gender, ethnicity, marital status, income, health, occupation, and religious affiliation, account for about 10 to 20 percent; and the remainder is a product of how a person thinks and acts. In other words, people have an inborn disposition that's set within a certain range, but they can boost themselves to the top of their happiness range or push themselves down to the bottom of their happiness range by their actions. This finding confirmed my own observations. It seems obvious that some people are more naturally ebullient or melancholic than others and that, at the same time, people's decisions about how to live their lives also affect their happiness.

The second question: What is "happiness"?

In law school, we'd spent an entire semester discussing the meaning of a "contract," and as I dug into my happiness research, this training kicked in. In scholarship, there is merit in defining terms precisely, and one positive psychology study identified fifteen different academic definitions of happiness, but when it came to my project, spending a lot of energy exploring the distinctions among "positive affect," "subjective well-being," "hedonic tone," and a myriad of other terms didn't seem necessary. I didn't want to get stuck in a question that didn't particularly interest me.

I decided instead to follow the hallowed tradition set by Supreme Court Justice Potter Stewart, who defined obscenity by saying "I know it when I see it," and Louis Armstrong, who said, "If you have to ask what jazz is, you'll never know," and A. E. Housman, who wrote that he "could no more define poetry than a terrier can define a rat" but that he "recognized the object by the symptoms it evokes."

Aristotle declared happiness to be the *summum bonum,* the chief good; people desire other things, such as power or wealth or losing ten pounds, because they believe they will lead to happiness, but their real goal is happiness. Blaise Pascal argued, "All men seek happiness. This is without exception. Whatever different means they employ, they all tend to this end." One study showed that, all over the world, when asked what they want most from life—and what they want most for their children—people answered that they want *happiness*. Even people who can't agree on what it means to be "happy" can agree that most people can be "happier," according to their own particular definition. I know when I feel happy. That was good enough for my purposes.

I came to another important conclusion about defining happiness: that the opposite of *happiness* is *unhappiness*, not *depression*. Depression, a grave condition that deserves urgent attention, occupies its own category apart from happiness and unhappiness. Addressing its causes and remedies was far beyond the scope of my happiness project. But even though I wasn't depressed and I wasn't going to attempt to deal with depression in my framework, there remained much ground to cover—just because I wasn't depressed didn't mean that I couldn't benefit from trying to be happier.

Having determined that it was possible to boost my happiness level and that I knew what it meant to be "happy," I had to figure out *how*, exactly, to make myself happier.

Could I discover a startling new secret about happiness? Probably not. People have been thinking about happiness for thousands of years, and the great truths about happiness have already been laid out by the most brilliant minds in history. Everything important has been said before. (Even that statement. It was Alfred North Whitehead who said, "Everything important has been said before.") The laws of happiness are as fixed as the laws of chemistry.

But even though I wasn't making up these laws, I needed to grapple with them for *myself*. It's like dieting. We all know the secret of dieting—eat better, eat less, exercise more—it's the application that's challenging. I had to create a scheme to put happiness ideas into practice in my life.

Founding Father Benjamin Franklin is one of the patron saints of self-realization. In his *Autobiography*, he describes how he designed his Virtues

Chart as part of a "bold and arduous Project of arriving at moral Perfection." He identified thirteen virtues he wanted to cultivate—temperance, silence, order, resolution, frugality, industry, sincerity, justice, moderation, cleanliness, tranquillity, chastity, and humility—and made a chart with those virtues plotted against the days of the week. Each day, Franklin would score himself on whether he practiced those thirteen virtues.

Current research underscores the wisdom of his chart-keeping approach. People are more likely to make progress on goals that are broken into concrete, measurable actions, with some kind of structured accountability and positive reinforcement. Also, according to a current theory of the brain, the unconscious mind does crucial work in forming judgments, motives, and feelings outside our awareness or conscious control, and one factor that influences the work of the unconscious is the "accessibility" of information, or the ease with which it comes to mind. Information that has been recently called up or frequently used in the past is easier to retrieve and therefore energized. The concept of "accessibility" suggested to me that by constantly reminding myself of certain goals and ideas, I could keep them more active in my mind.

So, inspired by recent science and by Ben Franklin's method, I designed my own version of his scoring chart—a kind of calendar on which I could record all my resolutions and give myself a daily ✓ (good) or X (bad) for each resolution.

After I designed my blank chart, however, it took me a long time to determine which resolutions should fill the boxes. Franklin's thirteen virtues didn't match the kinds of changes I wanted to cultivate. I wasn't particularly concerned with "cleanliness" (though, come to think of it, I could do a better job of flossing). What should *I* do to become happier?

First I had to identify the areas to work on; then I had to come up with happiness-boosting resolutions that were concrete and measurable. For example, everyone from Seneca to Martin Seligman agreed that friendship is a key to happiness, and sure, I wanted to strengthen my friendships. The trick was to figure out *how,* exactly, I could accomplish the changes I sought. I wanted to be specific, so I'd know exactly what I was expecting from myself.

As I reflected on possible resolutions, it struck me again how much my happiness project would differ from anyone else's. Franklin's top priorities included "Temperance" ("Eat not to Dulness. Drink not to Elevation") and "Silence" (less "Prattling, Punning and Joking"). Other people might resolve to start going to the gym, or to give up smoking, or to improve their sex lives, or to learn to swim, or to start volunteering—I didn't need to make those particular resolutions. I had my own idiosyncratic priorities, with many items included on the list that other people would have omitted and many items omitted from the list that other people would have included.

For example, a friend asked, "Aren't you going to start therapy?"

"No," I asked, surprised. "Why, do you think I should?"

"Absolutely. It's essential. You have to go to therapy if you want to know the root causes of your behavior," she answered. "Don't you want to know *why* you are the way you are and *why* you want your life to be different?"

I thought those questions over for a good while, and then I decided— well, no, not really. Did that mean I was superficial? I knew many people for whom therapy had been invaluable, but the issues I wanted to tackle were right there for me to see, and at this point, I wanted to discover what approach I'd take, on my own.

I wanted to focus on a different subject each month, and twelve months in the year gave me twelve slots to fill. Research had taught me that the most important element to happiness is social bonds, so I resolved to tackle "Marriage," "Parenthood," and "Friends." I'd also learned that that my happiness depended a great deal on my perspective, so I added "Eternity" and "Attitude" to my list. Work was crucial to my happiness, and also leisure, so I included the topics "Work," "Play," and "Passion." What else did I want to cover? "Energy" seemed like a basic ingredient for the success of the entire project. "Money" was a subject I knew I wanted to address. To explore some of the insights I'd come across in my research,

I added "Mindfulness." December would be a month in which I would try to follow all my resolutions perfectly—so that gave me my twelve categories.

But what subject should come first? What was the most important element in happiness? I hadn't figured that out yet, but I decided to tackle "Energy" first. A high level of energy would make keeping all my other resolutions easier.

Just in time for January 1, when I planned to start my project rolling, I completed my chart with dozens of resolutions to try in the coming year. For the first month, I'd attempt only January's resolutions; in February, I'd add the next set of resolutions to the January set. By December, I'd be scoring myself on the whole year's worth of resolutions.

As I worked to identify my resolutions, some overarching principles started to emerge. Distilling these principles turned out to be far more taxing than I expected, but after many additions and subtractions, I arrived at my Twelve Commandments:

TWELVE COMMANDMENTS

1. Be Gretchen.
2. Let it go.
3. Act the way I want to feel.
4. Do it now.
5. Be polite and be fair.
6. Enjoy the process.
7. Spend out.
8. Identify the problem.
9. Lighten up.
10. Do what ought to be done.
11. No calculation.
12. There is only love.

These Twelve Commandments, I predicted, would help me as I was struggling to keep my resolutions.

I also came up with a goofier list: my Secrets of Adulthood. These were the lessons I'd learned with some difficulty as I'd grown up. I'm not sure why it took me years to embrace the notion that over-the-counter medication actually would cure a headache, but it had.

SECRETS OF ADULTHOOD

People don't notice your mistakes as much as you think.

It's okay to ask for help.

Most decisions don't require extensive research.

Do good, feel good.

It's important to be nice to *everyone*.

Bring a sweater.

By doing a little bit each day, you can get a lot accomplished.

Soap and water remove most stains.

Turning the computer on and off a few times often fixes a glitch.

If you can't find something, clean up.

You can choose what you do; you can't choose what you *like* to do.

Happiness doesn't always make you feel happy.

What you do *every day* matters more than what you do *once in a while*.

You don't have to be good at everything.

If you're not failing, you're not trying hard enough.

Over-the-counter medicines are very effective.

Don't let the perfect be the enemy of the good.

What's fun for other people may not be fun for you—and vice versa.

People actually prefer that you buy wedding gifts off their registry.

You can't profoundly change your children's natures by nagging them or signing them up for classes.

No deposit, no return.

I had fun coming up with my Twelve Commandments and my Secrets of Adulthood, but the heart of my happiness project remained my list of resolutions, which embodied the changes I wanted to make in my life. When I stepped back to reflect on the resolutions, however, I was struck by their small scale. Take January. "Go to sleep earlier" and "Tackle a nagging task" didn't sound dramatic or colorful or particularly ambitious.

Other people's radical happiness projects, such as Henry David Thoreau's move to Walden Pond or Elizabeth Gilbert's move to Italy, India, and Indonesia, exhilarated me. The fresh start, the total commitment, the leap into the unknown—I found their quests illuminating, plus I got a vicarious thrill from their abandonment of everyday worries.

But my project wasn't like that. I was an unadventurous soul, and I didn't want to undertake that kind of extraordinary change. Which was lucky, because I wouldn't have been able to do it even if I'd wanted to. I had a family and responsibilities that made it practically impossible for me to leave for one weekend, let alone for a year.

And more important, I didn't want to reject my life. I wanted to change my life without changing my life, by finding more happiness in my own kitchen. I knew I wouldn't discover happiness in a faraway place or in unusual circumstances; it was right here, right now—as in the haunting play *The Blue Bird,* where two children spend a year searching the world for the Blue Bird of Happiness, only to find the bird waiting for them when they finally return home.

A lot of people took issue with my happiness project. Starting with my own husband.

"I don't really get it," Jamie said as he lay on the floor to do his daily back and knee exercises. "You're already pretty happy, aren't you? If you were really unhappy, this would make more sense, but you're not." He paused. "You're *not* unhappy, are you?"

"I *am* happy," I reassured him. "Actually," I added, pleased to have an opportunity to show off my new expertise, "most people are pretty happy—in a 2006 study, eighty-four percent of Americans ranked themselves as 'very happy' or 'pretty happy,' and in a survey of forty-five countries, on average, people put themselves at 7 on a 1 to 10 scale and at 75 on a 1 to 100 scale. I just took the Authentic Happiness Inventory Questionnaire myself, and on a range of 1 to 5, I scored a 3.92."

"So if you're pretty happy, why do a happiness project?"

"I *am* happy—but I'm not as happy as I should be. I have such a good life, I want to appreciate it more—and live up to it better." I had a hard time explaining it. "I complain too much, I get annoyed more than I should. I should be more grateful. I think if I felt happier, I'd behave better."

"Do you really think any of *this* is going to make a difference?" he asked, pointing to the printout of my first blank Resolutions Chart.

"Well, I'll find out."

"Huh," he snorted. "I guess so."

I ran into even more skepticism soon after, at a cocktail party. The usual polite chitchat devolved into a conversation more closely resembling a Ph.D. dissertation defense when a longtime acquaintance openly scoffed at the idea of my happiness project.

"Your project is to see if you can make yourself happier? And you're not even depressed?" he asked.

"That's right," I answered, trying to look intelligent as I juggled a glass of wine, a napkin, and a fancy version of a pig in a blanket.

"No offense, but what's the point? I don't think examining how an ordinary person can become happier is very interesting."

I wasn't sure how to answer. Could I tell him that one Secret of Adulthood is "Never start a sentence with the words 'No offense' "?

"And anyway," he persisted, "you're not a regular person. You're highly educated, you're a full-time writer, you live on the Upper East Side, your husband has a good job. What do you have to say to someone in the Midwest?"

"I'm from the Midwest," I said weakly.

He waved that away. "I just don't think you're going to have insights that other people would find useful."

"Well," I answered, "I've come to believe that people really can learn a lot from each other."

"I think you'll find that your experience doesn't translate very well."

"I'll do my best," I answered. Then I walked away to find someone else to talk to.

This guy, discouraging as he'd been, hadn't actually hit on my real worry about my project: Was it supremely self-centered to spend so much effort on my own happiness?

I gave this question a lot of thought. In the end, I sided with the ancient philosophers and modern scientists who argue that working to be happier is a worthy goal. According to Aristotle, "Happiness is the meaning and the purpose of life, the whole aim and end of human existence." Epicurus wrote, "We must exercise ourselves in the things which bring happiness, since, if that be present, we have everything, and, if that be absent, all our actions are directed toward attaining it." Contemporary research shows that happy people are more altruistic, more productive, more helpful, more likable, more creative, more resilient, more interested in others, friendlier, and healthier. Happy people make better friends, colleagues, and citizens. I wanted to be one of those people.

I knew it was certainly easier for me to be good when I was happy. I was more patient, more forgiving, more energetic, more lighthearted, and more generous. Working on my happiness wouldn't just make me happier, it would boost the happiness of the people around me.

And—though I didn't recognize this immediately—I started my happiness project because I wanted to *prepare*. I was a very fortunate person, but the wheel would turn. One dark night, my phone was going to ring, and I already had a notion about one particular phone call that might come. One of my goals for the happiness project was to prepare for adversity—to develop the self-discipline and the mental habits to deal with a bad thing when it happened. The time to start exercising, stop nagging, and organize our digital photos was when everything was going smoothly. I didn't want to wait for a crisis to remake my life.

1

[JANUARY]

Boost Energy

VITALITY

- Go to sleep earlier.
- Exercise better.
- Toss, restore, organize.
- Tackle a nagging task.
- Act more energetic.

Like 44 percent of Americans, I make New Year's resolutions—and usually don't keep them for long. How many times had I resolved to exercise more, eat better, and keep up with my e-mail in-box? This year, though, I was making my resolutions in the context of my happiness project, and I hoped that would mean that I'd do a better job of keeping them. To launch the new year and my happiness project, I decided to focus on boosting my energy. More vitality, I hoped, would make it easier for me to stick to all my happiness-project resolutions in future months.

In a virtuous circle, research shows, being

happy energizes you, and at the same time, having more energy makes it easier for you to engage in activities—like socializing and exercise—that boost happiness. Studies also show that when you feel energetic, your self-esteem rises. Feeling tired, on the other hand, makes everything seem arduous. An activity that you'd ordinarily find fun, like putting up holiday decorations, feels difficult, and a more demanding task, like learning a new software program, feels overwhelming.

I know that when I feel energetic, I find it much easier to behave in ways that make me happy. I take the time to e-mail the grandparents with a report from the pediatrician's checkup. I don't scold when Eliza drops her glass of milk on the rug just as we're leaving for school. I have the perseverance to figure out why my computer screen is frozen. I take the time to put my dishes in the dishwasher.

I decided to tackle both the *physical* and *mental* aspects of energy.

For my physical energy: I needed to make sure that I got enough sleep and enough exercise. Although I'd already known that sleep and exercise were important to good health, I'd been surprised to learn that happiness—which can seem like a complex, lofty, and intangible goal—was quite influenced by these straightforward habits. For my mental energy: I needed to tackle my apartment and office, which felt oppressively messy and crowded. Outer order, I hoped, would bring inner peace. What's more, I needed to clear away metaphorical clutter; I wanted to cross tasks off my to-do list. I added one last resolution that combined the mental and the physical. Studies show that by acting *as if* you feel more energetic, you can *become* more energetic. I was skeptical, but it seemed worth a try.

GO TO SLEEP EARLIER.

First: bodily energy.

A glamorous friend with a tendency to make sweeping pronouncements had told me that "Sleep is the new sex," and I'd recently been at a dinner party where each person at the table detailed the best nap he or she had ever had, in lascivious detail, while everyone moaned in appreciation.

Millions of people fail to get the recommended seven to eight hours of sleep a night, and one study revealed that along with tight work deadlines, a bad night's sleep was one of the top two factors that upset people's daily moods. Another study suggested that getting one extra hour of sleep each night would do more for a person's daily happiness than getting a $60,000 raise. Nevertheless, the average adult sleeps only 6.9 hours during the week, and 7.9 on the weekend—20 percent less than in 1900. Although people adjust to feeling sleepy, sleep deprivation impairs memory, weakens the immune system, slows metabolism, and might, some studies suggest, foster weight gain.

My new, not-exactly-startling resolution for getting more sleep was to *turn off the light.* Too often I stayed up to read, answer e-mails, watch TV, pay bills, or whatever, instead of going to bed.

Nevertheless, just a few days into the happiness project, although I practically fell asleep on Eliza's purple sheets as I was tucking her in, I wavered for a moment when Jamie proposed watching our latest Netflix DVD, *The Conversation.* I love movies; I wanted to spend time with Jamie; 9:30 P.M. seemed a ridiculously early hour to go to bed; and I knew from experience that if I started watching, I'd perk up. On the other hand, I felt exhausted.

Why does it often seem more tiring to go to bed than to stay up? Inertia, I suppose. Plus there's the prebed work of taking out my contact lenses, brushing my teeth, and washing my face. But I'd made my resolution, so resolutely I headed to bed. I slept eight solid hours and woke up an hour early, at 5:30 A.M., so in addition to getting a good night's sleep, I had the chance to do a peaceful block of work while my family was still in bed.

I'm a real know-it-all, so I was pleased when my sister called and complained of insomnia. Elizabeth is five years younger than I am, but usually I'm the one asking her for advice.

"I'm not getting any sleep," she said. "I've already given up caffeine. What else can I do?"

"Lots of things," I said, prepared to rattle off the tips that I'd uncovered in my research. "Near your bedtime, don't do any work that requires alert thinking. Keep your bedroom slightly chilly. Do a few prebed stretches. Also—this is important—because light confuses the body's circadian clock, keep the lights low around bedtime, say, if you go to the bathroom. Also, make sure your room is very dark when the lights are out. Like a hotel room."

"Do you really think it can make a difference?" she asked.

"All the studies say that it does."

I'd tried all these steps myself, and I'd found the last one—keeping our bedroom dark—surprisingly difficult to accomplish.

"What *are* you doing?" Jamie had asked one night when he caught me rearranging various devices throughout our room.

"I'm trying to block the light from all these gizmos," I answered. "I read that even a tiny light from a digital alarm clock can disrupt a sleep cycle, and it's like a mad scientist's lab in here. Our BlackBerrys, the computer, the cable box—everything blinks or glows bright green."

"Huh" was all he said, but he did help me move some things on the nightstand to block the light coming from our alarm clock.

These changes did seem to make falling asleep easier. But I often lost sleep for another reason: I'd wake up in the middle of the night—curiously, usually at 3:18 A.M.—and be unable to go back to sleep. For those nights, I developed another set of tricks. I breathed deeply and slowly until I couldn't stand it anymore. When my mind was racing with a to-do list, I wrote everything down. There's evidence that too little blood flow to the extremities can keep you awake, so if my feet were cold, I put on wool socks—which, though it made me feel frumpish, did seem to help.

Two of my most useful getting-to-sleep strategies were my own invention. First, I tried to get ready for bed well before bedtime. Sometimes I stayed up late because I was too tired to take out my contacts—plus, putting on my glasses had an effect like putting the cover on the parrot's cage. Also, if I woke up in the night, I'd tell myself, "I have to get up in two minutes." I'd imagine that I'd just hit the snooze alarm and in two minutes, I'd have to march through my morning routine. Often this was an exhausting enough prospect to make me fall asleep.

And sometimes I gave up and took an Ambien.

After a week or so of more sleep, I began to feel a real difference. I felt more energetic and cheerful with my children in the morning. I didn't feel a painful, never-fulfilled urge to take a nap in the afternoon. Getting out of bed in the morning was no longer torture; it's so much nicer to wake up naturally instead of being jerked out of sleep by a buzzing alarm.

Nevertheless, despite all the benefits, I still struggled to put myself to bed as soon as I felt sleepy. Those last few hours of the day were precious—when the workday was finished, Jamie was home, my daughters were asleep, and I had some free time. Only the daily reminder on my Resolutions Chart kept me from staying up until midnight most nights.

EXERCISE BETTER.

There's a staggering amount of evidence to show that exercise is good for you. Among other benefits, people who exercise are healthier, think more clearly, sleep better, and have delayed onset of dementia. Regular exercise boosts energy levels; although some people assume that working out is tiring, in fact, it boosts energy, especially in sedentary people—of whom there are many. A recent study showed that 25 percent of Americans don't get any exercise at all. Just by exercising twenty minutes a day three days a week for six weeks, persistently tired people boosted their energy.

Even knowing all these benefits, though, you can find it difficult to change from a couch potato into a gym enthusiast. Many years ago, I'd managed to turn myself into a regular exerciser, but it hadn't been easy. My idea of fun has always been to lie in bed reading. Preferably while eating a snack.

When I was in high school, I wanted to redecorate my bedroom to replace the stylized flowered wallpaper that I thought wasn't sufficiently sophisticated for a freshman, and I wrote a long proposal laying out my argument to my parents. My father considered the proposal and said, "All right, we'll redecorate your room. But in return, you have to do something four times a week for twenty minutes."

"What do I have to do?" I asked, suspicious.

"You have to take it or leave it. It's twenty minutes. How bad can it be?"

"Okay, I'll take the deal," I decided. "What do I have to do?"

His answer: "Go for a run."

My father, himself a dedicated runner, never told me how far I had to run or how fast; he didn't even keep track of whether I went for twenty minutes. All he asked was that I put on my running shoes and shut the door behind me. My father's deal got me to commit to a routine, and once I started running, I found that I didn't mind *exercising,* I just didn't like *sports.*

My father's approach might well have backfired. With *extrinsic motivation,* people act to win external rewards or avoid external punishments; with *intrinsic motivation,* people act for their own satisfaction. Studies show that if you reward people for doing an activity, they often stop doing it for fun; being paid turns it into "work." Parents, for example, are warned not to reward children for reading—they're teaching kids to read for a reward, not for pleasure. By giving me an extrinsic motivation, my father risked sapping my inclination to exercise on my own. As it happened, in my case, he provided an extrinsic motivation that unleashed my intrinsic motivation.

Ever since that room redecoration, I've been exercising regularly. I never push myself hard, but I get myself out the door several times a week. For a long time, however, I'd been thinking that I really should start strength training. Lifting weights increases muscle mass, strengthens bones, firms the core, and—I admit, most important to me—improves shape. People who work out with weights maintain more muscle and gain less fat as they age. A few times over the years, I'd halfheartedly tried lifting weights, but I'd never stuck to it; now, with my resolution to "Exercise better," it was time to start.

There's a Buddhist saying that I've found to be uncannily true: "When the student is ready, the teacher appears." Just a few days after I committed to my resolution to "Exercise better," I met a friend for coffee, and she mentioned that she'd started a great weight-training program at a gym in my neighborhood.

"I don't like the idea of working out with a trainer," I objected. "I'd feel self-conscious, and it's expensive. I want to do it on my own."

"Try it," my friend urged. "I promise, you'll love it. It's a superefficient way to exercise. The whole workout takes only twenty minutes. Plus"—she paused dramatically—"you don't *sweat*. You work out without having to shower afterward."

This was a major selling point. I dislike taking showers. "But," I asked doubtfully, "how can a good workout take only twenty minutes if you're not even sweating?"

"You lift weights at the very outer limit of your strength. You don't do many repetitions, and you do only one set. Believe me, it works. I love it."

In Daniel Gilbert's book *Stumbling on Happiness,* he argues that the most effective way to judge whether a particular course of action will make you happy in the future is to ask people who are following that course of action right now if they're happy and assume that you'll feel the same way. According to his theory, the fact that my friend raved about this fitness routine was a pretty good indicator that I'd be enthusiastic, too. Also, I reminded myself, one of my Secrets of Adulthood was "Most decisions don't require extensive research."

I made an appointment for the next day, and by the time I left, I was a convert. My trainer was terrific, and the atmosphere in the training room was much nicer than most gyms—no music, no mirrors, no crowds, no waiting. On my way out the door, I charged the maximum twenty-four sessions on my credit card to get the discount, and within a month, I'd convinced Jamie and my mother-in-law, Judy, to start going to the same gym.

The only disadvantage was that it was expensive. "It seems like a lot to spend for a twenty-minute workout," I said to Jamie.

"Would you rather get more for your money?" he asked. "We're spending more to get a shorter workout." Good point.

In addition to strength training, I wanted to start walking more. The repetitive activity of walking, studies show, triggers the body's relaxation response and so helps reduce stress; at the same time, even a quick ten-minute walk provides an immediate energy boost and improves mood—in fact, exercise is an effective way to snap out of a funk. Also, I kept reading that, as a minimum of activity for good health, people should aim to take 10,000 steps a day—a number that also reportedly keeps most people from gaining weight.

Living in New York, I felt as if I walked miles every day. But did I? I picked up a $20 pedometer from the running store near my apartment. Once I'd been clipping it onto my belt for a week, I discovered that on days when I did a fair amount of walking—walking Eliza to school *and* walking to the gym, for example—I hit 10,000 easily. On days when I stayed close to home, I barely cleared 3,000.

It was interesting to have a better sense of my daily habits. Also, the very fact of wearing a pedometer made me walk more. One of my worst qualities is my insatiable need for *credit*; I always want the gold star, the recognition. One night when I was in high school, I came home late from a party and decided to surprise my mother by cleaning up our messy kitchen. She came downstairs the next morning and said, "What wonderful fairy came in the night and did all this work?" and looked so pleased. More than twenty years later, I still remember that gold star, and I still want more of them.

This generally negative quality had a benefit in this circumstance; because the pedometer gave me credit for making an extra effort, I was more likely to do it. One morning I'd planned to take the subway to my dentist's appointment, but as I walked out the door, it occurred to me, "Walking to the dentist will take the same amount of time, and I'll get credit for the steps!" Plus, I think I benefited from the "Hawthorne effect," in which people being studied improve their performance, simply because of the extra attention they're getting. In this case, I was the guinea pig of my own experiment.

Walking had an added benefit: it helped me to think. Nietzsche wrote, "All truly great thoughts are conceived while walking," and his observation is backed up by science; exercise-induced brain chemicals help people think clearly. In fact, just stepping outside clarifies thinking and boosts energy. Light deprivation is one reason that people feel tired, and even five minutes of daylight stimulates production of serotonin and dopamine, brain chemicals that improve mood. Many times, I'd guiltily leave my desk to take a break, and while I was walking around the block, I'd get some useful insight that had eluded me when I was being virtuously diligent.

TOSS, RESTORE, ORGANIZE

Household disorder was a constant drain on my energy; the minute I walked through the apartment door, I felt as if I needed to start putting clothes in the hamper and gathering loose toys. I wasn't alone in my fight against clutter. In a sign that people are finding their possessions truly unmanageable, the number of storage units nationwide practically doubled in one decade. One study suggested that eliminating clutter would cut down the amount of housework in the average home by 40 percent.

To use the first month of my happiness project to tackle clutter seemed a bit small-minded, as if my highest priority in life were to rearrange my sock drawer. But I craved an existence of order and serenity—which, translated into real life, meant a household with coats hung in the closet and spare rolls of paper towels.

I was also weighed down by the invisible, but even more enervating, psychic clutter of loose ends. I had a long list of neglected tasks that made me feel weary and guilty whenever I thought of them. I needed to clear away the detritus in my mind.

I decided to tackle the visible clutter first, and I discovered something surprising: the psychologists and social scientists who do happiness research never mention clutter at all. They never raise it in their descriptions of the factors that contribute to happiness or in their lists of strategies to boost happiness. The philosophers, too, ignore it, although Samuel Johnson, who had an opinion about everything, did remark, "No money is better spent that what is laid out for domestic satisfaction."

By contrast, when I turned to popular culture, discussions of clutter clearing abounded. Whatever the happiness scientists might study, ordinary people are convinced that clearing clutter will boost their happiness—and they're "laying out money for domestic satisfaction" by buying *Real Simple* magazine, reading the *Unclutterer* blog, hiring California Closets, and practicing amateur feng shui. Apparently, other people, like me, believe that their physical surroundings influence their spiritual happiness.

I paced through our apartment to size up the clutter-clearing challenge I faced. Once I started really looking, I was amazed by how much clutter had accumulated without my realizing it. Our apartment was bright and pleasant, but a scum of clutter filmed its surface.

When I surveyed the master bedroom, for example, I was dismayed. The soft green walls and the rose-and-leaf pattern on the bed and curtains made the room calm and inviting, but stacks of papers were piled randomly on the coffee table and on the floor in the corner. Untidy heaps of books covered every available surface. CDs, DVDs, cords, chargers, coins, collar stays, business cards, and instruction booklets were scattered like confetti. Objects that needed to be put away, objects that didn't have a real place, unidentified lurking objects—they all needed to be placed in their proper homes. Or tossed or given away.

As I contemplated the magnitude of the job before me, I invoked my

Tenth Commandment: "Do what ought to be done." This comm distilled into one principle a lot of different strands of advice my had given me over the years. The fact is, I tend to feel overwhelmed by large tasks and am often tempted to try to make life easier by cutting corners.

We recently moved, and beforehand, I was panicking at the thought of everything that needed to be done. What moving company should we use? Where could we buy boxes? How would our furniture fit into our new apartment building's tiny service elevator? I was paralyzed. My mother had her usual matter-of-fact, unruffled attitude, and she reminded me that I should just do what I knew I ought to do. "It won't really be that hard," she said reassuringly when I called her for a pep talk. "Make a list, do a little bit each day, and *stay calm.*" Taking the bar exam, writing thank-you notes, having a baby, getting our carpets cleaned, checking endless footnotes as I was finishing my biography of Winston Churchill . . . my mother made me feel that nothing was insurmountable if I did what I knew ought to be done, little by little.

My evaluation of our apartment revealed that my clutter came in several distinct varieties. First was *nostalgic clutter,* made up of relics I clung to from my earlier life. I made a mental note that I didn't need to keep the huge box of materials I used for the "Business and Regulation of Television" seminar I taught years ago.

Second was self-righteous *conservation clutter,* made up of things that I've kept because they're useful—even though they're useless to me. Why was I storing twenty-three glass florist-shop vases?

One kind of clutter I saw in other people's homes but didn't suffer from myself was *bargain clutter,* which results from buying unnecessary things because they're on sale. I did suffer from related *freebie clutter*—the clutter of gifts, hand-me-downs, and giveaways that we didn't use. Recently my mother-in-law mentioned that she was getting rid of one of their table lamps, and she asked if we wanted it.

"Sure," I said automatically, "it's a great lamp." But a few days later,

I thought better of it. The lampshade wasn't right, the color wasn't right, and we didn't really have a place to put it.

"Actually," I e-mailed her later, "we don't need the lamp. But thanks." I'd narrowly missed some *freebie clutter*.

I also had a problem with *crutch clutter*. These things I used but knew I shouldn't: my horrible green sweatshirt (bought secondhand more than ten years ago), my eight-year-old underwear with holes and frayed edges. This kind of clutter drove my mother crazy. "Why do you want to wear *that*?" she'd say. She always looked fabulous, while I found it difficult not to wear shapeless yoga pants and ratty white T-shirts day after day.

I felt particularly oppressed by *aspirational clutter*—things that I owned but only aspired to use: the glue gun I never mastered, mysteriously specific silver serving pieces untouched since our wedding, my beige pumps with superhigh heels. The flip side of aspirational clutter is *outgrown clutter*. I discovered a big pile of plastic photo boxes piled in a drawer. I used them for years, but even though I like proper picture frames now, I'd held on to the plastic versions.

The kind of clutter that I found most disagreeable was *buyer's remorse clutter*, when, rather than admit that I'd made a bad purchase, I hung on to things until somehow I felt they'd been "used up" by sitting in a closet or on a shelf—the canvas bag that I'd used only once since I bought it two years ago, those impractical white pants.

Having sized up the situation, I went straight to the festering heart of my household clutter: my own closet. I've never been very good at folding, so messy, lopsided towers of shirts and sweaters jammed the shelves. Too many items were hung on the clothes rod, so I had to muscle my way into a mass of wool and cotton to pull anything out. Bits of socks and T-shirts hung over the edges of the drawers that I'd forced shut. I'd start my clutter clearing here.

So I could focus properly, I stayed home while Jamie took the girls to visit his parents for the day. The minute the elevator door closed behind them, I began.

I'd read suggestions that I should invest in an extra closet storage boxes that fit under the bed or in hangers that would hold four pairs of pants on one rod. For me, however, there was only one essential tool of clutter clearing: trash bags. I set aside one bag for throwaways and one for giveaways and dived in.

First, I got rid of items that no one should be wearing anymore. Good-bye, baggy yoga pants. Next I pulled out the items that, realistically, I knew I wouldn't wear. Good-bye, gray sweater that barely covered my navel. Then the culling got harder. I liked those brown pants, but I couldn't figure out what shoes to wear with them. I liked that dress, but I never had the right place to wear it. I forced myself to take the time to make each item work, and if I couldn't, out it went. I started to notice my dodges. When I told myself, "I would wear this," I meant that I didn't, in fact, wear it. "I have worn this" meant that I'd worn it twice in five years. "I could wear this" meant that I'd never worn it and never would.

Once I'd finished the closet, I went back through it once again. When I finished, I had four bags full of clothes, and I could see huge patches of the back of my closet. I no longer felt drained; instead, I felt exhilarated. No more being confronted with my mistakes! No more searching in frustration for a particular white button-down shirt!

Having cleared some space, I craved more. I tried any trick I could. Why had I been holding on to thirty extra hangers? I got rid of all but a few extra hangers, which opened up a considerable amount of space. I got rid of some shopping bags I'd kept tucked away for years, for no good reason. I'd planned only on sorting through hanging items, but, energized and inspired, I attacked my sock and T-shirt drawers. Instead of pawing around for items to eliminate, I emptied each drawer completely, and I put back only the items that I actually wore.

I gloated as I surveyed my now-roomy closet. So much space. No more guilt. The next day I craved another hit. "We're going to do something really fun tonight!" I said to Jamie in a bright voice as he was checking sports news on TV.

"What?" he said, immediately suspicious. He kept the remote control prominently in his hand.

"We're going to clear out your closet and drawers!"

"Oh. Well, okay," he said agreeably. I shouldn't have been surprised by his reaction; Jamie loves order. He turned off the TV.

"But we're not going to get rid of much," he warned me. "I wear most of this stuff pretty regularly."

"Okay, sure," I said sweetly. We'll see about that, I thought.

Going through his closet turned out to be fun. Jamie sat on the bed while I pulled hangers out of his closet, two at a time, and he, much less tortured than I, gave a simple thumbs-up or thumbs-down—except once, when he insisted, "I've never seen that pair of pants before in my life." He got rid of a giant bag of clothes.

Over the next few weeks, as I adjusted to my half-empty closet, I noticed a paradox: although I had far fewer clothes in front of me, I felt as though I had *more* to wear—because everything in my closet was something that I realistically would wear.

Also, having few clothing choices made me feel happier. Although people believe they like to have lots of choice, in fact, having too many choices can be discouraging. Instead of making people feel more satisfied, a wide range of options can paralyze them. Studies show that when faced with two dozen varieties of jam in a grocery store, for example, or lots of investment options for their pension plan, people often choose arbitrarily or walk away without making any choice at all, rather than labor to make a reasoned choice. I certainly felt happier choosing between two pairs of black pants that I liked rather than among five pairs of black pants, the majority of which were either uncomfortable or unfashionable—and which made me feel guilty for never wearing them, to boot.

Who knew that doing something so mundane could give me such a kick? By this point, I was jonesing for more of the clutter-clearing buzz, so while a pregnant friend opened her presents at a baby shower, I quizzed my fellow guests for new strategies.

"Focus on the dump zones," advised one friend. "You know, the dining room table, the kitchen counter, the place where everyone dumps their stuff."

"Right," I said. "Our biggest dump zone is a chair in our bedroom. We never sit in it, we just pile clothes and magazines on it."

"Junk attracts more junk. If you clear it off, it's likely to stay clear. And here's another thing," she continued. "When you buy any kind of device, put the cords, the manual, all that stuff in a labeled Ziploc bag. You avoid having a big tangle of mystery cords, plus when you get rid of the device, you can get rid of the ancillary parts, too."

"Try a 'virtual move,'" another friend added. "I just did it myself. Walk around your apartment and ask yourself—if I were moving, would I pack this or get rid of it?"

"I *never* keep anything for sentimental reasons alone," someone else claimed. "Only if I'm still using it."

These suggestions were helpful, but that last rule was too draconian for me. I'd never get rid of the "Justice Never Rests" T-shirt from the aerobics class I took with Justice Sandra Day O'Connor when I clerked for her, even though it never did fit, or the doll-sized outfit that our preemie Eliza wore when she came home from the hospital. (At least these items didn't take up much room. I have a friend who keeps twelve tennis racquets, left over from her days playing college tennis.)

When one of my college roommates visited New York, we waxed lyrical over coffee about the glories of clutter clearing.

"What in life," I demanded, "gives immediate gratification equal to cleaning out a medicine cabinet? Nothing!"

"No, nothing," she agreed with equal fervor. But she took it even further. "You know, I keep an empty shelf."

"What do you mean?"

"I keep one shelf, somewhere in my house, completely empty. I'll pack every other shelf to the top, but I keep one shelf bare."

I was struck by the poetry of this resolution. An empty shelf! And she had three children. An empty shelf meant possibility; space to expand; a luxurious waste of something useful for the sheer elegance of it. I had to have one. I went home, went straight to my hall closet, and emptied a shelf. It wasn't a big shelf, but it was empty. Thrilling.

I hunted through the apartment, and no object, no matter how small, escaped my scrutiny. I'd long been annoyed by the maddening accumulation of gimcracks that children attract. Glittery superballs, miniature flashlights, small plastic zoo animals . . . this stuff was everywhere. It was fun to have and the girls wanted to keep it, but it was hard to put it away, because where did it go?

My Eighth Commandment is "Identify the problem." I'd realized that often I put up with a problem for years because I never examined the nature of the problem and how it might be solved. It turns out that stating a problem clearly often suggests its solution. For instance, I hated hanging up my coat, so I usually left it slung on the back of a chair.

Identify the problem: "Why don't I ever hang up my coat?"

Answer: "I don't like fussing with hangers."

Solution: "So use the hook on the inside of the door!"

When I asked myself, "What's the problem with all these little toys?" I answered, "Eliza and Eleanor want to keep this stuff, but we don't have a place to put it away." Bingo. I immediately saw the solution to my problem. The next day, I stopped by the Container Store and bought five large glass canisters. I combed the apartment to collect toy flotsam and stuffed it in. Clutter cured! I filled all five jars. What I hadn't anticipated was that the jars looked great on the shelf—colorful, festive, and inviting. My solution was ornamental as well as practical.

A pleasant, unintended consequence of my clutter clearing was that it solved the "four-thermometer syndrome": I could never find our thermometer, so I kept buying new ones, and when my clutter clearing flushed them all out, we had *four* thermometers. (Which I never used, by the way; I felt the back of the girls' necks to see if they had a fever.) It's a Secret of Adulthood: if you can't find something, clean up. I discovered that although it seemed easier to put things away in general areas—the coat closet, any kitchen drawer—it was more satisfying when each item went in a highly specific location. One of life's small pleasures is to return something to its proper place; putting the shoe polish on the second shelf in the linen closet gave me the archer's satisfaction of hitting a mark.

I also hit on a few daily rules to help keep the apartment from constantly falling into disorder. First, following my Fourth Commandment, "Do it now," I started to apply the "one-minute rule"; I didn't postpone any task that could be done in less than one minute. I put away my umbrella; I filed a document; I put the newspapers in the recycling bin; I closed the cabinet door. These steps took just a few moments, but the cumulative impact was impressive.

Along with the "one-minute rule," I observed the "evening tidy-up" by taking ten minutes before bed to do simple tidying. Tidying up at night made our mornings more serene and pleasant and, in an added benefit, helped prepare me for sleep. Putting things in order is very calming, and doing something physical makes me aware of being tired. If I've been reading under the covers for an hour before turning out the light, I don't get the same feeling of luxurious comfort when I stretch out in bed.

As the clutter behind closed doors and cabinets began to diminish, I attacked visual clutter. For instance, we subscribe to a huge number of magazines, and we couldn't keep them neat. I cleared out a drawer, and now we keep magazines stacked out of sight, ready to grab before we head to the gym. I'd been keeping invitations, school notices, and various miscellanea posted on a bulletin board, but I pulled it all down and moved it into a file labeled "Upcoming events and invitations." I was no more or less organized than before, but our visual chaos dropped.

I'd dreaded doing the clutter clearing, because it seemed like such an enormous job, and it *was* an enormous job, but every time I looked around and saw the extra space and order, I registered a little jolt of energy. I was thrilled with the improved conditions in our apartment, and I kept waiting for Jamie to say, "Boy, everything looks terrific! You've done so much work, it's so much nicer!" But he never did. I love my gold stars, so that was disappointing, but on the other hand, he didn't complain about lugging five hundred pounds of stuff to the thrift store. And even if he didn't appreciate my efforts as much I'd expected, it didn't really matter; I felt uplifted and restored by my clutter clearing.

TACKLE A NAGGING TASK.

Unfinished tasks were draining my energy and making me feel guilty. I felt like a bad friend because I hadn't bought a wedding gift. I felt like an irresponsible family member because I'd never gotten a skin cancer check (and I have the superfair skin that comes with red hair). I felt like a bad parent because our toddler, Eleanor, needed new shoes. I had an image of myself sitting in front of a hive-shaped laptop, while reminders in the form of bees dive-bombed my head, buzzing, "Do me!" "Do me!" while I slapped them away. It was time for some relief.

I sat down and wrote a five-page to-do list. Writing the list was sort of fun, but then I had to face the prospect of doing tasks that I'd been avoiding—in some cases, for years. For the sake of morale, I added several items that could be crossed off with five minutes of effort.

Over the next several weeks, I doggedly tackled my list. I had my first skin cancer check. I got the windows cleaned. I got a backup system for my computer. I figured out a mystery cable bill. I took my shoes to be reheeled.

As I grappled with some of the more difficult items on the to-do list, though, I faced a discouraging number of "boomerang errands": errands that I thought I was getting rid of but then came right back to me. Eighteen months overdue, congratulating myself on crossing the task off the list, I went to the dentist to get my teeth cleaned, only to discover that I had decay under one filling. I had to return to the dentist the next week. Boomerang. After months of procrastination, I asked the building super to fix our bedroom wall light, but it turned out he couldn't do it. He ___ the number of an electrician. I called the electrician; he came, he ___ light off the wall, but he couldn't fix it. He told me about a repair shop. I took the light to the repair shop. A week later, I picked it up. Then the electrician had to come back to install it. Then the light worked again. Boomerang, boomerang, boomerang.

I had to accept the fact that some nagging tasks would never be crossed off my list. I would have to do them every day for the rest of my life. Finally I started wearing sunscreen every day—well, most days. Finally I started flossing every day—well, most days. (Although I knew that sun exposure can lead to cancer and unhealthy gums can lead to tooth loss, focusing on wrinkles and bad breath proved to be more motivating considerations.)

Sometimes, though, the most difficult part of doing a task was just deciding to *do it.* I began one morning by sending an e-mail that included only forty-eight words and took forty-five seconds to write—yet it had been weighing on my mind for at least two weeks. Such unfinished tasks were disproportionately draining.

An important aspect of happiness is managing your moods, and studies show that one of the best ways to lift your mood is to engineer an easy success, such as tackling a long-delayed chore. I was astounded by the dramatic boost in my mental energy that came from taking care of these neglected tasks.

ACT MORE ENERGETIC.

To feel more energetic, I applied one of my Twelve Commandments, "Act the way I want to feel." This commandment sums up one of the most helpful insights that I'd learned in my happiness research: although we presume that we *act* because of the way we *feel,* in fact we often *feel* because of the way we *act.* For example, studies show that even an artificially induced smile brings about happier emotions, and one experiment suggested that people who use Botox are less prone to anger, because they can't make angry faces. The philosopher and psychologist William James explained, "Action seems to follow feeling, but really action and feeling go together; and by regulating the action, which is under the more direct control of the will, we can indirectly regulate the feeling, which is not." Advice from every quarter, ancient and contemporary, backs up the observation that to change our feelings, we should change our actions.

Although a "fake it till you feel it" strategy sounded hokey, I found it extremely effective. When I felt draggy, I started to act with more energy. I sped up my walk. I paced while talking on the phone. I put more warmth and zest into my voice. Sometimes I feel exhausted by the prospect of spending time with my own children, but one tired afternoon, instead of trying to devise a game that involved my lying on the couch (I've managed to be astonishingly resourceful in coming up with ideas), I bounded into the room and said, "Hey, let's play in the tent!" It really worked; I did manage to give myself an energy boost by acting with energy.

By the end of January, I was off to a promising start, but did I feel happier? It was too soon to tell. I did feel more alert and calm, and although I still had periods when I felt overtaxed, they became less frequent.

I found that rewarding myself for good behavior—even when that reward was nothing more than a check mark that I gave myself on my Resolutions Chart—made it easier for me to stick to a resolution. Getting a bit of reinforcement did make a difference. I could see, however, that I'd have to remind myself continually to keep my resolutions. In particular, I noticed a decline in my order-maintaining zeal by the end of the month. I loved the big payoff of cleaning out a closet, but keeping the apartment tidy was a Sisyphean task that never stayed finished. Perhaps the "one-minute rule" and the "evening tidy-up" would keep me attacking clutter regularly, in small doses, so that it couldn't grow to its previous crushing proportions.

Nevertheless, I was astonished by the charge of energy and satisfaction I got from creating order. The closet that had been an eyesore was now a joy; the stack of papers slowly yellowing on the edge of my desk was gone. "It is by studying *little things*," wrote Samuel Johnson, "that we attain the great art of having as little misery, and as much happiness as possible."

2

[FEBRUARY]

Remember Love

MARRIAGE

- Quit nagging.
- Don't expect praise or appreciation.
- Fight right.
- No dumping.
- Give proofs of love.

One alarming fact jumps out from the research about happiness and marriage: marital satisfaction drops substantially after the first child arrives. The disruptive presence of new babies and teenagers, in particular, puts a lot of pressure on marriages, and discontent spikes when children are in these stages.

Jamie and I had been married for eleven years, and sure enough, the incidence of low-level bickering in our marriage increased significantly after our daughter Eliza was born. Until then, the phrase "Can't *you* do it?" had never crossed my lips. Over the last several years, I'd started doing too much complaining, nagging, and foot-dragging. It was time to do something about that.

As corny as it sounds, I've always felt that from the moment we were introduced in the library during law school, when I was a first-year and he was a second-year, Jamie and I have had an extraordinary love (the rose-colored pile jacket he was wearing that afternoon still hangs at the back of my closet). In recent years, though, I'd begun to worry that an accumulation of minor irritations and sharp words was making us less outwardly loving.

Our marriage wasn't in trouble. We showed our affection openly and often. We were indulgent with each other. We handled conflict pretty well. We didn't practice the behaviors that the marriage expert John Gottman calls the "Four Horsemen of the Apocalypse" for their destructive role in relationships: stonewalling, defensiveness, criticism, and contempt. Well, sometimes we indulged in stonewalling, defensiveness, and criticism, but *never* contempt, the worst behavior of all.

But we—*I*—had fallen into some bad habits that I wanted to change.

Working on my marriage was an obvious goal for my happiness project, because a good marriage is one of the factors most strongly associated with happiness. Partly this reflects the fact that happy people find it easier to get and stay married than unhappy people do, because happy people make better dates and easier spouses. But marriage itself also brings happiness, because it provides the support and companionship that everyone needs.

For me, as for most married people, my marriage was the foundation of all the other important choices in my life: where I lived, having kids, my friends, my work, my leisure. The atmosphere of my marriage set the weather for my whole life. That's why I'd decided not only to include marriage in my happiness project but also to tackle it early, in the second month.

Yet though my relationship with Jamie was the most important factor in shaping my daily existence, it was also, unfortunately, the relationship in which I was most likely to behave badly. Too often I focused on gripes and disputes, and I did quite a bit of blaming. If the lightbulbs were burned out, if I was feeling plagued by a messy apartment, or even if I felt discouraged about my work, I blamed Jamie.

Jamie is a funny mix. He has a sardonic side that can make him seem distant and almost harsh to people who don't know him well, but he's also very tender-hearted. (A good example: he loves movies that I find unbearably dark, such as *Open Water* and *Reservoir Dogs,* but he also loves sweet, sentimental movies—his favorite is *Say Anything.*) He drives me crazy by refusing to carry out various husbandly assignments, then surprises me by upgrading my computer without my asking. He makes the bed but never uses the clothes hamper. He's bad at buying presents for birthdays, but he brings home lovely gifts unexpectedly. Like everyone, he's a combination of good and not-so-good qualities, and the worst of my bad habits was to focus on his faults while taking his virtues for granted.

I had come to understand one critical fact about my happiness project: I couldn't change anyone else. As tempting as it was to try, I couldn't lighten the atmosphere of our marriage by bullying Jamie into changing his ways. I could work only on myself. For inspiration, I turned to the twelfth of my Twelve Commandments: "There is only love."

A friend of mine was the source of that commandment. She came up with the phrase when she was considering taking a high-pressure job where she'd be working for a notoriously difficult person. The person handling the hiring process told her, "I'm going to be honest with you. John Doe is very effective, but he's an extremely tough guy to work for. Think hard about whether you want this job." My friend really wanted the job, so she decided, "There is only love." From that moment on, she refused to think critical thoughts about John Doe; she never complained about him behind his back; she wouldn't even listen to other people criticize him.

"Don't your coworkers think you're a goody-goody?" I asked.

"Oh, no," she said. "They all wish they could do the same thing, too. He drives them crazy, but I can honestly say that I like John."

If my friend could do that for her boss, why couldn't I do it for Jamie? Deep down, I had only love for Jamie—but I was allowing too many petty issues to get in the way. I wasn't living up to my own standards of behavior, and then, because I felt guilty when I behaved badly, I behaved even worse.

Love is a funny thing. I'd donate a kidney to Jamie without a moment's hesitation, but I was intensely annoyed if he asked me to make a special stop at the drugstore to pick up shaving cream. Studies show that the most common sources of conflict among couples are money, work, sex, communication, religion, children, in-laws, appreciation, and leisure activities. Having a newborn is also particularly tough. However, these categories—as seemingly all-inclusive as they were—didn't quite capture my problem areas. I thought hard about my particular marriage, and the changes I could make to restore the tenderness and patience of our newlywed, prebaby days.

First, I needed to change my approach to household work. I was spending too much time handing out assignments and nagging, and not only was I nagging Jamie to do his work, I was nagging him to give me praise for *my* work. Also, I wanted to become more lighthearted, especially in moments of anger. A line by G. K. Chesterton echoed in my head: "It is easy to be heavy: hard to be light" (or, as the saying goes, "Dying is easy; comedy is hard"). And I wanted to stop taking Jamie for granted. Small, frequent gestures of thoughtfulness were more important than flowers on Valentine's Day, and I wanted to load Jamie with small treats and courtesies, praise and appreciation—after all, as my Secret of Adulthood holds, "What you do *every day* matters more than what you do *once in a while*."

Jamie didn't ask me what experiments I'd planned for the month, and I didn't tell him. I knew him well enough to know that although he realized that, in some ways, he was my lab rat, hearing about the details would make him feel self-conscious.

These resolutions were going to be tough for me—I knew that. I wasn't unrealistic enough to expect to be able to keep every resolution, every day, but I wanted to aim higher than I had. One reason I started my happiness project by raising my energy and clearing my clutter was that I knew I'd be more able to act lighthearted and loving if I didn't feel overwhelmed by mental or physical disorder. It seemed ridiculous, but already, having a tidier closet and getting more sleep was putting me into a happier and more peaceable frame of mind. The challenge would be to keep up with January's resolutions now that I was adding a new list of resolutions for February.

QUIT NAGGING.

Jamie hated being nagged, and I hated *being* a nag, yet I found myself doing it all too often. Studies show that the quality of a couple's friendship determines, in large part, whether they feel satisfied with their marriage's romance and passion, and nothing kills the feeling of friendship (and passion) more than nagging. Anyway, nagging doesn't work.

Our Valentine's cards gave me a chance to put this resolution to a test. As happens to many people, about five minutes after Eliza was born, I was possessed with an irresistible urge to send out yearly holiday cards. In a decision born more out of desperation rather than originality, I'd decided to make a tradition of sending cards in February for Valentine's Day, instead of in December, when life is crazy.

When it was time to send out the cards this year, as Jamie and I sat down to watch *Close Encounters of the Third Kind,* I got out the enormous stacks of envelopes and asked brightly, "Would you like to stuff or seal?"

He gave me a sad look and said, "Please don't make me."

I struggled to decide how to answer. Should I insist that he help? Should I tell him that it wasn't fair that I had to do all the work? That I'd done the hard part of ordering the cards and arranging for the photo (an adorable picture of Eleanor and Eliza in ballet clothes), and he was just helping with the easy part? On the other hand, I'd decided to do these cards to suit myself. Was it fair to ask him to help? Well, fairness didn't really matter. I'd rather finish the envelopes myself than feel like a nag.

"It's okay," I told him with a sigh. "Don't worry about it." I did feel a few twinges of resentment when I glanced at Jamie lounging back on the sofa, but I realized that I enjoyed *not* feeling like a nag more than I enjoyed watching TV without licking envelopes at the same time.

After the movie, Jamie looked over at me, where I sat surrounded by stuffed, sealed, and stamped red envelopes.

He put his hand on mine. "Will you be my Valentine?"

I was glad that I'd decided not to push it.

To make it easier to quit nagging, I made myself a checklist of antinagging techniques. First, because it's annoying to hear a hectoring voice, I found ways for us to suggest tasks without talking; when I put an envelope on the floor by the front door, Jamie knew he was supposed to mail it on his way to work. I limited myself to a one-word reminder. Instead of barking out, "Now remember, you promised to figure out what's wrong with the video camera before we go to the park!" I just said, "Camera!" as Jamie got up from lunch. I reminded myself that tasks didn't need to be done according to my schedule. I had to fight the urge to nag Jamie to retrieve the play slide from our basement storage, because once I decided Eleanor would enjoy it, I wanted it brought up immediately. But it wasn't really urgent. I did give myself credit for not indulging in the popular "It's for your own good" variety of nagging. I never bugged Jamie about taking an umbrella, eating breakfast, or going to the dentist. Although some people think that that kind of nagging shows love, I think that an adult should be able to decide whether or not to wear a sweater without interference from others.

The most obvious (and least appealing) antinagging technique, of course, was to do a task myself. Why did I get to decree that it was Jamie's responsibility to make sure we had plenty of cash on hand? Once I took over the job, we always had cash, and I was much happier. And when Jamie did a task, I didn't allow myself to carp from the sidelines. I thought he paid too much when he bought the replacement for the dud video camera, but it was his decision to make in his own way.

I also tried to be more observant and appreciative of all the tasks that Jamie did. I was certainly guilty of "unconscious overclaiming," the phenomenon in which we unconsciously overestimate our contributions or skills relative to other people. (It's related to the Garrison Keillor–named "Lake Wobegon fallacy," which describes the fact that we all fancy ourselves to be above average.) In one study, when students in a work group each estimated their contribution to the team, the total was 139 percent. This makes sense, because we're far more aware of what *we* do than what other people do: I complain about the time I spend paying bills, but I overlook the time Jamie spends dealing with our car.

I have a friend who has a radical solution. She and her husband *don't assign.* Even though they have four children, they have a tacit agreement never to say things such as "You need to take the kids to the birthday party" or "Fix the toilet, it's running again." Their system works because they both pitch in, but even so, I can't imagine living that way. It's an impossible ideal, yet inspiring.

DON'T EXPECT PRAISE OR APPRECIATION.

My examination of my nagging habit showed me that I also engaged in a more subtle form of nagging—nagging that concerned work that *I* did. I nagged Jamie to give me more praise.

With something like the Valentine's cards project, I realized that what I really wanted—even more than help—was for Jamie to say something such as "Wow, the photograph of the girls is terrific! You're doing a great job with these Valentine's cards!" I wanted that gold star stuck onto my homework.

Why did I have such a need for gold stars? Was it vanity that needed to be stoked? Was it insecurity that needed to be soothed? Whatever the

reason, I knew I should get over my need for Jamie to applaud the n
things I did, and, even more, I should get over my need for Jamie even
notice the nice things I did. So I made the resolution "Don't expect praise
or appreciation."

Until I started paying close attention, I hadn't appreciated how much
this need affected my behavior. One morning, I staggered into the kitchen
in my robe around 7:30 A.M. I'd been up for much of the night with
Eleanor, who had hardly slept; Jamie had got up with her around 6:00 so
I could go back to bed.

"Good morning," I mumbled as I cracked open a Diet Coke. I didn't
add any words of thanks for my luxurious extra ninety minutes of sleep.

Jamie waited a moment, then prompted, "I hope you appreciate that
I bought you some time this morning." He needs gold stars himself, even
though he isn't very good—to my mind—at handing them out.

I'd been concentrating about behaving better in my marriage. I'd been
patting myself on the back for learning so much. So did I say in a tender
voice, "Of course I appreciate it, thanks so much, you're my hero"? Did I
give Jamie a big hug of gratitude? Nope. Because Jamie neglected to give
me a gold star for staying up with Eleanor, I snapped, "I *did* appreciate it,
but you never show any appreciation when *I* let *you* sleep. Then you expect
a lot of gratitude when you let me sleep." Jamie's look made me wish I'd re-
acted differently. I remembered my Ninth Commandment: "Lighten up."

I put my arms around him. "I'm sorry. Really. I shouldn't have talked
that way, and I do appreciate getting the extra sleep this morning."

"You know," he said, "I really was trying to give you a treat. And I *do*
appreciate the fact that you let me sleep."

"Okay."

We hugged—for at least six seconds, which, I happened to know from
my research, is the minimum time necessary to promote the flow of oxy-
tocin and serotonin, mood-boosting chemicals that promote bonding. The
moment of tension passed.

This exchange led me to an important insight into how to manage myself better. I'd been self-righteously telling myself that I did certain chores or made certain efforts "for Jamie" or "for the team." Though this sounded generous, it led to a bad result, because I sulked when Jamie didn't appreciate my efforts. Instead, I started to tell myself, "I'm doing this *for myself.* This is what *I* want." *I* wanted to send out Valentine's cards. *I* wanted to clean out the kitchen cabinets. This sounded selfish, but in fact, it was less selfish, because it meant I wasn't nagging to get a gold star from Jamie or anyone else. No one else even had to notice what I'd done.

I remember talking to a friend whose parents had been very involved in the civil rights movement. "They always said," he told me, "that you have to do that kind of work for yourself. If you do it for other people, you end up wanting them to acknowledge it and to be grateful and to give you credit. If you do it for yourself, you don't expect other people to react in a particular way." I think that's right.

Nevertheless, for all my talk of giving up gold stars, I have to admit that I still thought it would be nice for Jamie to hand them out a bit more lavishly. Whether or not I *should* want them, I *do.*

FIGHT RIGHT.

Nagging was easier to address than some other behaviors I was trying to change. I faced a tougher challenge with my second priority: lightening my attitude. Marital conflicts fall into two categories: issues that can be clearly resolved and those that can't. Unfortunately, more conflicts fall into the open-ended "How should we spend our money?" and "How should we raise our children?" categories than into the easier "What movie should we see this weekend?" or "Where should we go on our vacation this summer?" category.

Some disagreement is inevitable and even valuable. Since Jamie and I were going to fight, I wanted to be able to have fights that were more fun, where we could joke around and be affectionate even while we were disagreeing.

I also wanted to conquer my own particular bosom enemy: *snapping.* Far too often, in a kind of one-sided minifight, I would lash out in sudden fits of temper that soured the household mood. I'd often wondered why anger—along with pride, greed, gluttony, lust, sloth, and envy—were the seven deadly sins, because they didn't seem as deadly as lots of other sins. It turns out that they're deadly sins not because of their gravity but because of their power to generate other, worse sins. They're the gateway sins to the big sins. Of the seven deadly sins, anger was certainly my nemesis.

Fighting style is very important to the health of a marriage; Gottman's "love laboratory" research shows that *how* a couple fights matters more than *how much* they fight. Couples who fight right tackle only one difficult topic at a time, instead of indulging in arguments that cover every grievance since the first date. These couples ease into arguments instead of blowing up immediately—and avoid bombs such as "You never . . ." and "You always . . ." They know how to bring an argument to an end, instead of keeping it going for hours. They make "repair attempts" by using words or actions to keep bad feelings from escalating. They recognize other pressures imposed on a spouse—a husband acknowledges that his wife feels overwhelmed by the demands of work and home; a wife acknowledges that her husband feels caught between her and his mother.

Here's an example of how *not* to fight right. Apparently, much as I hate to acknowledge it, I may snore from time to time. I hate to hear any mention of it, because snoring sounds so unattractive, but when Jamie joked about it one morning, I was trying to "be light," so I laughed along with him.

Then, a few weeks later, as we were listening to our favorite all-news radio station before the 6:30 alarm rang and I was reflecting groggily on how much more peaceful our bedroom was now that I'd cleared away so much mess, Jamie said in a sweet, kidding-around way, "I'll start the day with two observations. First, you snore."

I snapped. "So that's the first thing I have to hear in the morning?" I exploded. I practically threw the covers in his face as I got out of bed.

"That I *snore*. Can you think of nothing nicer to say?" I stormed across the room and started yanking clothes out of the closet. "If you want me to stop, give me a poke while I'm sleeping, but don't keep harping on it!"

Lesson learned? By laughing along with him, I'd made Jamie think that snoring was a good subject for a joke. I tried to be light, but I couldn't; I wish I could always laugh at myself easily, but in some situations, I can't, and I should have responded honestly, so I could avoid an eventual blowup. Jamie had had no warning that his comment was going to enrage me. So much for "Fight right." This time, I hadn't managed to keep my resolution—I couldn't even bring myself to apologize, I just wanted to forget about it—but next time, I'd do better (I hoped).

In marriage, it's less important to have many pleasant experiences than it is to have fewer unpleasant experiences, because people have a "negativity bias"; our reactions to bad events are faster, stronger, and stickier than our reactions to good events. In fact, in practically every language, there are more concepts to describe negative emotions than positive emotions.

It takes at least five positive marital actions to offset one critical or destructive action, so one way to strengthen a marriage is to make sure that the positive far outweighs the negative. When a couple's interactions are usually loving and kind, it's much easier to disregard the occasional unpleasant exchange. I had a feeling, however, that it would take more than five marital actions, on both our parts, to offset the negative force of our snoring exchange.

Fighting right made a big difference to my happiness, because the failure to fight right was a significant source of guilt in my life. As Mark Twain observed, "An uneasy conscience is a hair in the mouth." When Jamie did something annoying and I snapped at him, and then I felt bad about snapping, I blamed it on *him*. But in fact, I realized, a major cause of my bad feelings wasn't Jamie's behavior but rather my guilt about my reaction to his behavior; fighting right eliminated that guilt and so made me happier.

One day when I repeatedly failed to fight right helped me to see this point clearly. For Presidents Day weekend, we went on a little vacation with Jamie's parents. My in-laws, Judy and Bob, are wonderful grandparents with whom to vacation—helpful, easygoing, with a reasonable tolerance for chaos—but they like to have plenty of time when traveling, and in our rush to get out the door to meet them, I let myself get too hungry. Just as we were leaving the apartment, I realized I was famished, and I gave myself a quick fix by digging into an enormous heart-shaped box of M&M's that Eliza had gotten for Valentine's Day.

Eating all that candy made me feel guilty and a little sick, and I couldn't keep from making nasty remarks. The worse I behaved, the guiltier I felt, and that made me behave worse.

"Jamie, please get those papers out of my way."

"Eliza, stop leaning on me, you're hurting my arm."

"Jamie, can't you get that bag?"

Even after we arrived at the hotel, having made a wrong start, I couldn't shake my bad feelings.

"Are you okay?" Jamie asked me at one point.

"Sure, I'm fine," I mumbled, temporarily chastened, but my bad mood soon reasserted itself.

That night, after Eliza and Eleanor went to sleep, the adults could finally have a sustained conversation. We drank our after-dinner coffee (even after years as part of this family, I still marvel at Judy's and Bob's ability to drink espresso *with caffeine* after dinner) and talked about a recent *New York Times* article about VX-950, a hepatitis C drug in trials.

We cared a lot about those trials. Jamie jokes about being a "broken toy" with his bad knee, his impressive scar from childhood surgery, and occasional back spasms, but his major broken part is his liver. He has hepatitis C.

As chronic and potentially fatal conditions go, hepatitis C has some good points. It's not contagious except through direct blood contact. Jamie has no apparent symptoms and found out that he has hepatitis C only through a blood test. One day he'll develop cirrhosis and his liver will stop functioning and he'll be in very big trouble, but for now, he's perfectly fine. Also, when it comes to health problems, misery loves company; if a lot of people share your ailment, drug companies work hard to find a cure. About 3 million people in the United States have hepatitis C, along with 170 million or so worldwide, so it's an active area of research, and Jamie's doctors estimate that new, effective treatments are likely to be approved within five to eight years. Hepatitis C has a very long course—of the people who develop cirrhosis, most don't get it for twenty or thirty years.

Thirty years sounds like a very long time, but Jamie picked up hepatitis C through a blood transfusion during a heart operation when he was eight years old, before screening for hepatitis C began. And now he's thirty-eight.

The one treatment now available, pegylated interferon plus ribavirin, didn't work for Jamie, despite an unpleasant year of flulike symptoms, pills, and weekly shots. Now we just have to hope that Jamie manages to hang on to his liver until researchers find new treatments. In addition to cirrhosis leading to liver failure, itself not an attractive prospect, hepatitis C also makes liver cancer far more likely. Thank goodness for liver transplants—though a transplanted liver is no picnic and, scarily, not always possible to get. (Like the old joke about the restaurant: "The food is terrible!" "Yes, and the portions are so small.")

So we were all very interested in the *Times* piece's description of possible new treatments. My father-in-law, Bob, found the article encouraging, but every time he made a comment, I countered it.

"According to the article, the research is very promising," he said.

"But both of Jamie's liver doctors told us that it's going to be at least five years, if not more, for a drug to be approved," I answered.

"The article suggests that they're making great strides," he answered mildly. Bob never becomes argumentative.

"But they're still a very long way from getting it on the market." I often become argumentative.

"This field of research is enormously active."

"But the time horizon is very long."

Etc., etc., etc.

It's not often that I find myself telling Bob that he's being overly optimistic. He emphasizes the importance of rational, probabilistic decision making, and he practices this discipline himself, with yellow notepads with "pros" and "cons" columns, a habit of gathering multiple viewpoints, a detached "Markets go up, markets go down" outlook. In this situation, however, he chose to take an optimistic view of the evidence. Why argue with him? I didn't agree with his view, but I'm no doctor, what did I know?

My new aspirations for my behavior were high but not unreasonable. I knew that my combativeness and pedantry in this conversation came not from petty irritation but from a desire to protect myself against false hopes. Bob was taking the positive route, and I would have felt better if I'd let the issue go without arguing. I'm sure I made Bob, and certainly Jamie, feel worse by saying discouraging things, and being quarrelsome just made me feel bad. Fight right—not just with your husband but with everyone.

On a less lofty note, I also learned not to eat half a pound of M&M's on an empty stomach.

NO DUMPING.

For my research on learning how to "Fight right," I had acquired an extensive library of books on marriage and relationships.

"Anyone who looks at our shelves is going to think that our marriage is in trouble," Jamie observed.

"Why's that?" I asked, startled.

"Look what you've got here. *The Seven Principles for Making Marriage*

Work. Love Is Never Enough. Babyproofing Your Marriage. Uncoupling. One Man, Hurt. I'd be worried myself if I didn't know what you were working on."

"But this material is great," I said. "There's so much fascinating research."

"Sure, but people don't bother to read these books unless they have *issues.*"

Maybe Jamie was right, but I was happy that I'd had a reason to study the latest findings about marriage and relationships. I'd learned a lot. For example, there's an intriguing difference in how men and women approach intimacy. Although men and women agree that sharing activities and self-disclosure are important, women's idea of an intimate moment is a face-to-face conversation, while men feel close when they work or play sitting alongside someone.

So when Jamie asked, "Do you want to watch *The Shield?*" I understood that in his eyes, watching TV together counted as true quality time, not we're-just-sitting-in-a-room-watching-TV-not-talking-to-each-other time.

"Great idea!" I answered. And, as it turned out, while lying in bed watching a TV show about a rogue cop in L.A. didn't sound very romantic, it *felt* romantic once we were cozily settled in against the pillows.

Perhaps because men have this low standard for what qualifies as intimacy, both men and women find relationships with women to be more intimate and enjoyable than those with men. Women have more feelings of empathy for other people than men do (though women and men have about the same degree of empathy for animals, whatever that means). In fact, for both men and women—and this finding struck me as highly significant—the most reliable predictor of not being lonely is the amount of contact with women. Time spent with men doesn't make a difference.

Learning about this research made a difference in my attitude toward Jamie. I love him with all my heart, and I know he loves me, and I know that I can absolutely trust and confide in him, yet I often felt frustrated because he never wanted to have long heart-to-heart discussions. In particular, I wished that he would take more interest in my work. My sister,

Elizabeth, is a TV writer, and I envy her having her writing partner, Sarah. Practically daily, she and Sarah have marathon conversations about their writing and career strategies. I don't have a partner or any colleagues with whom to discuss work issues, so I wanted Jamie to fill that role for me.

Also, I expected to be able to dump all my insecurities into Jamie's lap. I'd start conversations with enticing openers such as "I'm worried that I'm not living up to my potential" or "I'm doing a bad job of networking" or "What if my writing is no good?" Jamie, remarkably, didn't want to have these conversations, and that made me angry. I wanted him to help me work through my feelings of anxiety and self-doubt.

Learning that men and women both turn to women for understanding showed me that Jamie wasn't ignoring me out of lack of interest or affection; he just wasn't good at giving that kind of support. Jamie wasn't going to have a long discussion about whether I should start a blog or how I should structure my book. He didn't want to spend hours pumping up my self-confidence. He was never going to play the role of a female writing partner, and it wasn't realistic to expect him to do it. If I needed that kind of support, I should figure out another way to get it. My realization didn't change his behavior—but I stopped feeling so resentful.

I'd also noticed that the more upset I felt, the less Jamie seemed to want to talk about it.

"You know," I said to him one night, "I'm feeling anxious. I wish you'd try to help me feel better. The worse I feel, the less you seem to want to talk to me."

"I just can't stand to see you unhappy," he answered.

Light again dawned. It wasn't perversity that kept Jamie from being a sympathetic listener; not only was he constitutionally less oriented to having long heart-to-heart conversations, he also tried to avoid any topic that got me upset, because he found it so painful to see me feeling blue. Now, that didn't let him off the hook altogether—sometimes I needed a sympathetic listener, even if he didn't feel like playing that role—but at least I understood his perspective.

Our conversation started me thinking about how my happiness affected Jamie and others. I'd heard the aphorism "Happy wife, happy life" or, put another way, "If Mama ain't happy, ain't nobody happy." At first I'd thought that sounded great—yippee, it's all about pleasing *me*!—but if these sayings are true, it's a tremendous responsibility.

I'd wondered whether my happiness project was selfish, because it seemed self-indulgent to concentrate on my own happiness. True, I do make other people happy when I tend to my own happiness—I was trying not to snap at Jamie and to laugh at his jokes. But it went beyond that. By being happy myself, I was better able to try to make other people happier.

Happy people generally are more forgiving, helpful, and charitable, have better self-control, and are more tolerant of frustration than unhappy people, while unhappy people are more often withdrawn, defensive, antagonistic, and self-absorbed. Oscar Wilde observed, "One is not always happy when one is good; but one is always good when one is happy."

Happiness has a particularly strong influence in marriage, because spouses pick up each other's moods so easily. A 30 percent increase in one spouse's happiness boosts the other spouse's happiness, while a drop in one spouse's happiness drags the other down. (Not only that: I was fascinated to learn that in a phenomenon known as "health concordance," partners' health behaviors tend to merge, as they pick up good or bad habits from each other related to eating, exercising, visiting doctors, smoking, and drinking.)

I know that Jamie wants me to be happy. In fact, the happier I seem to be, the more Jamie tries to make me happy, and when I'm unhappy—for whatever reason—Jamie goes into a funk. So, as part of my attempt to be happy, I resolved, "No dumping," especially on Jamie. I would bring up my worries if I really needed Jamie's counsel or support, but I wouldn't dump my minor troubles on him.

I had an opportunity to live up to my resolution one Sunday morning. It was a rare moment of calm. Jamie was cleaning up the mess he'd created while whipping up pancakes, Eliza was absorbed in *Harry Potter and the Goblet of Fire,* Eleanor was covering every page of a Scooby-Doo coloring book with green crayon, and I was going through the mail. I opened an innocent-looking letter from our credit card company to discover that because of a security breach on its end, our main credit card had been canceled, and we'd been issued a new card and number.

I was furious. Now I'd have to go into every account that relied on that credit card number to update it. I hadn't kept a list, so I had no idea how I was going to figure out which accounts needed to be changed. Our automatic toll pass, our Amazon account, my gym membership . . . what else? The statement was so matter-of-fact too; no apology, no little perk to acknowledge the corporate fault or the inconvenience to cardholders. This was the kind of chore that made me crazy: it took up precious time and mental energy, yet when it was done, I was no better off than before I started it.

"I can't *believe* this!" I fumed to Jamie. "They've canceled our credit card because of *their* mistake!" I was prepared to launch into a full diatribe when the thought flashed through my mind: "No dumping." I paused. Why should I spoil a peaceful moment with my irritation? Hearing someone complain is tiresome whether you're in a good mood or a bad one and whether or not the complaining is justified. I took a deep breath and stopped in mid-rant. "Oh, well" was all I said, in a tone of forced calm.

Jamie looked at me with surprise, then relief. He probably knew what an effort it had taken for me to restrain myself. When I got up to get more coffee, he stood up to give me a hug, without saying anything.

GIVE PROOFS OF LOVE.

I've never forgotten something I read in college, by Pierre Reverdy: "There is no love; there are only proofs of love." Whatever love I might feel in my heart, others will see only my actions.

When I looked back at my Resolutions Chart, I could see that some entries, such as "Toss, restore, organize" boasted a row of cheerful check marks, while other resolutions were dotted with X marks. I was doing a lot better with "Go to sleep earlier" than with "Don't expect praise or appreciation." Fortunately, "Give proofs of love" seemed like the kind of action that could easily become a pleasant habit.

Some ways of showing my love were easy. Because people are 47 percent (how do they come up with these statistics?) more apt to feel close to a family member who often expresses affection than to one who rarely does, I started telling Jamie "I love you" at every turn and putting "ILY" at the end of my e-mails. I also started hugging Jamie more—as well as other people in my life. Hugging relieves stress, boosts feelings of closeness, and even squelches pain. In one study, people assigned to give five hugs each day for a month, aiming to hug as many different people as they could, became happier.

Some things I was already doing right. Because I didn't want every one of my e-mails to Jamie to contain some irksome question or reminder, I'd gotten into the habit of sending him enjoyable messages, with interesting news or funny stories about the girls.

One day when I walked by Jamie's office building in midtown on my way to a meeting, I stopped to call him on my cell phone.

"Are you at your desk?" I asked.

"Yes, why?"

"Look down at the steps of St. Bartholomew's." The church was right across the street from Jamie's office. "Do you see me waving to you?"

"Yes, look, there you are! I'm waving back."

Taking the time to give that silly, affectionate wave filled me with good feelings that lasted for hours.

These were small gestures, but they made a surprisingly big shift in the tone of our interactions. I had an opportunity to make a larger gesture, too, because my mother-in-law, Judy, had a significant birthday coming up.

Parents and in-laws play a big part in our lives. My parents, Karen and Jack Craft, live in Kansas City, where I grew up, but one or both of my parents visit every few months, and we go to Kansas City to stay with them at least twice a year. These visits are of the intense, what-should-we-all-do-today? variety. Jamie's parents live just around the corner. Literally. There's one lone skinny town house between their apartment building and our apartment building. When we're walking around the neighborhood, we often see them heading toward us, on their way to get coffee or to stop by the market—Judy with her silver hair and beautiful scarves, Bob with his stiff gait and wool cap.

Fortunately for our marriage, Jamie and I agree on the importance of our relationships with our two sets of parents, so it was natural for me to be thinking about Judy's birthday. If we'd asked Judy how she'd like to celebrate, she would have said she didn't care. However, if you want to know how people would like to be treated, it's more helpful to look at how they themselves *act* than what they *say*. Judy is one of the most reliable people I've ever met; she never forgets an obligation, fails to do something she says she'll do, or misses an important date. And though she insists that exchanging birthday or holiday gifts isn't important to her, no one gives more thoughtful and beautifully wrapped presents. She even gives us wedding-anniversary presents that track the traditional theme for each year: for our fourth, "fruits and flowers" anniversary, she gave us a beautiful quilt with a fruits and flowers design; for our tenth, "tin/aluminum" anniversary, she gave us ten boxes of aluminum foil.

Jamie, his father, and his brother, Phil, aren't good at planning birthday celebrations. In the past, I would have made a few reminder comments as Judy's birthday loomed, nagged at Jamie to make plans, then had a smug I-told-you-so attitude when the birthday wasn't celebrated properly. My happiness project work hadn't all been in vain, however, and I saw the solution to the problem: *I* would take charge.

I knew the kind of party Judy would like. She definitely wouldn't want a surprise party, and she'd prefer a family party at home. She valued thoughtfulness far more than lavishness, so homemade gifts that showed forethought would mean more to her than anything store-bought, and she'd like a home-cooked meal more than dinner in a fancy restaurant. Fortunately, my brother-in-law, Phil, and his wife, Lauren, are gifted chefs who run a catering company, so a meal could be both home-cooked *and* fancy.

A vision came to me as if in a dream; then I needed authority to execute it.

I called my father-in-law at the office. "Hi, Bob. I'm calling to talk about plans for Judy's birthday."

"That's a little far off, don't you think?"

"Not really, not if we want to plan something special. And I think we should."

Pause.

"Well," he said slowly, "I'd been thinking—"

"Because I have an idea, if you'd like to hear what I think might be fun."

"Oh yes," he said with relief, "what do you have in mind?"

Bob immediately signed on to my plan. He's a very good sport about dealing with many kinds of tiresome family tasks and obligations, but this kind of project didn't play to his strengths. In fact, everyone in the family cooperated happily. They wanted Judy to have a wonderful birthday, too; they just weren't inclined to do the kind of planning it would require.

In pursuit of my vision, I took complete control. A few days before the party, I sent around an e-mail to Jamie, Bob, Phil, and Lauren—and, to their credit, I didn't get a single snarky e-mail in response:

Hello all—Judy's birthday party is just four days away.

We want a PILE of WRAPPED presents. This means you! One is not enough!

Bob: Eliza and I wrapped your present. Are you bringing champagne?

Jamie: have you bought the present from you and me?

Phil and Lauren: what are you making for dinner—is there anything special I need to have on hand? what time do you need to arrive? white wine or red wine with the food? Did you say you were making menu cards? I think Judy would think that was hilarious.

Everyone: I know I'd open myself up for family scorn if I instructed
everyone that it was inappropriate to wear your I-just-rolled-off-the-
couch-to-amble-over-to-your-party clothes. So I won't say a word about
that. Just remember that it is the sense of occasion and thoughtfulness
that will make it a great night.

This will be fun! xx g

I did a lot of preparation for this party. Eliza and I went to the "Our
Name Is Mud" pottery store, where Eliza decorated dinner plates with
theater themes, reflecting her grandmother's passion. We spent a pleasant
hour (yes, hour) scrolling through the Colette's Cakes Web site to choose
the prettiest cake. Jamie and I shot a DVD of Eliza singing a selection of
Judy's favorite songs, with Eleanor toddling through the action.

On the night of the party, before everyone was due to arrive at 6:30 P.M.,
I began my anxious last-minute tidying. My mother loves to entertain, and
from her I inherited a propensity to preparty jitters, which we call "hostess
neurosis"; experienced family members know to drift out of sight lest they
be conscripted into sudden vacuuming. But when Jamie emerged from
hiding at 6:29 P.M., he was wearing khakis, a plaid shirt, and no shoes.

I took a moment; then, careful to use a light tone, I remarked, "I wish
you were wearing something a little nicer."

Jamie looked as if *he* took a moment, then answered, "I'll put on a
nicer pair of pants, is that okay?" Then he went up and changed his pants
and his shirt and put on shoes, too.

The evening unfolded exactly as I'd hoped. Before the adults sat down
for dinner, the granddaughters ate chicken salad sandwiches—Judy's favorite—with their grandmother. We presented the birthday cake while the
girls were still awake so they could sing "Happy Birthday" and eat a piece.
Then we packed the girls off to bed, and the adults sat down to eat (Indian
food, Judy's favorite).

"This was really a perfect evening," Judy said as everyone stood up
to go. "I loved everything about it. My presents, the food, the cake—
really, everything was wonderful." It was obvious that Judy really did

enjoy the party, and everyone was pleased to have played a part, but I think I enjoyed it most of all. I was *so happy* that it had turned out just right.

The party underscored the truth of the third of my Twelve Commandments: "Act the way I want to feel." Although I might have predicted that organizing the party would make me feel resentful, in fact, acting in a loving way amplified my loving feelings toward everyone in the family, particularly Judy.

I must admit, however, that at times before the party, I felt that Jamie and the others weren't appreciative enough. I was happy to do the planning, and I would've been annoyed if anyone else had tried to take over, but still I wanted my gold star. I wanted Jamie, Bob, or Phil to say, "Wow, Gretchen, you're really putting together a terrific evening! Thanks so much for your brilliant, creative, and thoughtful planning!" That wasn't going to happen—so let it go. Do it *for myself.*

But Jamie knows me very well. While Judy was opening her gifts, Jamie pulled a box from a shelf and handed it to me.

"This is for you," he said.

"For me?" I was surprised and pleased. "Why do I get a present?" Jamie didn't answer, but I knew.

I opened the box to find a beautiful necklace made of polished wooden beads. "I love it!" I said as I tried it on. Maybe I shouldn't have needed the recognition, but Jamie was right, I did.

One of the great joys of falling in love is the feeling that the most extraordinary person in the entire world has chosen *you*. I remember being astonished when, after I pointed out my new boyfriend, Jamie, to my law school roommate, she admitted, "I've never seen him before." I honestly couldn't imagine that everyone's eyes weren't drawn to him every time he walked down the hallway or into the dining hall.

Over time, however, spouses start to take each other for granted. Jamie is my fate. He's my soul mate. He pervades my whole existence. So, of course, I often ignore him.

The more readily you respond to a spouse's bids for attention, the stronger your marriage—but it's easy to fall into bad habits. Too often I hear myself murmuring "Mmm-hmmm," with my eyes glued to the book I'm reading as Jamie makes a joke or starts a conversation. Also, marriage has a strange muffling effect on some kinds of deep communication. Most married people have probably had the experience of hearing their spouse make a startling revelation to a stranger at a barbecue; it's hard to have reflective, probing conversations during the tumult of daily life.

I'd fallen into the bad marriage habit of being less considerate of Jamie than I was of other people. As part of my resolution to "Give proofs of love," I tried to think of small treats or courtesies for Jamie. One night when some friends came over, after taking everyone else's drink order, I added, "How about you, Jamie? What would you like?" Usually I just worry about taking care of the guests, so Jamie looked surprised but pleased. His travel toiletry kit was falling apart, so I bought him a new one and loaded it with travel supplies. I left the new *Sports Illustrated* out on the table, so he'd see it when he walked in the door from work.

One way to make sure that you're paying attention to your spouse is to spend time alone together, and marriage experts universally advise that couples have frequent child-free "date nights." One of my happiness project challenges, however, was to figure out what recommendations to ignore, and I couldn't work up any enthusiasm for "date nights." Jamie and I seem to go out a lot, to various school, work, or friend functions, and we like to stay home when we can. I dreaded the thought of adding another item to the schedule.

Plus I figured Jamie would never go along with it.

Jamie surprised me when I floated the idea. "We can if you want," he said. "It might be fun to go see a movie or have dinner, the two of us. But we go out so much, it's nice to stay in." I agreed, but it made me happy that even though he didn't want to do it, he agreed with the goal.

In addition to ignoring some expert advice, I also sought the advice of nonexperts. One night, when my book group didn't have much to say about the book we'd picked, I asked for my friends' suggestions about marriage.

"You should both go to bed at the same time," said one friend. "No matter what, something good will come of it. You'll get more sleep or have sex or have a conversation."

"Before I got married, my boss told me that the secret to a strong marriage is to leave at least three things unsaid each day."

"My husband and I never criticize each other for more than one thing at a time."

"My Quaker grandparents, who were married seventy-two years, said that each married couple should have an outdoor game, like tennis or golf, and an indoor game, like Scrabble or gin, that they play together."

When I got home, I told Jamie that rule, and the next day he brought home a backgammon set.

I'd been working on giving proofs of love when I decided to push myself to the highest level of proof: a Week of Extreme Nice.

What was "Extreme Nice"? It was an extreme sport, like bungee jumping or skydiving, that stretched me beyond my ordinary efforts, that showed me new depths within myself. All done in the comfort of my own home. For a week, I was *extremely nice* to Jamie. No criticism! No snapping! No nagging! I even offered to drop his shoes off at the shoe-repair shop before he asked me!

Extreme Nice reminded me to aim for a high standard of behavior. It's not right that I show more consideration to my friends or family than to Jamie, the love of my life. We wouldn't be able to live together forever without a disagreement, but I should be able to go more than a week without nagging him. In a way, of course, the entire month of February was an exercise in Extreme Nice, because all my resolutions work Jamie's benefit. But for this week, I was going to take my niceness dramatic new level.

Too often I focused on the things that annoyed me: Jamie postponed making scheduling decisions; he didn't answer my e-mails; he didn't appreciate what I do to make our lives run smoothly. Instead, I should have thought about all the things I love about him. He's kind, funny, brilliant, thoughtful, loving, ambitious, sweet, a good father, son, and son-in-law, bizarrely well informed on a wide range of subjects, creative, hardworking, magnanimous. He kisses me and says, "I love you," every night before we go to sleep, he comes to my side at parties and puts his arm around me, he rarely shows irritation or criticizes me. He even has a full head of hair.

On the first morning of Extreme Nice, Jamie asked tentatively, "I'd like to get up and go to the gym and get it over with. Okay?" He's compulsive about going to the gym.

Instead of giving him a pained look or a grudging "Okay, but go ahead and go now so you can get back soon, we promised the girls we'd go to the park," I said, "Sure, no problem!"

It wasn't easy.

A moment of reframing helped. How would I feel if Jamie never wanted to go to the gym—or worse, if he *couldn't* go? I have a gorgeous, athletic husband. How *lucky* I am that he wants to go to the gym.

During the week of Extreme Nice, when Jamie sneaked into our bedroom to take a nap, I let him sleep while I made lunch for Eliza and Eleanor; I kept our bathroom tidy instead of leaving bottles and tubes scattered over the counter; he rented *The Aristocrats,* and I said, "Great!" I stopped leaving Popsicle wrappers all over the apartment. As pathetic as it is to report, each of these instances took considerable restraint on my part.

Because of Extreme Nice, when I discovered one night that Jamie had thrown away *The Economist* and the *Entertainment Weekly* that I hadn't read yet, I didn't badger him about it. When I woke up the next morning, I saw how insignificant it was and was relieved I hadn't indulged in a scene.

I'd always followed the adage "Don't let the sun go down on your anger," which meant, in practical terms, that I scrupulously aired every annoyance as soon as possible, to make sure I had my chance to vent my bad feelings before bedtime. I was surprised to learn from my research, however, that the well-known notion of anger catharsis is poppycock. There's no evidence for the belief that "letting off steam" is healthy or constructive. In fact, studies show that aggressively expressing anger doesn't relieve anger but amplifies it. On the other hand, not expressing anger often allows it to disappear without leaving ugly traces.

Extreme Nice also started me thinking about the degree to which Jamie and I accepted orders from each other. It's safe to say that married people spend a lot of time trying to coax each other into performing various chores, and the ability to cooperate in tackling daily tasks is a key component of a happy marriage. Often I wish I could tell Jamie, "Call the super" or "Unload the dishwasher," and have him obey me unhesitatingly. And I'm sure he wishes he could say, "Don't eat outside the kitchen" or "Find the keys to the basement storage room," and have *me* obey *him.* So I tried to do cheerfully whatever he asked me to do, without debate.

As the days went by, I did feel a bit of resentment when Jamie never seemed to notice that he was the winner of a Week of Extreme Nice. Then I realized that I should be *pleased* that he didn't notice, because it showed that the Week of Extreme Nice wasn't a shocking improvement over our regular, unextreme lives.

The Week of Extreme Nice proved the power of my commandment to "Act the way I want to feel" because I was treating Jamie extremely nicely, I found myself feeling more tender toward him. Nevertheless, although it was a valuable experiment, I was relieved when the week was over. I couldn't keep up the intensity of being that Nice. My tongue hurt because I'd bitten it so often.

·   ·   ·

As I was filling in my Resolutions Chart on the last afternoon of February, I was struck by the significance of the chart to my happiness project. The process of constantly reviewing my resolutions and holding myself accountable each day was already having a big effect on my behavior, and it wasn't even March yet. I'd made dozens of resolutions in my life—every New Year since I was nine or ten years old—but keeping the Resolutions Chart was allowing me to live up to my resolutions more faithfully than I'd even been able to do before. I'd heard the business school truism "You manage what you measure," and I could see how this phenomenon worked in my case.

The end of February brought me another important realization as well. For a long time, I'd been puzzling to come up with an overall theory of happiness, and one afternoon, after many false starts, I arrived at my earth-shattering happiness formula.

It hit me while I was on the subway. I was reading Bruno Frey and Alois Stutzer's *Happiness and Economics,* and I looked up for a moment to ponder the meaning of the sentence "It has been shown that pleasant affect, unpleasant affect, and life satisfaction are separable constructs." Along the same lines, I'd just read some research that showed that happiness and unhappiness (or, in more scientific terms, positive affect and negative affect) aren't opposite sides of the same emotion—they're distinct and rise and fall independently. Suddenly, as I thought about these ideas and about my own experience so far, everything slipped into place, and my happiness formula sprang into my mind with such a jolt that I felt as if the other subway riders must have been able to see a lightbulb appearing above my head.

To be happy, I need to think about feeling good, feeling bad, and feeling right.

So simple, yet so profound. It looks like something you might read on the cover of a glossy magazine, but it had taken enormous effort to come up with a framework that ordered and distilled everything I'd learned.

To be happy, I needed to generate more positive emotions, so that I increased the amount of joy, pleasure, enthusiasm, gratitude, intimacy, and friendship in my life. That wasn't hard to understand. I also needed to remove sources of bad feelings, so that I suffered less guilt, remorse, shame, anger, envy, boredom, and irritation. Also easy to understand. And apart from feeling more "good" and feeling less "bad," I saw that I also needed to consider *feeling right*.

"Feeling right" was a trickier concept: it was the feeling that I'm living the life I'm supposed to lead. In my own case, although I'd had a great experience as a lawyer, I'd been haunted by an uncomfortable feeling—that I wasn't doing what I was "supposed" to be doing. Now, though my writing career can be a source of "feeling bad" as well as "feeling good," I do "feel right."

"Feeling right" is about living the life that's right for you—in occupation, location, marital status, and so on. It's also about virtue: doing your duty, living up to the expectations you set for yourself. For some people, "feeling right" can also include less elevated considerations: achieving a certain job status or material standard of living.

After the first few minutes, the ecstasy of discovering my formula wore off, and I realized that it wasn't quite complete. It was lacking some important element. I searched for a way to account for the fact that people seem programmed to be striving constantly, to be stretching toward happiness. For example, we tend to think that we'll be slightly happier in the future than we are in the present. And a sense of purpose is very important to happiness. But my formula didn't account for these observations. I searched for the missing concept—was it striving? Advancement? Purpose? Hope? None of these words seemed right. Then I thought of a line from William Butler Yeats. "Happiness," wrote Yeats, "is neither virtue nor pleasure nor this thing nor that, but simply growth. We are happy when we are growing." Contemporary researchers make the same argument: that it isn't goal attainment but the process of striving after goals—that is, growth—that brings happiness.

Of course. Growth. Growth explains the happiness brought by training for a marathon, learning a new language, collecting stamps; by helping children learn to talk; by cooking your way through every recipe in a Julia Child cookbook. My father was a great tennis player and played a lot when I was growing up. At some point, he started playing golf and, over time, gave up tennis. I asked him why. "My tennis game," he explained, "was gradually getting worse, but my golf game is improving."

People are very adaptable, and we quickly adjust to a new life circumstance—for better or worse—and consider it normal. Although this helps us when our situation worsens, it means that when circumstances improve, we soon become hardened to new comforts or privileges. This "hedonic treadmill," as it's called, makes it easy to grow accustomed to some of the things that make you "feel good," such as a new car, a new job title, or air-conditioning, so that the good feeling wears off. An atmosphere of growth offsets that. You may soon take your new dining room table for granted, but tending your garden will give you fresh joy and surprise every spring. Growth is important in a spiritual sense, and I do think that material growth is gratifying as well. As much as folks insist that money can't buy happiness, for example, it's awfully nice to have more money this year than you had last year.

So I arrived at my final formula, and it struck me as so important that I named it the First Splendid Truth—I'd have to trust that I'd have at least one more Splendid Truth by the time the year was over. The First Splendid Truth: *To be happy, I need to think about feeling good, feeling bad, and feeling right, in an atmosphere of growth.*

I called Jamie the minute I got home. "At last!" I said. "I have my happiness formula! It's just one sentence long, and with it, I can tie together all the studies, all the loose ends that were driving me crazy."

"That's great!" said Jamie, very enthusiastically. Pause.

"Don't you want to hear the formula?" I hinted. I had decided not to expect Jamie to play the role of my female writing partner—but sometimes he just was going to have to do his best.

"Of course, right!" he said. "What's the formula?"

Well, he was trying. And maybe it was my imagination, but it seemed to me that now that I was trying harder, Jamie was trying harder, too. I couldn't put my finger on what was different exactly, but he seemed more loving. He wasn't much interested in talking about happiness—in fact, he felt like a bit of a martyr to my inexhaustible enthusiasm for the subject—but he had started replacing the dead lightbulbs without waiting for me to bug him, and he seemed to be answering my e-mails more diligently. He bought us the backgammon set. He asked me for my happiness formula.

When thinking about happiness in marriage, you may have an almost irresistible impulse to focus on your spouse, to emphasize how he or she should change in order to boost your happiness. But the fact is, you can't change anyone but yourself. A friend told me that her "marriage mantra" was "I love Leo, just as he is." I love Jamie just as he is. I can't make him do a better job of doing household chores, I can only stop myself from nagging—and that makes me happier. When you give up expecting a spouse to change (within reason), you lessen anger and resentment, and that creates a more loving atmosphere in a marriage.

3

MARCH

Aim Higher

WORK

- Launch a blog.
- Enjoy the fun of failure.
- Ask for help.
- Work smart.
- Enjoy now.

Happiness is a critical factor for work, and work is a critical factor for happiness. In one of those life-isn't-fair results, it turns out that the happy outperform the less happy. Happy people work more hours each week—and they work more in their free time, too. They tend to be more cooperative, less self-centered, and more willing to help other people—say, by sharing information or pitching in to help a colleague—and then, because they've helped others, others tend to help them. Also, they work better with others, because people prefer to be around happier people, who are also less likely to show the counterproductive behaviors of burnout, absenteeism, counter- and nonproductive work, work disputes, and retaliatory behavior than are less happy people.

Happier people also make more effective leaders. They perform better on managerial tasks such as leadership and mastery of information. They're viewed as more assertive and self-confident than less happy people. They're perceived to be more friendly, warmer, and even more *physically* attractive. A study showed that students who were happy as college freshmen were earning more money in their midthirties—without any wealth advantage to start. Being happy can make a big difference in your work life.

Of course, happiness also matters to work simply because work occupies so much of our time. A majority of Americans work seven or more hours each day, and time spent on vacation is shrinking. Also, work can be a source of many of the elements necessary for a happy life: the atmosphere of growth, social contact, fun, a sense of purpose, self-esteem, recognition.

Whenever I feel blue, working cheers me. Sometimes when I sink into a bad mood, Jamie says, "Why don't you go to your office for a while?" Even if I don't feel like working, once I plunge in, the encouraging feeling of getting something accomplished, the intellectual stimulation, and even the mere distraction lift me out of my crabbiness.

Because work is so crucial to happiness, another person's happiness project might well focus on choosing the right work. I, however, had already been through a major happiness quest career shift. I'd started out in law, and I'd had a great experience. But when my clerkship with Justice O'Connor drew to a close, I couldn't figure out what job I wanted next.

During this time, I visited the apartment of a friend who was in graduate school studying education, and I noticed several thick textbooks lying around her living room.

"Is this what they make you read for your program?" I asked, idly flipping through the dense, dull pages.

"Yes," she said, "but that's what I read in my spare time, anyhow."

For some reason, that casual answer shocked me to attention. What did *I* do in my spare time? I asked myself. As much as I liked clerking, I never spent one second more on legal subjects than I had to. For fun, I was writing a book (which would later become *Power Money Fame Sex*), and it occurred to me that perhaps I could write books for a living. Over the next several months, I became convinced that that was what I wanted to do.

I'm a very ambitious, competitive person, and it was wrenching to walk away from my legal credentials and start my career over from the beginning. Being editor in chief of *The Yale Law Journal*, winning a legal writing prize—inside the world of law, these credentials mattered a lot. Outside the world of law, they didn't matter at all. My ambition, however, was also a factor in leaving the law. I'd become convinced that passion was a critical factor in professional success. People who love their work bring an intensity and enthusiasm that's impossible to match through sheer diligence. I could see that in my co-clerks at the Supreme Court: they read law journals for fun, they talked about cases during their lunch hours, they felt energized by their efforts. I didn't.

Enthusiasm is more important to mastery than innate ability, it turns out, because the single most important element in developing an expertise is your willingness to practice. Therefore, career experts argue, you're better off pursuing a profession that comes easily and that you love, because that's where you'll be more eager to practice and thereby earn a competitive advantage.

I love writing, reading, research, note taking, analysis, and criticism. (Well, I don't actually love *writing*, but then practically no writer actually loves the writing part.) My past, when I thought back, was littered with clues that I wanted to be a writer. I'd written two novels, now locked in a drawer. I've always spent most of my free time reading. I take voluminous notes for no apparent reason. I majored in English. And the biggest clue: I was writing a book in my free time.

Why hadn't it occurred to me sooner to think about writing for a living? There are probably several reasons, but the most important is the fact that it's often hard for me to "Be Gretchen." Erasmus observed, "The chief happiness for a man is to be what he is," and although that sounds easy enough, it has always been difficult for me. That's why "Be Gretchen" is the first of my Twelve Commandments.

I have an idea of who I *wish* I were, and that obscures my understanding of who I actually am. Sometimes I pretend even to myself to enjoy activities that I don't really enjoy, such as shopping, or to be interested in subjects that don't much interest me, such as foreign policy. And worse, I ignore my true desires and interests.

"Fake it till you feel it" was an effective way to change my mood in the moment, as I followed my Third Commandment to "Act the way I want to feel," but it isn't a good governing principle for major life decisions. By "faking it," I could become engaged in subjects and activities that didn't particularly interest me, but that enthusiasm paled in comparison to the passion I felt for the subjects in which I naturally found myself interested.

Self-knowledge is one of the qualities that I admire most in my sister. Elizabeth never questions her own nature. In school, I played field hockey (even though I was a terrible athlete), took physics (which I hated), and wished that I were more into music (I wasn't). Not Elizabeth. She has always been unswervingly true to herself. Unlike many smart people, for example, she never apologized for her love of commercial fiction or television—an attitude vindicated by the fact that she started her career writing commercial young-adult novels (my favorites among her early works include *The Truth About Love* and *Prom Season*) and then became a TV writer. I sometimes wonder if I would have become a writer if Elizabeth hadn't become a writer first. I remember talking to her while I was struggling with my decision.

"I worry about feeling *legitimate*," I confessed. "Working in something like law or finance or politics would make me feel legitimate."

I expected her to say something like "Writing *is* legitimate" or "You can switch to something else if you don't like it," but she was far more astute.

"You know," she said, "you've always had this desire for legitimacy, and you'll have it forever. It's probably why you went to law school. But should you let it determine your next job?"

"Well . . ."

"You've already done highly legitimate things, like clerking on the Supreme Court, but do you feel legitimate?"

"Not really."

"So you probably never will. Okay. Just don't let that drive your decisions."

I took one more legal job—at the Federal Communications Commission—then decided to try to start a career as a writer. It was daunting to take the first step toward an unfamiliar, untested career, but this switch was made easier by the fact that Jamie and I were moving from Washington, D.C., to New York City and Jamie had decided to make a career shift, too. While I'd been reading a book about how to write a book proposal, he'd been taking a night class in financial accounting. I still remember the day we decided to stop paying our bar fees.

Leaving law to become a writer was the most important step I ever took to "Be Gretchen." I'd decided to do what I wanted to do, and I ignored options that, no matter how enticing they might be for other people, weren't right for me.

So if my goals for this month didn't include a reevaluation of my work, what did they include? I wanted to bring more energy, creativity, and efficiency to my work life. No one loves the familiar and the routine more than I do, but I decided to stretch myself to tackle a work challenge that would force me to navigate unfamiliar territory. I would think about ways to work more efficiently by packing more reading and writing into each day—and also more time spent with other people. And perhaps most important, I would take care to remind myself to remember how lucky I was to be as eager for Monday mornings as I was for Friday afternoons.

LAUNCH A BLOG.

My research had revealed that challenge and novelty are key elements to happiness. The brain is stimulated by surprise, and successfully dealing with an unexpected situation gives a powerful sense of satisfaction. If you do new things—visit a museum for the first time, learn a new game, travel to a new place, meet new people—you're more apt to feel happy than people who stick to more familiar activities.

This is one of the many paradoxes of happiness: we seek to control our lives, but the unfamiliar and the unexpected are important sources of happiness. What's more, because novelty requires more work from the brain, dealing with novel situations evokes more intense emotional responses and makes the passage of time seem slower and richer. After the birth of his first child, a friend told me, "One reason that I love having a new baby is that time has slowed down. My wife and I felt like our lives were speeding by, but the minute Clara was born, it was like time stood still. Each week has been like an era, so much happens."

So how was I going to incorporate novelty and challenge into my happiness project? I wanted to choose a goal related to other things I liked to do—no violin lessons or salsa-dancing classes for me, no matter what the experts said. At the point when I was trying to figure this out, my literary agent suggested that I start a blog.

"Oh, I wouldn't know how to do that," I answered. "It's too technical. I can barely figure out how to use TiVo."

"These days, it's pretty easy to set up a blog," she said. "Think about it. I bet you'd really enjoy it."

She'd planted the idea in my mind, and I decided to give it a try. Reading the research on the importance of challenge to happiness had convinced me that I should stretch myself to tackle a large, difficult goal. Not only that—if I did manage to start a blog, it would connect me with other people with similar interests, give me a source of self-expression, and allow me a way to try to convince others to start their own happiness projects.

But despite the promise of a big happiness payoff, I felt apprehensive. I worried about the time and effort a blog would consume, when I already felt pressed for time and mental energy. It would require me to make decisions that I didn't feel equipped to make. It would expose me daily to public criticism and failure. It would make me feel stupid.

Then, around this time, I happened to run into two acquaintances who had blogs of their own, and together they gave me the few pieces of key advice that I needed to get started. Maybe these providential meetings were a product of cosmic harmony—"when the student is ready, the teacher appears"—or maybe they were examples of the efficacy of articulating my goals. Or maybe I just got lucky.

"Use TypePad," my first adviser suggested. "That's what I use." She kept a blog about restaurants and recipes. "And keep it simple—you can add features later, as you figure out what you're doing."

"Post every day, that's absolutely key," insisted my second adviser, who ran a law blog. Oh dear, I thought with dismay, I'd planned to post three times a week. "And when you send an e-mail to alert someone to a post you've made, include the entire text of your post, not just the link."

"Okay," I answered uncertainly. "So, to follow up on that . . . sounds like I should plan to send e-mails about my posts to other bloggers?" Such a thing had never occurred to me.

"Um, *yes*," he answered.

After three weeks of confused poking around on the Internet, cautiously, almost furtively, I opened an account on TypePad. Just this step—before I'd even made one decision about the blog—filled me with anxiety and elation. I kept reminding myself of one of my Secrets of Adulthood: "People don't notice your mistakes as much as you think." Even if I did something wrong on the blog, it wouldn't be a disaster.

Each day, I spent an hour or so working on it, and slowly the blank template supplied by TypePad started to take shape. I filled in the

"About" section that described me. I wrote a description of the blog to appear in the header. I put in links to my books. I added my Twelve Commandments. I sort of figured out what "RSS" was and added an RSS button. Finally, on March 27, I took a deep breath and wrote a "blog post" for the first time.

Today is the first day of the Happiness Project blog.

Now, what is the Happiness Project?

One afternoon, not too long ago, I realized with a jolt that I was allowing my life to flash by without facing a critical question: was I happy?

From that moment, I couldn't stop thinking about happiness. Was it mostly a product of temperament? Could I take steps to be happier? What did it even mean to be "happy"?

So The Happiness Project blog is my memoir of one year in which I test-drive every principle, tip, theory, and research-study result I can find, from Aristotle to St. Thérèse to Benjamin Franklin to Martin Seligman to Oprah. What advice actually works?

That very fact that I've started this blog makes me happy, because now I've achieved one of my chief goals this month (just in time, too). I set myself a task, worked toward it, and achieved it.

Preparing to launch the blog reminded me of two of my Secrets of Adulthood:

1. It's okay to ask for help.
   When trying to get started, I floundered until I thought to do the obvious: ask for advice from friends with blogs.
2. By doing a little bit each day, you can get a lot accomplished.
   We tend to overestimate how much we can accomplish in an hour or a week and underestimate how much we can accomplish in a month or a year, by doing just a little bit each day. "A small daily task, if it be really daily, will beat the labours of a spasmodic Hercules."—Anthony Trollope

Since then I've posted six days a week, every week.

Seeing that first post hit the screen gave me an enormous rush of triumph. I couldn't believe I'd managed to do it. The experts had certainly been correct about the happiness effect of novelty, challenge, and an atmosphere of growth.

However, I quickly discovered that even after I'd launched it, my blog remained an excellent source of happiness through challenge. To put it more baldly, it often drove me crazy with frustration. The more I did, the more I wanted to do. I wanted to add images. I wanted to drop the word "typepad" out of my URL. I wanted to podcast. I wanted to add live links to my TypeLists. As I was trying to solve these problems, I'd find myself overwhelmed with nasty feelings of ignorance and helplessness. The image wasn't loading. The images were too small. The links weren't working. Suddenly every word was underlined.

As I struggled to master these tasks, I felt rushed and anxious when I couldn't figure something out right away, until I hit upon a way to help myself slow down: I "put myself in jail." "I'm in jail," I'd tell myself. "I'm locked up with nowhere to go and nothing to do except the task in front of me. It doesn't matter how long it takes, I have all the time I want." Of course, this wasn't true, but telling myself that I had all the time I needed helped me to focus.

As I worked on the blog, I often had to remind myself to "Be Gretchen" and to be faithful to *my* vision of my project. Many kind, smart people gave me advice. One person encouraged me to "stick with irony," and several people suggested that I comment frequently on news items. One friend, in all sympathy, told me that the phrase "The Happiness Project" was no good and made the pitch for "Oh Happy Day."

"I can't really imagine changing the name," I said uncertainly. "It's been the Happiness Project right from the first moment I thought of the idea."

He shook his head. "It's not too late to change!"

Another friend had a different suggestion. "You should explore your conflicts with your mother," he urged. "Everyone's interested in that."

"Good point . . . but I don't really have much conflict with my mother," I said, regretting my close relationship with my mother for the first time ever.

"Huh," he answered. Clearly he thought I was in massive denial.

All these suggestions were sound and very well intentioned, and each time I got a new piece of advice, I'd worry; one of the biggest challenges posed by my blog was the doubt raised by my own inner critic. Should I recast the Happiness Project? Did the word "project" sound difficult and unappealing? Was it egocentric to write so much about my own experience? Was my earnest tone too preachy? Very likely! But I didn't want to be like the novelist who spent so much time rewriting his first sentence that he never wrote his second. If I wanted to get anything accomplished, I needed to keep pushing ahead without constantly second-guessing myself.

The gratifying thing was that once I'd launched it, people responded enthusiastically to my blog just as it was. At first I didn't even know enough to be able to track my traffic, but little by little, I figured out how to monitor it. I remember the shock of delight I got when I'd checked Technorati, the leading blog monitor, for the first time—and discovered that I'd made it into the Technorati Top 5000, without even knowing it. Because I'd launched the blog as part of my personal happiness project, I hadn't expected it actually to attract an audience, so its slowly expanding success was an unanticipated pleasure—and a great contributor to the atmosphere of growth in my life.

One reason that challenge brings happiness is that it allows you to expand your self-definition. You become larger. Suddenly you can do yoga or make homemade beer or speak a decent amount of Spanish. Research shows that the more elements make up your identity, the less threatening it is when any one element is threatened. Losing your job might be a blow to your self-esteem, but the fact that you lead your local alumni association gives you a comforting source of self-respect. Also, a new identity brings you into contact with new people and new experiences, which are also powerful sources of happiness.

That's how it worked for me. My blog gave me a new identity, new skills, a new set of colleagues, and a way to connect with people who shared my interest. I'd expanded my vision of the kind of writer I could be. I had become a blogger.

ENJOY THE FUN OF FAILURE.

As I was pushing myself on the blog, I wanted to extend myself in other parts of my work, too. I wanted to nudge myself out of my comfort zone into my stretch zone. But wasn't that resolution inconsistent with "Be Gretchen"?

Yes and no. I wanted to develop *in my natural direction*. W. H. Auden articulated this tension beautifully: "Between the ages of twenty and forty we are engaged in the process of discovering who we are, which involves learning the difference between accidental limitations which it is our duty to outgrow and the necessary limitations of our nature beyond which we cannot trespass with impunity." Starting my blog, for example, made me feel anxious, but deep down, I knew I could do it and would very likely enjoy it, once I'd overcome the initial intimidating hurdles.

Pushing myself, I knew, would cause me serious discomfort. It's a Secret of Adulthood: Happiness doesn't always make you feel happy. When I thought about why I was sometimes reluctant to push myself, I realized that it was because I was afraid of failure—but in order to have more success, I needed to be willing to accept more failure. I remembered the words of Robert Browning: "Ah, but a man's reach should exceed his grasp, or what's a heaven for?"

To counteract this fear, I told myself, *"I enjoy the fun of failure."* It's *fun* to fail, I kept repeating. It's part of being ambitious; it's part of being creative. If something is worth doing, it's worth doing badly.

And in fact this mantra helped me. The words "the fun of failure" released me from my sense of dread. And I did fail. I applied to the prestigious writing colony Yaddo, and I wasn't accepted. I pitched a column to *The Wall Street Journal,* and although it looked promising, the editors ultimately told me there was no room for it. I was dismayed by the sales report for *Forty Ways to Look at JFK,* which didn't sell nearly as well as *Forty Ways to Look at Winston Churchill* ("I don't want to be flip," my agent said comfortingly, "but maybe you can use this disappointment for your happiness project"). I talked to a friend about starting a biography reading group, but the idea fizzled out. I submitted an essay for the back page of *The New York Times Book Review,* but it was rejected. I talked to a friend about teaming up to do webcasts, but that didn't work out. I sent innumerable e-mails to try to get links to my blog, most of which were ignored.

At the same time, risking failure gave me the opportunity to score some successes. I was invited to contribute to the enormously popular Huffington Post blog, and I started to get picked up by huge blogs such as Lifehacker, Lifehack, and Marginal Revolution. I was invited to join the LifeRemix blog network. I wrote a piece about money and happiness for *The Wall Street Journal.* I started going to a monthly writers' meeting. In the past, I think I might have shied away from pursuing these goals, because I wouldn't have wanted to deal with rejection.

Friends told me about similar shifts in thinking that had helped them. One friend said that in his office, whenever crisis strikes, he tells everyone, "This is the *fun* part!" Although I wasn't even halfway through my happiness project, I could already appreciate that feeling happier made it easier for me to risk failure—or rather, made it easier for me to embrace the *fun of failure.* A goal like launching a blog was much easier to tackle when I was in a happy frame of mind. Then, once the blog was launched, it became an engine of happiness itself.

ASK FOR HELP.

Despite the fact that "It's okay to ask for help" is one of my Secrets of Adulthood, I constantly had to remind myself to ask for help. I often had the immature and counterproductive impulse to pretend to know things that I didn't know.

Perhaps because I was constantly reviewing my goal and my resolutions in March, I came up with a novel way to ask for help: I pulled together a strategy group. I had recently met two writers, Michael and Marci. Each of us was working on a book, each of us was trying to be smart about our project and our overall career, each of us was an extroverted type working alone much of the time and eager for conversation. When I discovered that, coincidentally, Michael and Marci knew each other, I had an inspiration.

In February, I'd identified a problem. I wished I had a writing partner, someone with whom I could discuss writing and career strategy. I'd let Jamie off the hook, mostly, but maybe Michael, Marci, and I could form a group that would help fill that need. Benjamin Franklin, along with twelve friends, formed a club for mutual improvement that met weekly for forty years. Maybe we could form a group, with a slightly narrower mission than "mutual improvement."

I tentatively floated the idea in an e-mail to Michael and Marci. To my surprised gratification, they both immediately embraced the idea. Michael suggested a structure for our meetings. "How about every six weeks, for two hours? Twenty minutes of catch-up conversation, then thirty minutes each to talk about our individual concerns, with a ten-minute break in the middle." Marci and I embraced this highly defined structure, which was a good indication that the three of us were well matched.

"And we should give ourselves a name," Marci said, only half joking. "And what kind of group *are* we?"

We decided to call ourselves MGM, after our initials, and we decided that we were a "writers' strategy group." We didn't talk about actual writing very much, though sometimes one of us circulated a chapter or two; we spent most of our time talking about strategy. Should Michael hire a virtual assistant? Was Marci spending too much time touring for her book? Should Gretchen send out a happiness project newsletter? The group was an instant success. Sitting with two other energetic, encouraging, smart writers for a few hours exhilarated me. Also, as with groups such as Weight Watchers and Alcoholics Anonymous, and with my Resolutions Chart, we gave one another a sense of accountability.

Only after we'd met a few times did I stumble on some career-building articles that suggested forming a "community of aspirants" or, in less elaborate terms, a "goals group." Shoot, I'd thought I'd invented the idea.

WORK SMART.

Turning aside from lofty ambition to prosaic details, I figured that I'd work better if I spent some time thinking about how to boost my efficiency. At the very least, I could make my day feel calmer. I felt as if I never had enough time for all the work I wanted to do.

I started paying close attention to how I spent my days. Were there pockets of time that I was wasting? Could I find the equivalent of loose change under the sofa, like an overlooked habit of watching a *Law & Order* rerun every night? Alas, I was running pretty close to efficiency. If I was watching a rerun, I was paying bills at the same time. Nevertheless, considering the way I spent my time yielded some good results.

I changed the way I thought about productive time. In the past, I'd believed that I couldn't sit down and write productively unless I had at least three or four hours with no interruptions. Often, that was hard to arrange, and I felt inefficient and frustrated. To test that assumption, for a few weeks, I added a note on my Resolutions Chart to remind myself of what I'd worked on each day. It didn't take me long to see that I did better when I had *less* time. Not several hours but ninety minutes turned out to be the optimally efficient length of time—long enough for me to get some real work done but not so long that I started to goof off or lose concentration. As a consequence, I began to organize my day into ninety-minute writing blocks, separated by different non-writing tasks: exercising, meeting someone, making a phone call, tinkering with my blog.

Also, although I'd always considered fifteen minutes to be too short a period in which to get anything done, I started to push myself to squeeze in an extra fifteen minutes somewhere during the day. This was often wedged in between two appointments or at the very end of the workday. It did, indeed, boost my productivity. Fifteen minutes a day, several times a week, was not insignificant—fifteen minutes was long enough to draft a blog post, to make notes on research that I'd been reading, or to answer some e-mails. As I'd found in January, when I started applying the "one-minute rule" and the "evening tidy-up," small efforts, made consistently, brought significant results. I felt more in control of my workload.

I halfheartedly considered trying to get up early each day to work for an hour or so before my family awoke. Anthony Trollope, the nineteenth-century writer who managed to be a prolific novelist while also revolutionizing the British postal system, attributed his productivity to his habit of starting his day at 5:30 A.M. In his *Autobiography,* he notes, "An old groom, whose business it was to call me, and to whom I paid £5 extra for the duty, allowed himself no mercy." Which suggests that it's not easy to get out of bed at 5:30 A.M.—especially if you don't have an old groom on hand to shake you awake. Nope, 6:30 A.M. was as early as I could push it.

I found a small way to make my office more pleasant. At a party at someone's house, I smelled a scent so lovely that I walked around the room sniffing until I found the source: a Jo Malone Orange Blossom candle. Although I never buy this sort of thing, when I got home, I ent straight to the computer and ordered one for myself, and I started the habit of burning it in my office. Though I sometimes mocked the scented-candle-pushing brand of happiness building, I discovered that there is something nice about working in an office with a candle burning. It's like seeing snow falling outside the window or having a dog snoozing on the carpet beside you. It's a kind of silent presence in the room and very pleasant.

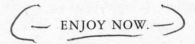

ENJOY NOW.

As I worked, and especially when I was pushing myself to do things that made me slightly uncomfortable, I kept reminding myself of my resolution to "Enjoy now." As a writer, I often found myself imagining some happy future: "When I sell this proposal . . ." or "When this book comes out . . ."

In his book *Happier,* Tal Ben-Shahar describes the "arrival fallacy," the belief that when you arrive at a certain destination, you'll be happy. (Other fallacies include the "floating world fallacy," the belief that immediate pleasure, cut off from future purpose, can bring happiness, and the "nihilism fallacy," the belief that it's not possible to become happier.) The arrival fallacy is a fallacy because, though you may anticipate great happiness in arrival, arriving rarely makes you as happy as you anticipate.

First of all, by the time you've arrived at your destination, you're expecting to reach it, so it has already been incorporated into your happiness. Also, arrival often brings more work and responsibility. It's rare to achieve something (other than winning an award) that brings unadulterated pleasure without added concerns. Having a baby. Getting a promotion. Buying a house. You look forward to reaching these destinations, but once you've reached them, they bring emotions other than sheer happiness. And of course, arriving at one goal usually reveals another, yet more challenging goal. Publishing the first book means it's time to start the second. There's another hill to climb. The challenge, therefore, is to take pleasure in the "atmosphere of growth," in the gradual progress made toward a goal, in the present. The unpoetic name for this very powerful source of happiness is "pre-goal-attainment positive affect."

When I find myself focusing overmuch on the anticipated future happiness of arriving at a certain goal, I remind myself to "Enjoy now." If I can enjoy the present, I don't need to count on the happiness that is (or isn't) waiting for me in the future. The fun part doesn't come later, *now* is the fun part. That's another reason I feel lucky to enjoy my work so much. If you're doing something that you don't enjoy and you don't have the gratification of success, failure is particularly painful. But doing what you love is itself the reward.

When I thought back on the experience of writing my Churchill biography, for example, the most thrilling moment came when I was sitting at a study table at the library where I do most of my writing and I read two lines from Churchill's speech to the House of Commons on June 4, 1940: "We shall go on to the end . . . we shall defend our island, whatever the cost may be." As I read, the thought occurred to me, "Churchill's life fits the pattern of classical tragedy." This realization gave me such an ecstatic shock of recognition that tears welled up in my eyes. I spent the next several days testing my theory, and the more I read, the more excited I became. The requirements of a classical tragedy are very stringent, yet I was able to prove that Churchill's life met every one of them. Ah, *that* was the fun part.

But the arrival fallacy doesn't mean that pursuing goals isn't a route to happiness. To the contrary. The goal is necessary, just as is the process toward the goal. Friedrich Nietzsche explained it well: "The end of a melody is not its goal; but nonetheless, if the melody had not reached its end it would not have reached its goal either. A parable."

To enjoy now, there was something else I was going to have to master: my dread of criticism. Too much concern about whether I was getting praise or blame, too much anticipatory anxiety about what my detrac tors would say—those kinds of fears spoiled my pleasure in my work and, what's more, probably weakened my work.

I'd had a chance to tackle this very issue, during my preparation stage for the happiness project, when *The Washington Post* published a critical review of my biography *Forty Ways to Look at JFK*. At that point, I'd learned a lot of happiness theories and I'd identified my Twelve Commandments, but I hadn't put much into practice.

The review made me feel depressed, defensive, and angry; I wished that I felt secure, open to criticism, with benevolent feelings toward the reviewer. I decided to apply my Third Commandment, to "Act the way I want to feel." Would it really work in this extreme case? I made myself do something I did *not* want to do. I sent a friendly e-mail to the reviewer, in order to show *myself* that I was confident enough to take criticism graciously and able to respond without attack or self-justification. It took me a very, very long time to compose that e-mail. But guess what—it worked. The minute I sent it, I felt better.

Hello David Greenberg—

As you can imagine, I read with interest your review of my book on Wednesday.

While writing, I have the disheartening habit of composing negative reviews—imagining how I'd criticize the very work I'm doing. Your review hit three of my dark themes—gimmick, arbitrary, obvious. You criticized me most where I criticized myself. In brighter moments, I was satisfied that I captured some of the insight I felt I gained into Kennedy, and I'm sorry I wasn't able to convey that to you.

If I write another "forty ways" biography, I'm sure I'll benefit from your comments. For example, I debated about whether to reiterate the material from my Churchill book about why the number "forty," the tradition of multiple ways of seeing (Wallace Stevens, Monet, *Rashomon*—alas, I didn't read Julian Barnes's brilliant *Flaubert's Parrot* until after I'd written my Churchill book), etc.—but it struck me as somehow pompous to go over all that again. Now I see that of course it's frustrating to the reader not to see that argument set forth afresh.

Good luck with your work, and best wishes, Gretchen Rubin

The minute I pushed "send," I felt terrific. No matter what David Greenberg did, I'd changed myself. I felt magnanimous, open to criticism, sending good wishes to someone who had hurt me. I didn't even care if I got a reply. But I did. I got a very nice response.

> Dear Gretchen (if I may),
>
> Thanks for your note. I admire and applaud you for taking the review in stride and for making the overture to me. I know that when I received mixed or critical reviews of my book, I certainly didn't react with such aplomb. But on such occasions, more experienced authors reminded me that any review is just one person's opinion, and in the end the reviews vanish with the next day's papers while the books endure (which is why we write books, in part). In any event, whether or not you felt my comments were apt, I hope you considered the tone and treatment to be respectful and fair.
>
> Again, it was good of you to write, and I return the good wishes to you in your work and pursuits.
>
> Sincerely,
>
> David Greenberg

Having an effective strategy to deal with criticism of my work made it easier to enjoy the process of working. Also, this exchange had an added benefit, one that I, as the one being reviewed, didn't consider at first. We often dislike those whom we've hurt, and I bet David Greenberg wasn't very pleased to see my name pop up in his e-mail in-box. By initiating a friendly exchange, I showed that I bore no hard feelings and let him off the hook. If we were ever introduced at some cocktail party, we could meet on friendly terms.

Nevertheless, even while I was writing about happiness and focused precisely on the issue of handling criticism, I never did manage entirely to "Enjoy now" with no anxiety about the future. I spent a lot of time arguing with imaginary critics of my happiness project.

"You have it easy," one whispered in my ear. "No cocaine, no abuse, no cancer, no divorce, no three-hundred-pound weight loss . . . you didn't even have to quit smoking!"

"What about the millions of people who go to bed hungry?" another added. "What about people who suffer from real depression?"

"You don't care about plumbing the depths of your psyche."

"You're not spiritual enough."

"The idea of a one-year experiment is stale."

"You just talk about yourself."

Oh, well, I told myself, if it's not one thing, it's another. If I do my project my way, I'm unspiritual and gimmicky; if I tried to do it a different way, I'd be inauthentic and fake. Might as well "Be Gretchen."

March's focus on work and happiness highlighted a tricky issue: the relationship between ambition and happiness. There's a common belief that happiness and ambition are incompatible. Many ambitious people I've known seem eager to claim that they aren't happy, almost as a way to emphasize their zeal, in echo of Andrew Carnegie's observation "Show me a contented man, and I'll show you a failure."

Perhaps the happiness-thwarting feelings of dissatisfaction, competitiveness, and jealousy are necessary goads for ambition. If I remained ambitious, was it impossible to be happy? If my project made me happier, would I become complacent? Was the arrival fallacy an important mechanism to keep me striving?

Studies show that many creative, influential people in the arts and public life score above average in "neuroticism" (i.e., they have a greater propensity to experience negative emotions); this discontent arguably urges them to higher achievement. Other studies, however, show that people tend to think more flexibly and with more complexity when they're feeling happy.

But whatever a wide-ranging study might show about the connection between ambition and happiness generally, I realized that for my own part, I was much more likely to take risks, reach out to others, and expose myself to rejection and failure when I felt happy. When I felt unhappy, I felt defensive, touchy, and self-conscious. For example, if I'd been feeling unhappy, I doubt I would have proposed forming a writers' strategy group. I wouldn't have wanted to open myself up to rejection or failure.

"So," Jamie asked one night at the end of March, as we were getting ready for bed, "do you think your project is making any difference?"

"Oh yes," I said without hesitation, "it's working. Can't you see a change?"

"I *think* so," he said. "But it's hard to tell from the outside. You've always seemed pretty happy to me."

I was pleased to hear him say that, because the more I learned about happiness, the more I realized how much my happiness influenced the people around me.

"I feel a little blue today myself," he sighed.

"You do? Why?" I said, crossing the room to put my arms around him. (As I'd learned last month, a hug is cheering.)

"I don't know. I just felt low all day."

I opened my mouth to start firing probing questions, but it was obvious that Jamie didn't really feel like talking.

"Well," I said instead, "let's turn off the light. If you're feeling down, you'll feel better after a good night's sleep."

"Did you read a study about that?"

"Nope, I offer that little nugget of wisdom on my own authority."

"Well," he said, "I think you're right. Let's go to sleep."

It worked.

4

[APRIL]
(*Lighten Up*)

PARENTHOOD

- Sing in the morning.
- Acknowledge the reality of people's feelings.
- Be a treasure house of happy memories.
- Take time for projects.

M y children are a tremendous source of happiness. They've given me some of the high points of my life and also many of the small moments that make the days happier. I'm not alone in this. Many people have told me that the very happiest moments of their lives have been the births of their children.

Of course, my children are also a tremendous source of worry, irritation, expense, inconvenience, and lost sleep. In fact, some happiness experts argue that although parents—like me—insist that their children are a major source of happiness, this belief isn't true. One study that examined a group of women's emotions during their daily activities showed that they found "child care" only slightly more pleasant than commuting. Marital satisfaction nose-dives after the first child is born and picks up again once the children leave home. From my own experience, I knew that Jamie and I squabbled far more often once we had kids, we had fewer adventures, and we had less time for each other.

Nevertheless, despite these findings, I had to reject the experts' argument that children don't bring happiness. Because they do. Not always in a moment-to-moment way, perhaps, but in a more profound way. After all, in a poll where people were asked, "What one thing in life has brought you the greatest happiness?" the most common answer was "children" or "grandchildren" or both. Were all these people mired in self-deception?

In many ways, the happiness of having children falls into the kind of happiness that could be called fog happiness. Fog is elusive. Fog surrounds you and transforms the atmosphere, but when you try to examine it, it vanishes. Fog happiness is the kind of happiness you get from activities that, closely examined, don't really seem to bring much happiness at all— yet somehow they do.

I identified fog happiness during a party. My host was bustling around the kitchen, juggling the preparation and presentation of the three major dishes he was serving to thirty people.

"Are you having fun at your own party?" I asked him, when I probably should have gotten out of his way.

"Mm, not really right now," he said distractedly. "I'll have fun when it's over." Really, when? I wondered. Doing the dishes? Rearranging the furniture? Carrying sticky bottles of wine to the recycling bin? Where and when, exactly, was the fun?

That started me thinking. Many activities that I consider enjoyable aren't much fun while they're happening—or ahead of time or afterward. Throwing a party. Giving a performance. Writing. When I stop to analyze my emotions during the various stages of these activities, I see procrastination, dread, anxiety, nervousness, annoyance at having to do errands and busywork, irritation, distraction, time pressure, and anticlimax. Yet these activities undoubtedly make me "happy." And so it is with raising children. At any one time, the negative may swamp the positive, and I might wish I were doing something else. Nevertheless, the experience of having children gives me tremendous fog happiness. It surrounds me, I see it everywhere, despite the fact that when I zoom in on any particular moment, it can be hard to identify.

Before I actually gave birth, the aspect of parenthood that intimidated me most was its irreversibility. Spouse, job, work, location—most of the big decisions in life can be reconsidered. Change might be difficult and painful, but it's possible. But a baby is different. A baby is irrevocable. Once Eliza was born, however, I never gave another thought to the irreversibility of parenthood. I sometimes miss the freedom and leisure of my pre-Mommy days, but I never regret having children; instead, I worry about being a good enough parent. My standards for parenting aren't especially high: I never fuss much about whether my daughters' food is organic or whether their rooms are tidy. But when I started my happiness project, I was uneasy about the fact that I wasn't living up to my own standard of behavior. I lost my temper, I didn't make enough time for fun, I knew I didn't appreciate enough this fleeting time in my children's lives. Though the stages of diapers and dress-up clothes and car seats seem interminable, they pass quickly, and too often, I was so focused on checking off the items of my to-do list that I forgot what really mattered.

Eliza, bright-eyed and snaggle-toothed at seven years old, is even-tempered, loving, and oddly sensible for a child. She's wildly creative and loves any kind of imaginative play or homemade project. Apart from the occasional histrionic sulking fit, she's a delight. Eleanor, at age one, with her dimples, her big blue eyes, and her never-growing hair, is a darling toddler. She has a wide emotional range—she laughs easily, and she cries easily. She's friendly to everyone, fearless, very determined, and already frustrated by not being able to keep up with Eliza.

My goal for April, the month dedicated to parenthood? To become more tender and playful with my two daughters. I wanted a peaceful, cheerful, even joyous atmosphere at home—and I knew that nagging and yelling weren't the way to achieve that. I had two healthy, affectionate little girls, and I wanted my actions as a parent to rise to the level of that good fortune. I wanted to stop my quick bursts of temper—I indulged in that behavior all too often, and then, because it made me feel bad, I behaved even worse. I wanted to be more lighthearted. I wanted to take steps to preserve the happy memories from this time.

Eliza was old enough to grasp, dimly, that I was writing a book about happiness, but I didn't tell her that I was working on my parenting skills. As a child, I would have been shocked to learn that my parents gave any thought to how they behaved as parents; they seemed all-wise, practically all-powerful, without any self-doubt. Eliza, I figured, would be unnerved by the notion that I was questioning my actions as a mother.

But although I didn't tell her what I was doing, April Fool's Day conveniently presented me with an opportunity to keep some of my resolutions on the very first day of the month.

The night before, I'd put a bowl of Cheerios and milk in the freezer, and on the morning of April 1, I presented it to Eliza with a spoon—and watched as she tried, unsuccessfully, to dig in. Her puzzled look was hilarious.

"April Fool's!" I said.

"Really?" she answered, thrilled. "It's a real April Fool's joke? Great!" She examined the bowl closely, then ran to show it to Jamie. She got a big kick out of the prank.

The night before, I'd already gotten into bed when I realized that I'd forgotten to prepare the bowl, and I'd been tempted to drop the whole idea. I remembered my goals for April, though, and hauled myself out of bed. When morning came, I was so happy that I'd taken the time to set up the joke. The fact is, life is more fun when I keep my resolutions.

SING IN THE MORNING.

In a family, it's worth the effort to find ways to get mornings running smoothly, because while mornings set the tone for everyone's days, they also tend to be stressful as adults try to get themselves organized while also chivvying their children to get ready. From a conversation with Eliza, I got the idea of my resolution to "Sing in the morning."

"What did you do at school today?" I'd asked her.

"We talked about how our parents wake us up in the morning."

"What did you say?" I prodded, with curiosity and trepidation.

"With a good-morning song."

Why she said this, I don't know, because I'd done that only a few times in her whole life. After hearing her comment, though, I vowed to make a habit of it. (This conversation also reminded me that just as adults counsel themselves not to do anything that they wouldn't want reported in the newspaper, parents shouldn't do anything they wouldn't want featured in an essay displayed on the wall for Parent Night.)

As soon as I started, I saw that singing in the morning really had a cheering effect. I'd become a true believer of the "Act the way I want to feel" commandment; by *acting* happy, I made myself *feel* happy. After singing a verse of "I've Got a Golden Ticket," I found it easier to resist slipping into a hectoring tone.

Singing in the morning reminded me to follow my Ninth Commandment, to "Lighten up." I tried to free-ride off my children's laughter—Eleanor especially has always been unusually quick to laugh, even for a little kid—by pushing myself to enter into the mood, to have at least one moment of pure fun with Eliza and Eleanor each day, to laugh at Jamie's playfulness, and to take a light tone even when I'm chastising, nagging, or fending off complaints.

Easier said than done. On day three of my resolution, I woke up with a swollen, sore eyelid. I'm casual about most health-related matters, but because I'm so nearsighted that I'm legally blind, I take any eye problem very seriously. I'm prone to sties, but this didn't look like a sty.

Singing in the morning was the farthest thing from my mind.

Because Jamie was traveling on business, I couldn't leave the girls with him while I did some amateur medical diagnosis. Eliza is allowed to watch cartoons in the morning until Eleanor comes to the kitchen (I know, I shouldn't let her, but I do), so I sent her to the TV and left Eleanor singing to herself in her crib while I checked Internet health sites. I poked around until I assured myself that this was probably nothing serious.

By then, Eleanor was roaring "Up, up! Mama!" so I went in to rescue her. She pointed to her diaper and said, "Hurts."

When I took off her diaper, I discovered an angry diaper rash. I also discovered that we had only one lone baby wipe left in the entire apartment. As I changed her diaper, using every inch of the sole wipe, Eliza, still in her favorite cherry-printed nightgown, came charging in.

"It's 7:18, and I haven't even eaten breakfast!" she wailed in accusation. Eliza hates to be late; in fact, she hates to be on time; she likes to be *early*. "I'm supposed to be done eating and getting dressed by 7:20! We're going to be late!"

Did I burst into cheering song? Did I laugh in a merry but comforting way? Did I murmur reassuringly, "Don't worry, sweetheart, we have plenty of time"?

No. I snarled in my most menacing voice, *"Wait a minute!"* She backed off and started sobbing.

It took every ounce of my willpower not to keep yelling more, but after that first terrible moment, I managed to hold back. I gave Eliza a quick hug and said, "You go get dressed while I make breakfast. We still have plenty of time until school starts." ("Make breakfast" in this case meant spreading crunchy peanut butter on toast.) We did in fact have plenty of time. Because of Eliza's concern for promptness, our mornings have a sizable cushion—especially since January, when I began doing the evening tidy-up. Even after the commotion, we managed to make an on-time departure.

The effort to stop yelling taxed my self-control to the uttermost, but as we walked to school, I realized how much more pleasant our morning had been than it would have been had I kept yelling. As we walked down the street, I started singing "Oh, What a Beautiful Morning," until an embarrassed Eliza hushed me up.

The most effective way to lighten up—but also the most difficult, because a whining child sucks every particle of humor out of my head—is to make a joke. One morning when Eliza whined, *"Why* do I have to go to class today? I don't want to go to tae kwon do," I wanted to snap back, "You always say you don't want to go, but then you have fun," or "I don't like to hear all this grumbling." Instead, even though it wasn't easy, I sang out, "'I don't want to *go* to tae kwon *do'*—you're a *poet* and you don't *know it!"* After a minute I added, "I don't give a *snap* about going to *tap."*

Eliza answered, "I want to *stop* going to *hip-hop."*

I hate every kind of bathroom humor, but she loves it, so I whispered, "I don't give a *fart* about going to *art."*

She thought this was hilarious, then added, "I'd rather *pass gas* than to go to *science class."* We laughed until our stomachs hurt, and she didn't mention tae kwon do again. This technique worked better than telling her to buck up, and it was certainly more fun.

I hit on another rather Pollyannaish strategy that, to my astonishment, really worked to keep me in a "Sing in the morning" frame of mind, all day long: I "reframed" a particular chore by deciding that I *enjoyed* doing it.

For example, as Eleanor's birthday approached, I dreaded doing all the little errands—ordering the Baskin-Robbins ice cream cake (a Rubin family tradition), taking the girls to the party store to choose paper plates, buying presents, and making invitations for our family birthday party. I begrudged the time I spent on it. Then I told myself, "I *love* making plans for Eleanor's birthday! How fun! I'll never have a baby this young again!" And . . . it really did change my attitude. I also reframed by imagining that someone had offered to take over the task from me. Would I let someone else plan Eleanor's party? Nope. That realization also changed my attitude toward the task.

A friend of mine told me that when his sons were five and three years old, they woke up at six every morning. On the weekends, week after week, he and his wife tried to persuade them to go back to sleep or to play quietly—with no success.

So finally he gave up. He'd let his wife stay in bed, and he'd get the boys dressed and out the door. He'd stop for coffee, then the three of them would head for the park, and he'd watch them play for an hour before they returned home for breakfast.

These days his boys sleep late on the weekends, and now, my friend told me, those mornings are some of his clearest and happiest memories of that period. The morning light, the quiet park, his little boys racing across the grass.

The days are long, but the years are short.

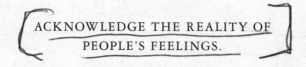

ACKNOWLEDGE THE REALITY OF
PEOPLE'S FEELINGS.

As part of my research for the month, I reread, for the fourth time, the collected works of the world's greatest parenting experts, Adele Faber and Elaine Mazlish, and in particular their two masterpieces, *Siblings Without Rivalry* and *How to Talk So Kids Will Listen and Listen So Kids Will Talk*. I discovered these books when a friend of mine mentioned that two friends of *hers* had the best-behaved children she'd ever seen. So when I met that couple, I asked for their secret—and they swore by *How to Talk So Kids Will Listen*. I ordered it that night, and I became an instant follower of Faber and Mazlish.

What's different about their books is that they're packed with practical advice and examples. So many parenting books belabor the arguments about the importance of the goals—as if anyone is disputing that children should be well behaved, respectful, able to tolerate frustration, self-directed, and so on. Fine, but what do you do when your child throws a tantrum in the cereal aisle?

The most important lesson from Faber and Mazlish's books is simple and as applicable to adults as to children: we should acknowledge the reality of people's feelings. In other words, don't deny feelings such as anger, irritation, fear, or reluctance; instead, articulate the feeling and the other person's point of view. Sounds simple, right? Wrong. I had no idea how often I contradicted my children's assertions of their feelings until I tried to quit. Too often, I said things like "You're not afraid of clowns," "You can't possibly want more Legos, you never play with the ones you have," "You're not hungry, you just ate."

Crazily enough, I discovered, just repeating what my child was saying, to show that I appreciated her point of view, was often enough to bring peace. Instead of saying to Eleanor, "Don't whine, you love to take a bath!" I said, "You're having fun playing. You don't want to take a bath now, even though it's time." This strategy was astoundingly effective—which suggested to me that much of children's frustration comes not from being forced to do this or that but rather from the sheer fact that they're being ignored.

So what strategies could I use to help show my children that I was acknowledging their feelings?

Write it down.

For some reason, the simple act of writing something down makes a big impression on my children, even the preliterate Eleanor. To restore peace, it can be enough to whip out pen and paper and announce, "I'm going to write that down. 'Eleanor does not like to wear snow boots!'"

Don't feel as if I have to say anything.

Eliza can be a bit of a sulker. Sometimes I pull her onto my lap and cuddle her for five minutes, and when we get up, she's cheerful again.

Don't say "no" or "stop."

Instead, I try to give information that shows that although I understand their desire, I have a reason for not granting it: "You'd like to stay, but we have to go home because Daddy forgot his keys." Studies show that 85 percent of adult messages to children are negative—"no," "stop," "don't"—so it's worth trying to keep that to a minimum. Instead of saying, "No, not until after lunch," I try to say, "Yes, as soon as we've finished lunch."

Wave my magic wand.

"If I had a magic wand, I'd make it warm outside so we didn't have to wear coats." "If I were Ozma, I'd make a box of Cheerios appear right now." This shows that I understand what my kids want and would accommodate them if I could.

Admit that a task is difficult.

Studies show that people tend to persevere longer with problems they've been told are difficult as opposed to easy. I'd been doing the opposite with Eleanor. Thinking I was being encouraging, I'd say, "It's not tough to pull off your socks, just give it a try." I switched to saying things such as "Socks can be tough to get off. Sometimes it helps to push down the back part over your ankle, instead of pulling on the toe."

Not long after I'd made my cheat sheet, I had a chance to put these principles to work.

One Saturday, Jamie and I were talking in our bedroom when Eliza burst in crying. We knew it was real crying and not fake crying, because Eliza has a very convenient "tell" when she's staging her tears. If she balls up her hands and holds them to her eyes, like an actress in a melodrama, she's faking. This time, her hands were down, so we knew she was really upset.

I pulled her onto my lap, and she sobbed into my shoulder, "People always pay attention to Eleanor, but nobody ever pays any attention to *me*."

Jamie and I looked at each other with worried expressions, and Jamie gave me the look that means "I have no idea what to do, can you handle this one?"

Just in time, I remembered my resolution, "Acknowledge other people's feelings." Although I knew that it wasn't factually true that no one ever paid any attention to Eliza, I managed to restrain my first impulse, which was to argue, "What about the five games of Uno I played with you last night?" and "You *know* everyone loves you just as much as Eleanor."

Instead, I said, "Wow, that hurts your feelings. You feel ignored." That seemed to help. I rocked her for a few minutes in silence, then added, "You feel like people pay more attention to Eleanor." "Yes," she said quietly, "so what should I do?" Instead of groping for some facile solution, I said, "That's a tough question. You, Daddy, and I will give it some serious thought."

When we stood up, she threw her arms around my waist and gave me a big hug, one that felt more needy than grateful. I figured she needed some reassurance. I put my arms around her and said, "No matter what, you know that you're our most precious, darling Eliza, and no one would ever forget about you or think that someone else is more important than you."

"Come on, Eliza, let's go see if my bread dough has risen," Jamie said. "You can punch it down." She took his hand and skipped off!

Experts say that denying bad feelings intensifies them; acknowledging bad feelings allows good feelings to return. That sure seemed to be what happened with Eliza. This was a real happiness breakthrough: not only

was this approach more effective in soothing Eliza, it was far more gratifying to *me* to act in a loving way, instead of giving in to my impulse to act
in a dismissive or argumentative way.

Jamie is skeptical of child-rearing "techniques," and he hasn't glanced
inside a book about parenting since he tossed aside *What to Expect When
You're Expecting* after the first chapter, but even he started to use this
strategy. I watched one morning when, after Eleanor threw herself, kicking
and screaming, onto the floor, he picked her up and said soothingly, "You're
frustrated. You don't want to wear your shoes, you want to wear your ruby
slippers." And she *stopped crying.*

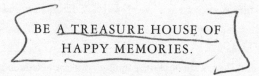

BE A TREASURE HOUSE OF HAPPY MEMORIES.

Sometimes the importance of some bit of happiness-related research or
advice won't hit me when I'm reading about it; only later do I grasp that I
stumbled across something essential.

One piece of wisdom that didn't resonate with me initially was the
importance of keeping happy memories vivid. But as I mulled over this
principle, I realized the tremendous value of mementos that help prompt
positive memories. Studies show that recalling happy times helps boost
happiness in the present. When people reminisce, they focus on positive
memories, with the result that recalling the past amplifies the positive
and minimizes the negative. However, because people remember events
better when they fit with their present mood, happy people remember
happy events better, and depressed people remember sad events better.
Depressed people have as many nice experiences as other people—they just
don't recall them as well.

With this knowledge in mind, I vowed to take steps to help everyone
in the family to experience happy times more vividly. Jamie loves looking
at photo albums and has a secret sentimental streak for things like out-

grown baby clothes, but he's not going to put in the time necessary to pull memorabilia together. If I wanted a treasure house of happy memories for my family, I needed to be the one to build it.

I stopped resenting the tedious hours I spend maintaining our family photo albums. I use these albums as a family diary, to capture little family jokes or funny incidents as well as the usual round of birthday party, Thanksgiving dinner, and vacation scenes. Photos help me recall happy details that once seemed unforgettable: how Jamie used to make rice pudding all the time; how tiny our four-pound Eliza was when she was born; and how Eleanor loved to show off her belly button. Without photographs, would we remember the fall afternoon when we wandered through Central Park with Eliza dressed as a "lovely fairy" or Eleanor's ecstasy the first time we put her in a swing?

Not a chance.

Beyond the taking of photographs, another way to accomplish this goal was to embrace my role as the family reporter, to spread family cheer. We have two sets of extremely engaged grandparents, and the two who live around the corner are as eager for information as the pair who lives in Kansas City. I made more of an effort to e-mail informational notes with updates from the pediatrician's visit, reports on school events, or funny things that happened. Now that I'm a parent myself, I realize how much the happiness of parents depends on the happiness of their children and grandchildren. By sending around a quick, fun e-mail, I can give everyone in the family a lift (and also myself—do good, feel good). As I'd learned in February, even Jamie likes to get e-mails during the day with interesting bits of family news.

With this in mind, when I joined Jamie in our bedroom after tucking Eleanor in for the night, I said, "I don't think I've told you about Eleanor's new good-night ritual. Now when I'm done rocking Eleanor, I carry her to the window, and she says, 'Good night, world.'"

"Does she really?" he asked in a tender voice. Without my resolution, I might never have bothered to mention it.

Resolving to be a "treasure house of happy memories" also got me thinking about the importance of family traditions. Family traditions make occasions feel special and exciting. They mark the passage of time in a happy way. They provide a sense of anticipation, security, and continuity. Studies show that family traditions support children's social development and strengthen family cohesiveness. They provide connection and predictability, which people—especially children—crave. I know that I enjoy a holiday more when I know exactly what we're going to do and when we're going to do it.

At the same time, because family traditions usually involve special decorations, special food, a special sequence of events, and participation by certain people, most traditions (other than the tradition of ordering a pizza during the Super Bowl) involve a fair amount of trouble and are a potential source of guilt, resentment, anger, and disappointment.

I was right to start my happiness project with a focus on energy. When I felt energetic, I enjoyed putting up decorations, getting out the video camera, and all the rest. When I felt low, everything seemed like a burden. Last year, I kept putting off buying a pumpkin for Halloween, and we ended up *not getting one at all*. Eliza and Eleanor didn't seem to mind, but I was shocked by myself. That counts as Mommy malpractice in my book.

But even though we didn't have a pumpkin, I did manage to keep up our family's personal Halloween tradition. Every Halloween, I take a picture of Eliza and Eleanor in their costumes, put the photo in a Halloween-themed picture frame, and add it to our Halloween photo gallery. I also give a copy to each pair of grandparents, so they have their own set. This tradition takes a fair amount of effort, but it's fun to have a set of holiday photos that we put out for just one week of the year, it gives a sense of family continuity, and it's an excuse to give a present to the grandparents—that's a lot of happiness bang for the buck.

My desire to be a treasure house of happy memories gave rise, however, to a problem. I didn't know what to do with my children's various keepsake papers, such as those Halloween pictures. I wanted the girls to have their own copies. Where should I put them? I also wanted both girls to have a copy of their yearly birthday party invitations, the family Valentine's cards, family wedding invitations, class photos, and so on—but where to keep all the stuff? Making little stacks in out-of-the-way cabinets and pinning papers to the bulletin board, as I'd been doing, wasn't a good long-term solution.

A friend told me that she kept scrapbooks of such items for each of her kids, but my heart sank at the thought. I was barely keeping up with our family photo albums. Then my Eighth Commandment started flashing inside my head: "Identify the problem." What was the problem? I wanted to save all these mementos for Eliza and Eleanor, but I didn't know where to put them. I wanted a convenient, inexpensive, attractive way to store them that would keep them organized without taking up too much room.

Instead of moving various piles around the apartment, as I usually did when confronted with this kind of problem, I forced myself to sit and think. Convenient. Inexpensive. Attractive. Organized. Paper storage.

And just like that, I thought of a solution. *File boxes.* I bought two the very next day. Instead of buying ugly cardboard file boxes, I splurged and bought a slightly fancier version from an upscale office supply store. The boxes were a pleasing tan color, covered with a woven fabric, with proper wooden handles. I fitted out each one with a pack of hanging files.

I started with Eliza. After gathering up a lot of loose memorabilia from around the apartment, I made a folder for each year of school, past and future, in which I put her birthday party invitation, a copy of the photo I took each year on the first day of school, the program from the school holiday party, some characteristic work, our family Valentine's card, a camp photo, and so on. Then I did the same with the few items I had for Eleanor.

These boxes make it easy to store these mementos neatly, and they'll make great keepsakes for the girls when they're older. How fun to imagine that when they're fifty years old, they'll be able to look back at their birthday party invitations from nursery school! I was so pleased with the system that I started a box for Jamie and me too, divided by year.

As I thought about the various traditions we observed, it occurred to me that I didn't need to wait for traditions to emerge spontaneously. A "new tradition" may be a bit of an oxymoron, but that shouldn't stop me from inventing a tradition that I wished we had.

Jamie came up with a great one: Polite Night. He suggested that every Sunday night, we set the table properly, enforce good manners, and have a nice meal together. Calling it "Polite Night" was my brilliant stroke. It turned out to be a very useful exercise and a lot of fun.

Also, when she was little, I'd started the tradition of Eliza and her grandmother taking a weekly music class together, and when Eleanor was old enough she started a weekly class, too. Judy is deeply involved in music and theater, and having this weekly date means that grandmother and granddaughter see each other at least once a week, in a context that allows Judy to impart her enthusiasm for music to the girls. Then I thought— what about their grandfather? He needed a grandchild tradition of his own, so I invented one. I proposed that a few times each year, during her vacations, Eliza would visit her grandfather at his office for lunch. He thought it was a terrific idea, and these lunches have been a great success.

I have no idea how Jamie and I started this, but we have a family tradition of yelling "Family love sandwich!" and scooping up the girls in a big tight hug. Our version of a secret handshake.

I wondered what traditions other people might observe, so on my blog, I asked readers for ideas from their families. Some of my favorites:

·   ·   ·   ·   ·   ·   ·   ·   ·   ·   ·   ·

When I was a kid and wanted my three younger sisters to help me clean the house—I invented a game called "Cleaning Company." (I had no idea there actually were such companies.) I'd pretend the phone was ringing ("Prrring! Prrring!") with hand to ear holding an invisible receiver. ("Hello, Cleaning Company. What's that you say? You need us to come over right now and clean your house for a party? We'll be right over, ma'am.") Then, I'd clap my hands together excitedly and announce to my sisters, "Sounds like another job for Cleaning Company!" We'd pretend to pile into an imaginary car and drive over to our living room ("vroom-vrooming" all around the house first—we were all still in elementary school so this was pretty fun for us). Then, we'd start cleaning whichever room we'd been assigned to briskly while repeatedly singing, "Cleaning Company! Cleaning Company! Woo woo!" with a raise of our hands (or feet if our hands were full) with every "Woo woo!" Pretty crazy, huh?

As a micro family—single mom of one kid—the little traditions are extra important to us because a lot of "normal" falls between the cracks. We have "adventures" regularly—it started off when my daughter was very small and it was to glamourize our errands. Now, we plan it out a bit—a map or agenda to pick the route, bring along the camera, "adventure" clothes (my daughter loves hats), and a snack or dish we haven't had before.

When my husband and I travel away from our children, we like to bring home little presents. But instead of just handing them over when we return, I make sure to pick the presents early in the trip, then allow my children to ask for clues. Each child gets one clue per day, and they have tremendous fun coming up with the questions, coordinating with each other about who will ask what, keeping a list of the clues that have been revealed, debating amongst themselves, etc. The gift itself brings them much less fun than the guessing game.

My brother has a tradition with his family. Every once in a while, they have "Pirate Dinner." They cover the table entirely in newspaper and eat with no plates, napkins, or utensils—just hands! He says that his kids have to follow rules and proper table etiquette all the time, so why not give them a break every now and then?

•   •   •   •   •   •   •   •   •   •   •   •

I couldn't wait to suggest Pirate Dinner to my girls. What a great idea.

TAKE TIME FOR PROJECTS.

Traditions often involve projects. Celebrating every family birthday, sending out a family Valentine's card, decorating an elaborate gingerbread house (actually, we make the houses out of graham crackers and tubs of Duncan Hines frosting)—these things are fun, but they take time, energy, planning, and patience. Inevitably, boomerang errands are involved. Out of the urge to simplify my life, I sometimes feel reluctant to undertake ambitious family projects, but at the same time, I know that these projects are a highlight of childhood—and adulthood.

Once I'd resolved to "Take time for projects," I made a purchase that I'd been considering for a long time: I ordered a laminator. The minute it arrived, I knew it had been worth the splurge. So many possible projects! First up: Mother's Day presents for the grandmothers. Under my direction, Eliza made a list of "Ten Reasons I Love Bunny" (her nickname for my mother) and "Ten Reasons I Love Grandma." As she dictated, I typed up her list; then she chose a different font for each item—playing with fonts on my computer is one of her favorite things to do. Then we printed the two lists out and let Eleanor scribble on them, to add her personal touch. And then to the laminator! Suddenly these modest pieces of paper were transformed into personalized place mats. What next? Book covers, bookmarks, cards of useful phone numbers.

Inspired by the success of the laminator, I experimented with the glue gun that I'd had for years but never used. An opportunity presented itself one evening when, after Eleanor had gone to sleep, Eliza announced that she was supposed to make a "scrappy cap" to bring to school.

"What's a scrappy cap?" I asked.

"It's from Julie Andrews Edwards's book, *The Last of the Really Great Whangdoodles*," Eliza explained. "It's a hat that reflects our imagination."

Now, in this situation, I knew perfectly well that as a parent, I should let my child take the lead while I merely helped gently and unobtrusively to guide her thinking.

But instead of doing that, I leaped to my feet and said, "I know what to do! Quick, run and get a baseball cap."

While she ran to get a hat, I studied the glue gun directions and plugged it in. Then I pulled down the jars of little bitty toys that I'd collected in January.

"Now what?" panted Eliza as she arrived with her cap.

"Dump out the stuff in the jars and see what reflects your imagination. Then we'll glue them onto this cap with a glue gun."

"Oh, I love glue guns," she said. "My teacher uses them."

Eliza began combing through the mounds of toys to pick her favorites. One by one, we carefully glued them onto the hat.

"I didn't expect this to be so *fun*," Eliza said happily at one point. It took hours because she wanted to debate the merits of every single gimcrack, but that was fine. *Take time for projects.*

Sometimes family projects pop up unexpectedly. For example, I didn't expect picking Eliza's birthday cake to turn into a "project." I figured that I'd ask, as I'd asked before, "Chocolate or vanilla? Flower decorations or princesses?" and Eliza would choose. Instead, as Eliza's birthday approached, she became utterly preoccupied with her cake. The guest list, the decorations, the activities—all these considerations paled in comparison to the question of the composition and decoration of the cake. Before my happiness project, I would have pressed her to decide quickly, so I could get the item crossed off my to-do list. But my research revealed that a key to happiness is squeezing out as much happiness as possible from a happy event.

We've all heard of Dr. Elisabeth Kübler-Ross's five stages of grief: denial, anger, bargaining, depression, and acceptance. By contrast, I realized, happiness has four stages. To eke out the most happiness from an experience, we must *anticipate* it, *savor* it as it unfolds, *express* happiness, and *recall* a happy memory.

Any single happy experience may be amplified or minimized, depending on how much attention you give it. For instance, if I call my parents to tell them about a funny thing that happened in the park that day, I relive the experience in my mind as I express it. Although it's true that taking photographs sometimes makes it hard to savor a moment when it's happening, in the future, having pictures will help me recall a happy time.

Eliza's birthday cake gave us plenty of opportunities to enjoy the "anticipation" stage. She asked me to bring home a Baskin-Robbins brochure, and we went over every word. We visited the Baskin-Robbins Web site, where Eliza pondered the list of ice cream flavors. We made a pilgrimage to the Baskin-Robbins store, so Eliza could sample the flavors and pore over the book of possible cake decorations. At last, I thought, she'd made her decisions. Nope.

"Mom," she asked a few days later, "can we go back to Baskin-Robbins to look at the cake book again?"

"Eliza, we spent an hour in there already. Plus your birthday is still a month away."

"But I want to look at the book!"

Before the happiness project, I would have resisted, but now I understand that this errand isn't birthday party inefficiency but the *very fun itself*. It's my Sixth Commandment: <u>Enjoy the process.</u> Eliza will enjoy eating the cake for only five minutes, but she can have hours of enjoyment from planning the cake. In fact, in what's known as "rosy prospection," anticipation of happiness is sometimes greater than the happiness actually experienced. All the more reason to revel in anticipation.

"Okay," I relented, "if you want, we can stop off after school on Friday."

Doing these kinds of projects showed me another way that children boost happiness: they reconnect us with sources of "feeling good" that we've outgrown. Left to my own devices, I wouldn't work on homemade Mother's Day gifts, pore over Baskin-Robbins cake designs, memorize *Is*

Your Mama a Llama?, or go to the Central Park boat pond on Saturday afternoons. I wouldn't watch *Shrek* over and over or listen to Laurie Berkner's music. I wouldn't visit amusement parks or the Museum of Natural History. I wouldn't use food coloring to make Rainbow Yogurt Surprise in a shot glass. Nevertheless, I honestly do enjoy these activities with my children. I don't just enjoy their pleasure—which I do, and that also makes me happy—I also experience my own sincere enjoyment of activities that I would otherwise never have considered.

On the last day of April, as I did at the end of every month, I paused to evaluate my progress before gearing up for the next month's resolutions. Soul-searching seems like an activity that should be undertaken by a woodland stream or at least in a quiet room, but this particular session of self-evaluation took place as I was riding the subway downtown. As we slowly lurched through the local stops, I asked myself, "Well, am I feeling any happier? Am I *really*?"

I happened to be in a blue mood that morning. "If I'm honest with myself," I thought dejectedly, "the fact is, I'm no different. Same old Gretchen, no better and no worse, nothing new and improved. I've been telling myself I'm happier, but I haven't really changed." Studies show that people who go to psychotherapy or to programs to lose weight, stop smoking, start exercising, or whatever usually believe they've changed a lot but in fact show only a modest benefit; apparently, after spending so much money, time, and effort, people think, "Wow, I *must* have changed for the better," even if they haven't changed that much. "That's probably why *I've* been telling myself that I'm happier," I thought, "when in fact my project hasn't been working at all." As I got off the subway, I couldn't shake my feelings of futility and gloom.

After a two-hour meeting, I was back on the subway and headed home in a more cheerful mood (thus confirming happiness research that shows that people get a mood boost from contact with others). I resumed my argument with myself. "Am I happier?" This time my answer was a little different: "No, but also yes." True, my fundamental nature hadn't changed. It wasn't realistic to think that I could bring about that kind of change in just four months or even by the end of the year. Yet something had changed. What?

Finally I put my finger on it. In moments when I was in "neutral," as when riding the subway, I was the same familiar Gretchen. The difference was that, although my nature was unchanged, I had more happiness in my life each day; my resolutions had added more sources of fun, engagement, and satisfaction and had also eliminated some significant sources of bad feelings, such as guilt and anger. Through my actions, I was successfully pushing myself to the high end of my inborn happiness range.

I could tell that my happier mood affected the household atmosphere. It's true that "if Mama ain't happy, ain't nobody happy," and it's also true that "if Daddy ain't happy, ain't nobody happy" and that "you're only as happy as your least happy child." Each member of a family picks up and reflects everyone else's emotions—but of course I could change no one's actions except my own.

On a less sublime note, after evaluating my progress I decided to give up wearing the pedometer. It had been a useful exercise, but I was getting tired of strapping it to my waistband every morning, and I'd almost dropped it in the toilet several times. The pedometer had served its purpose of helping me to evaluate and improve my walking habits, and it was time to put it into retirement.

5

MAY

Be Serious About Play

LEISURE

- Find more fun.
- Take time to be silly.
- Go off the path.
- Start a collection.

May, the beginning of springtime, seemed like the right time to *work* on my *play*—that is, the activities I did in my free time because I wanted to do them, for their own sake, for my own reasons, and not for money or ambition. In an irony that didn't escape me, I prepared to work doggedly at fun and to be serious about joking around.

The writer Jean Stafford scoffed, "Happy people don't need to have fun," but in fact, studies show that the absence of feeling bad isn't enough to make you happy; you must strive to find sources of feeling good. One way to feel good is to make time for play—which researchers define as an activity that's very satisfying, has no economic significance, doesn't create social harm, and doesn't necessarily lead to praise or recognition. Research shows that regularly having fun is a key factor in having a happy life; people who have fun are twenty times as likely to feel happy.

I had two goals for the month: I wanted to have more fun, and I wanted to use my leisure to cultivate my creativity. Play wasn't merely idle time but an opportunity to experiment with new interests and to draw closer to other people.

I was very fortunate that the activities that I did for work were, for the most part, versions of the same activities that I did for fun. There were many persuasive arguments against taking busman's holidays, but I always wanted to do the same things on the weekend that I did during the week. I knew exactly what the photographer Edward Weston meant when he noted in his daybook that he'd spent the day in "a holiday of work, but work which was play."

As I saw in March, novelty is an important source of happiness; it's also an important element in creativity. I tend to stick to the familiar, so I wanted to push myself toward new experiences and new ideas that attracted me.

I needed to take my leisure more seriously. I'd always assumed that having fun was something in my life that would flow naturally, so I didn't think about shaping it or getting the most out of it—but although having fun sounded simple, it wasn't. When I asked my blog readers about their ideas about fun, several readers responded.

· · · · · · · · · · ·

Making things is something that I get fun out of. I'm a great fan of crafts, but I find the fun is far increased when I am making a present for someone. This Christmas, I have a pretty ambitious project in mind for the boyfriend, but I know he'll love it and the challenge is giving me so much fun, as well as the anticipation that he'll appreciate it. Coming up with ideas myself is an intellectual challenge, followed by the mechanically creative challenge of realising them, and this is a combination which I find very fulfilling and fun.

Reading overseas blogs, including yours of course, is fun to me. Every weekday morning I read them over coffee (since I live in the Far East, they are updated while I'm asleep). Needless to say, it helps to learn foreign language (in my case, English). But what I find fun most is to find a person who has a similar taste, way of thinking, etc., in a different culture.

Books are a great source of joy and fun for me—collecting them, reading them, looking them up on the internet. It gives me great pleasure to open a "new" book whether it was previously used or fresh off the press.

My weekly Latin class is a whole lot of fun for me. I have been meeting for four years now with a few other individuals to sight-read Latin, review grammar, and talk about whatever comes up in conversation. I fell in love with the Latin language in high school and never had the opportunity to pursue further study until now. And that has made me very, very happy.

What's fun for me? ANYTHING creative . . . anything! The BEST fun is the kind of coloring book that has a very complex picture on only one side of the page . . . and a new box of beautifully sharpened colored pencils. Next best . . . a piece of stamped material and the colored cotton floss required to complete the embroidery.

Here's a tough one: I do not find it particularly fun to sit on the floor and play with my children with their toys. I love cooking with them, reading to them, talking to them, watching movies with them, going on walks with them, and taking them to age-appropriate places. My idea of a really good time is to pick my five-year-old up from school and go out for a snack. But I don't find playing with Polly Pockets (with the older one) or Little People (with the younger one) particularly fun. And I feel very guilty about that at times.

For me fun is . . . debating, tinkering (e.g., inside the guts of hardware or software), building (hardware/software), reading blogs (all kinds), telling my kids stories of my youth.

Seriously, I have come to the realisation that I don't have fun anymore. I have got to do something about this before I become a glum, boring, sad person!

· · · · · · · · · · · · · · ·

Like that last commenter, I wanted to bring more fun into my life.

FIND MORE FUN

When I thought about fun, I realized to my surprise that I didn't have a good sense of what I found fun. Only recently had I grasped one of my most important Secrets of Adulthood: just because something was fun for someone else didn't mean it was fun for *me*—and vice versa. There are many things that other people enjoy that I don't.

I love the *idea* of playing chess, going to a lecture on international markets, doing crossword puzzles, getting a pedicure, eating dinner at a hot new restaurant, or having a subscription to the opera or season tickets to the Knicks. I can see exactly why other people enjoy these activities. I wish I enjoyed them. But I don't. Some blog readers experienced the same tension:

· · · · · · · · · · · · · ·

Over the last few years, I've started figuring out what I really find fun. I realized I had a lot of stuff and activities in my life that I didn't enjoy. These were things that others find fun, but they just weren't to me. Accepting that what others find fun won't necessarily be fun for me felt like a huge breakthrough. It's hard enough to stay in touch with what's fun for you without thinking that you should like something that others find fun. For instance, I enjoy movies, but there are cheaper activities that I enjoy much more. So, I have gradually cut them out of my life. I will go occasionally with a friend, but I don't watch nearly as many as I used to and I used to watch a couple a week.

My husband posed this question to me a year or so ago—"What do you find fun?" and I had to think long and hard about it. Most of my pleasures are quiet and solitary. I love to be absorbed in a good book; I love to do needlework; I love to make jewelry. I've given myself permission to say that that's okay. I do love to play board games, though, especially with my children.

My understanding of fun is definitely not the same as other people's. I enjoy solitary, quiet things. Even the sports I enjoy are quiet ones. Reading is fun, both books and blogs. Computer programming is fun. Diving and mountain climbing are fun. Yoga is fun. Shopping, on the other hand, which girls are supposed to enjoy, is definitely NOT fun. Parties are generally not fun either.

* * *

I tended to overrate the fun activities that I didn't do and underrate my own inclinations. I felt like the things that other people enjoyed were more valuable, or more cultured . . . more, well, *legitimate*. But now it was time to "Be Gretchen." I needed to acknowledge to myself what I enjoyed, not what I *wished* I enjoyed. If something was really fun for me, it would pass this test: I looked forward to it; I found it energizing, not draining; and I didn't feel guilty about it later.

I told a friend about my quest, and she said, "Gosh, if I had something fun I wanted to do, I'd feel frustrated, because I wouldn't have time for it. I don't want to add anything else to my plate." This struck me as a bleak view—but it was something I might well have said myself in the past. My happiness project had shown me that I was better off saying "I have plenty of time to have fun!"

But what, exactly, did I find fun? What did I *want* to do? I couldn't think of much. Well, there was one thing: I really loved reading children's literature. I've never quite figured out what I get from children's literature that I don't get from adult literature, but there's something. The difference between novels for adults and novels for children isn't merely a matter of cover design, bookstore placement, and the age of the protagonist. It's a certain quality of atmosphere.

Children's literature often deals openly with the most transcendent themes, such as the battle between good and evil and the supreme power of love. These books don't gloss over the horror and fascination of evil, but in the end, in even the most realistic novels, good triumphs. Novelists for adults don't usually write that way; perhaps they fear being seen as sentimental or priggish or simplistic. Instead, they focus on guilt, hypocrisy, the perversion of good intentions, the cruel workings of fate, social criticism, the slipperiness of language, the inevitability of death, sexual passion, unjust accusation, and the like. These are grand literary themes. Yet I also find it enormously satisfying to see good prevail over evil, to see virtue vindicated and wrongdoing punished. I love didactic writing, whether by Tolstoy or Madeleine L'Engle.

What's more, in keeping with this good-versus-evil worldview, children's literature often plunges a reader into a world of archetypes. Certain images have a queer power to excite the imagination, and children's literature uses them with brilliant effect. Books such as *Peter Pan, The Golden Compass,* and *The Blue Bird* operate on a symbolic level and are penetrated with meanings that can't be fully worked out. Adult novels do sometimes have this atmosphere, but it's much rarer. I love to return to the world of stark good and evil, of talking animals and fulfilled prophecies.

But my passionate interest in kidlit didn't fit with my ideas of what I wished I were like; it wasn't grown up enough. I wanted to be interested in serious literature, constitutional law, the economy, art, and other adult subjects. And I *am* interested in those topics, but I somehow felt embarrassed by my love of J. R. R. Tolkien, E. L. Konigsberg, and Elizabeth Enright. I repressed this side of my personality to such a degree that when one of the Harry Potter books came out, I didn't buy it for several days. I'd fooled even myself into thinking that I didn't care.

If I was going to "Be serious about play," I needed to embrace this suppressed passion and have more fun with it. But how? While I was trying to figure that out, I had lunch with an acquaintance who was a polished, intimidating, well-established literary agent. We were having a "we'd like to become friends but haven't figured out how yet" kind of conversation when I mentioned how much I loved Stephen King's *The Stand.* Now, I felt as though this was a bit of a risk, because I feared she might be the kind of person who would disdain Stephen King.

"I love Stephen King, and I love *The Stand,*" she said. Then she added, "But it's not as good as Harry Potter."

"Oh, do you like Harry Potter?"

"I'm *obsessed* with Harry Potter."

Eureka, I'd found a kindred spirit. We talked about nothing but Harry Potter for the rest of lunch. As we talked, it occurred to me: I knew a third person who also loved children's literature. Could we start a book group?

"Let me float an idea by you," I said tentatively as we were paying. "Do you think you might want to start a children's literature reading group?"

"A reading group, for reading children's books? Like what?"

"Whatever we want. *The Giver, The Secret Garden, James and the Giant Peach,* whatever. We could take turns meeting for dinner."

"Sure, that could be fun," she said enthusiastically. Fortunately. If she'd said no, I'm not sure I would have asked anyone else. "I have a friend who might be interested in joining, too."

So I sent out a few e-mails and started asking around. Once I spoke up, I was startled to discover that I already knew and liked many people who shared my passion. Because I'd never mentioned my interest, I'd never known about theirs.

For our first meeting, I sent around an e-mail inviting everyone to my apartment for dinner to discuss C. S. Lewis's *The Lion, the Witch and the*

Wardrobe. At the end of the e-mail, I included a quotation from Lewis's brilliant essay "On Three Ways of Writing for Children":

> When I was ten, I read fairy tales in secret and would have been ashamed if I had been found doing so. Now that I am fifty I read them openly. When I became a man I put away childish things, including the fear of childishness and the desire to be very grown up.

This apologia didn't mean much to anyone else in the group, because they'd never tried to squash their interest in children's literature. Why had I? No more.

From our very first meeting, this group was a huge source of fun for me. I loved the people, I loved the books, I loved the discussions. I loved the fact that many of the people in the group didn't have children, so there was no question about the fact that we were reading children's literature *for ourselves.* I loved our kidlit tradition that the dinner's host must serve some food that tied in with the book. This started when I served Turkish delight for dessert at the first meeting, because Turkish delight plays a significant role in *The Lion, the Witch and the Wardrobe.* At our next meeting, we drank Tokay, the wine that appears at a key moment in Philip Pullman's *The Golden Compass* (I was surprised to discover that Tokay was real; I'd assumed it was part of Lyra's world). For Lewis Carroll's *Alice's Adventures in Wonderland,* we ate mock turtle soup and treacle tart; for Blue Balliett's *Chasing Vermeer,* the blue M&M's that are the signature candy eaten by Petra and Calder; for Louisa May Alcott's *Little Women,* Meg's blancmange, which Jo takes to Laurie the first time they meet. At the dinner to discuss Louis Sachar's *Holes,* we ate Dunkin' Donuts doughnut holes—for the pun.

Studies show that each common interest between people boosts the chances of a lasting relationship and also brings about a 2 percent increase in life satisfaction. This group gave me a bunch of new friends and a lift in life satisfaction that felt much higher than 2 percent. Also, it was fun just being part of a new group. Group membership makes people feel closer and brings a significant boost in personal confidence and happiness.

By contrast, around the same time, I was elected to the Council on Foreign Relations. Interesting subject, interesting group, and so very *legitimate*. Which group brought me more pleasure? Which helped me form new relationships? Kidlit. I'm passionate about Winston Churchill, I'm passionate about John Kennedy, but the truth is, I'm not passionate about foreign relations—so that group didn't form as solid a basis for fun for me.

So once again, one of my resolutions led me right back to my First Commandment, "Be Gretchen." I had to know and pursue what was truly fun *for me*. That was the road that led to happiness. But what else, beside the children's literature reading group, could I do for fun? I was stumped. Was I so cheerless and dull that I couldn't think of a single other thing?

One thing that's both good and bad about living in New York City is the sense that I could be doing so much—going to the ballet, going to an off-off-Broadway play, taking a graphic design class, shopping in Williamsburg, eating in Astoria. But I almost never do those things, so the possibilities are exciting, but also a reproach. I've been haunted for years by a public service poster I saw just one time, in the subway. It was a photo of a Chinese food take-out container sitting on top of two videos. The caption read, "If this is how you spend your time, why are you living in New York?"

Fun abounded in New York City, if only I had the largeness of spirit to tap into it.

I told a friend that I was trying to have more fun, and instead of pointing me toward the "Goings On About Town" column in *The New Yorker*, she asked me a question: "What did you like to do when you were a child? What you enjoyed as a ten-year-old is probably something you'd enjoy now."

That was an intriguing idea. I remembered that Carl Jung, when he was thirty-eight years old, had decided to start playing with building blocks again, to tap into the enthusiasm he'd felt as an eleven-year-old. What had I done for fun as a child? No chess, no ice-skating, no painting. I worked on my "Blank Books." For my tenth birthday, my uncle had given me a book that looked like an ordinary book but with blank pages, titled *Blank Book*. Now such books can be bought anywhere, but when I got this one, I'd never seen anything like it. Before long, I'd bought several more.

I turned my Blank Books into commonplace books filled with clippings, memorabilia, notes from school friends, cartoons, lists, snatches of information that interested me. Jokes cut from my grandparents' back copies of *Reader's Digest* sometimes found their way in. A special series of my Blank Books were illustrated books of quotations. Every time I read a quotation I liked, I'd write it on a slip of paper, and when I saw a picture in a magazine that I liked, I'd cut it out, and I created my books by matching the quotations to the pictures.

Keeping up with my Blank Books was the main leisure activity of my childhood. Every day after school, I sat on the floor sorting, cutting, matching, copying, and pasting while I watched TV.

I set off to replicate this experience. I was eager to give it a try, plus I'd thought of another potential benefit: I'd noticed that many of the most creative people are inveterate keepers of scrapbooks, inspiration boards, or other magpie creations. Twyla Tharp, for example, dedicates a file box to every project she begins, and as she works on the dance, she fills the box with the material that inspired her. Having some kind of physical way of preserving information keeps good ideas vivid and creates unexpected juxtapositions.

I bought a huge scrapbook and started looking for items to include. A motley assortment emerged: a portrait of Princess Diana made of tiny photographs of flowers; a review from *The New York Review of Books* about Books of Hours; a photograph of an artwork by Portia Munson called *Pink Project* (1994), made of a table covered by pink objects; a map of the counties of England, which I wished I'd had when I was writing my Churchill biography; one playing card from the pack I took from my grandparents' house after they both died, decorated with a Thomas Kinkade–like picture of a water mill.

Working on my new Blank Book made me look at magazines and newspapers in a different way. If something caught my attention, I'd think, "Why am I looking at this for a second time? Is it worth keeping for my Blank Book?" I was a less passive recipient of information. I also liked the process of cutting, placing, and pasting, so familiar from my childhood.

All this thinking about fun made me realize that I had to make time for it. Too often, I'd give up fun in order to work. I often felt so overwhelmed by tasks that I'd think, "The most fun would be to cross some items off my to-do list. I'd feel so much better if I could get something accomplished." I felt virtuous when I delayed gluing pictures into my scrapbook in order to deal with my e-mail.

In fact, though, turning from one chore to another just made me feel trapped and drained. When I took the time to do something that was truly fun for me, to reread *The Phantom Tollbooth* for the fifteenth time, for instance, or to call my sister, I felt better able to tackle my to-do list. Fun is energizing.

But I have to admit it—being Gretchen and accepting my true likes and dislikes bring me a kind of sadness. I will never visit a jazz club at midnight, hang out in artists' studios, jet off to Paris for the weekend, or pack up to go fly-fishing on a spring dawn. I won't be admired for my chic wardrobe or be appointed to a high government office. I'll never stand in line to buy tickets to the Ring Cycle. I love fortune cookies and refuse to try foie gras.

It makes me sad for two reasons. First, it makes me sad to realize my limitations. The world offers so much!—so much beauty, so much fun, and I am unable to appreciate most of it. But it also makes me sad because, in many ways, I wish I were different. One of my Secrets of Adulthood is "You can choose what you do; you can't choose what you *like* to do." I have a lot of notions about what I wish I liked to do, about the subjects and occupations that I wish interested me. But it doesn't matter what I wish I were like. I am Gretchen.

When I posted on my blog about the "sadness of a happiness

project," I was astounded by the response. I'd thought it unlikely that my sentiments would resonate with anyone else, but dozens of people commented.

* * * * * * * * * * * * * *

This post really resonates with me. Because this is exactly what's been on my mind lately.

I'm currently going through a period of major change, and as always, they make you think.

And I realize, I will never be an astronaut. I will never know what it's like to be someone else, live a different life. Like you say, the world is so big, and I wonder if I'm missing out.

I will never be an F-1 racer. I will never be a supermodel. I will never know what it's like to fight in a war. To be a dancer on a cruise ship. To be a dealer in Las Vegas.

Not because they are entirely impossible to achieve. But because I can't dance (I tried). I can't take G forces (I can't even ride a roller coaster). I am not tall or pretty enough. I hate physics and maths, so I can't be an astronaut.

This is less about whether I CAN actually do any of those things, but more about whether I'd actually want to do them. Or to be dedicated enough to work towards them.

I will never be that person.

It has taken me decades to even accept that the hairstyles I like can't be done with my actual hair.

I don't remember the exact date, but I remember the incident very clearly:

One day—I was about 34 years old—it dawned on me: I can DO ANY-THING I want, but I can't DO EVERYTHING I want.

Life-changing.

I think most of us feel the same way. I'm a college student, majoring in English and trying to figure out what path to take. I'm an English major because I like to read. There are so many things I can do that involve books, but I'm undecided. I think almost daily I grieve for my limitations (I will probably never set foot in any club), but my passions give me such joy.

I followed your lead and one of my commandments is to "Be Catherine." I would rather spend the night reading a great book than dancing in a club, I love children's books and check out dozens every time I go to the library. I think by knowing who we are as people and being ourselves, we can start making the world better.

I remember when I turned 25, and realised I'd never be a Rhodes Scholar. The fact that I'd never wanted to be such, never applied or even looked into it, was beside the point. It was the closing of an option. I'm now looking down the barrel of not having the opportunity to have children. Always thought I'd think about it/decide what I wanted when I met my future husband. Still haven't met him (if he exists!) but time waits for no ovary.

It's part of being human, isn't it? And more particularly so in the world we live in—we see so much of what other people do, have, are . . . But then there's the majority of humanity who have SO MUCH LESS than us— we are the rich, privileged west. That usually sobers me up when I start comparing my material situation to that of others who have X Y or Z.

I look at people ten years younger than me earning 6-figure incomes in corporate jobs and I think "I wish I wanted to do that," but I'm an artist at heart and my path to financial security is a different one. I fought it for years and was insanely unhappy. Now I'm following the artistic path, am flat broke, worry about money nearly all the time, but am insanely happy (except when I get the moments of wishing I could make life easier for myself and follow the crowd).

It's so true . . . and I do think about those things sometimes, especially as I'm getting older. There are no "do overs" and some things just aren't going to happen. It does make me a little sad sometimes. I just have to embrace what is. :)

I relate to what you say here, more than I'd like to admit. I'd like to be this really cool, easygoing person who gets along with everyone, but that isn't me—not really. I don't feel comfortable in strange situations and I get more uptight about things than I like, and I make friends slowly.

I WANT to be different and am pretty good at pretending, but it can be hard to deny that inside I am shy. In the same way, I'd like my husband to change, sometimes, and I have to remind myself that is unfair and unrealistic. Plus I love him, just the way he is.

I actually lost a friendship because I couldn't tell the difference between what I sometimes wished I was and what I was actually willing to become. I always had a touch of envy for those women who go out, in grand style, enjoying their cosmopolitans and discussing high fashion. I had a friend, however, who actually became that, and decided she was no longer interested in me because I didn't become that person. I wonder to this day if I am partially to blame for that, as I probably led her to believe that I was willing to go in that direction.

But the thing is . . . when given the choice, I'd much rather stay home. I'm such a homebody, and I really don't enjoy crowds, bars, or getting all dolled up, to be honest. Thanks for this post . . . it makes me realize that perhaps I can learn to be ok with being me . . . just as I am.

Ah, the constant tug between striving and accepting. I've never figured this out, except to say that it seems like a balance of necessary opposites. And yes it can be sad, while being busy and running out and fulfilling all things on my dreams/desires list I am not just accepting myself as is and letting me be me as is. I'm pushing myself. And yet if I don't push myself I find I can be dissatisfied with things about me and my life. I figure there is a time for both pursuing and accepting.

For me, I always wanted to start my own business. I pursued the idea of "being a businessman." However, whenever I tried to do things I thought businessmen "should" do, I would not be really happy. I would read certain magazines or do different things. Instead I try and make no plan on how to be a businessman and just do what sounds interesting, appealing, or "feels" like the right next step. I find I am still trending in a direction towards starting my own tech business but in a different way than I thought I should and it feels great at every step. Looking back, I feel the things I "should" have done were not the things that brought me towards my goal anyway and were taking me away from it (and wasting a ton of time).

You also mention the idea of regret for not appreciating something that you think must have some beauty, which you cannot see. I understand this as well, but maybe instead of focusing your mind on this, you look at those things that do have a beauty to you now and look at them more and more. Everything has its own beauty. Some appeal to us more than others.

Our lives are in the space between Isaiah Berlin's "We are doomed to choose and every choice may entail an irreparable loss" and Borges's Garden of Forking Paths, where every choice produces a quantum explosion of alternate futures. Ich bin ein Berliner for the most part, have a hard time seeing past the irreparable losses.

•   •   •   •   •   •   •   •   •   •   •   •

Seeing this response was comforting. I realized that just as clearing away my nostalgic clutter and my aspirational clutter in January had opened up more space for the possessions I really use in the present, relinquishing my fantasies of what I wished I found fun allowed me more room to do the things that I did find fun. Why worry about jazz clubs when I really wanted to design my own Book of Hours? Be Gretchen.

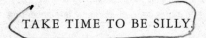

TAKE TIME TO BE SILLY

Preoccupied with my work, distracted by my running mental to-do lists, I'd become more humorless than I used to be. Many of my resolutions were aimed at gaining control of my temper, but that wasn't enough. A happy atmosphere isn't created merely by the absence of nagging and yelling but also by jokes, games, and tomfoolery.

One day while I was trying to prod everyone to put the groceries away as efficiently as possible, Jamie started showing off his juggling prowess with three oranges. Eliza and Eleanor were thrilled. I was annoyed.

"Come on, team!" I scolded. "Let's get this done. Jamie, put those oranges away and get the other bag." But we weren't in any hurry—only later did it occur to me that I should have enjoyed the moment and allowed the chore to be fun. Had I really become such a killjoy? The next time we were all unpacking groceries, I used two clementines to make goggle eyes at Eleanor and Eliza. They screamed with delight, Jamie laughed, and the groceries eventually got put away.

Studies show that in a phenomenon called "emotional contagion," we unconsciously catch emotions from other people—whether good moods or bad ones. Taking the time to be silly means that we're infecting one another with good cheer, and people who enjoy silliness are one third more likely to be happy.

As I went through my day, I looked for opportunities to see the ridiculous side of things, to enter into the spirit of Eliza and Eleanor's play, and to goof around. Instead of getting impatient when Eleanor wants to play the game "Where's Eleanor?" for the millionth time, I should try to have as much fun as she's having.

GO OFF THE PATH.

Diana Vreeland said, "The eye must travel." One of the things I admire most about my mother is her adventurousness—she's always eager to go new places and have new experiences; she's not intimidated by new situations; she's constantly developing new areas of mini-expertise just because she's interested in something. I wanted to be more like that, and my resolution to "Go off the path" was meant to push me to encounter the unexpected thoughts, unfamiliar scenes, new people, and unconventional juxtapositions that are key sources of creative energy—and happiness. Instead of always worrying about being efficient, I wanted to spend time on exploration, experimentation, digression, and failed attempts that didn't always *look* productive. But how should I do this?

In addition to the major interests that became the subjects of my books, I had lesser interests that I often shoved aside to concentrate on my "official" subjects. So, for instance, because I was working on my happiness project, I allowed myself to read anything related to happiness, but I ignored my extraneous interests. Now I wanted to goad myself into exploring these neglected byways. I discovered, however, that I'd been so diligent about ignoring these interests that I couldn't call any to mind when I tried to pursue them. I started keeping an "Interest Log" to get a better sense of what naturally caught my attention. When I read a newspaper article with special curiosity, stopped to look at a book in the bookstore, or became particularly engaged in a conversation, I noted the subject in my log.

A hodgepodge emerged: Saint Thérèse of Lisieux, obesity, cognitive bias, Francis Galton, organ donation, winter counts, Joseph Cornell, biography, people's relationships with objects, child development, photography, Zen koans, any kind of character analysis, methods of presentation of information, book design, and artists from the Golden Age of Illustration. I soon lost interest in my Interest Log, but I did push myself to pursue anything that caught my attention, to read at whim. I read Christopher Alexander's *A Pattern Language,* Edward Tufte's *The Visual Display of Quantitative Information,* the complete essays of George Orwell, Scott McCloud's *Understanding Comics*, the letters of Flannery O'Connor, biographies of Tolstoy, and every single book written by L. M. Montgomery.

Matthew Arnold wrote, "All knowledge is interesting to a wise man," and I often thought that if I took some time to learn more about the political situation in the Middle East, the architecture of Louis Sullivan, or the legacy of John Marshall, I would find these subjects very interesting. And probably I would. But then I think—well, I'd like to like Bach's music more than I do, and I could probably make myself like it better if I tried, but I don't like having to try to make myself like things. I want to spend more time on the things that I already like.

Along with following my jumble of interests, I searched for other ways to "Go off the path." I skimmed newspaper sections that I usually skipped. I disciplined myself to look into the windows of stores instead of walking by, oblivious. I started carrying a camera everywhere, to sharpen my eye.

Each Monday in the month of May, I bought three new magazines—ones that I would never have read otherwise. The first Monday, I wandered into a magazine shop near my gym that I'd walked by a thousand times, and I discovered a magazine gold mine. Racks lined the room from floor to ceiling, and more piles fanned out across the floor. Three times, I walked to an unfamiliar subject area, shut my eyes, and pulled out a magazine at random. After making sure that I hadn't accidentally picked up a porn magazine, I headed for the cash register. I ended up buying *Equus* (a special issue on "the Healthy Horse"), *Paper Crafts Gourmet* ("Easy ideas for food, cards & more!"), and *Fresh Outlook* ("The premier Christian magazine: spirit, body, life, home, business").

That night I looked at each of them from cover to cover. Never before had I thought about the challenges of taking a sick horse to a horse hospital or about hoof care. I'd never given any thought to the strangely fascinating life cycle of horse parasites. I did remain puzzled, however, by why a magazine store in midtown Manhattan stocked a magazine aimed at horse owners. I was intrigued by the text of *Paper Crafts Gourmet*'s sample invitation for a "Mocktail Party"—"Join us for dinner and mocktails with a Caribbean flair as we celebrate our 13th anniversary." I understood, of course, that some people don't drink alcohol. Is it the case that people in social sets where most people don't drink—observant Mormons, say—a host would serve "mocktails"? In *Fresh Outlook,* a Bible quotation grabbed my attention. All day long, I'd been annoyed by something a friend had done. I really wanted to criticize that person. I knew that if I did I'd feel remorseful afterward, but I was itching to pour out my irritation to some sympathetic ear. Then I came to a magazine page that had almost no text on it, so the words stood out in sharp relief: "Where there is no wood, the fire goes out; and where there is no talebearer, strife ceases." Proverbs 26:20. Point taken.

Each Monday, I have to admit, I dreaded reading the unfamiliar magazines. It felt like work and a waste of time, not like fun. But every week, I was glad that I'd done it. I always found something useful, provocative, or amusing. It was a painless (though slightly pricey) way to get new and unexpected ideas into my brain.

I intended to read a poem every night, but I never managed to make myself start that program. I'm sure it would have been worthwhile, but it seemed like too much work. Maybe I'll do that if I ever undertake a Happiness Project II.

START A COLLECTION.

I'd always wished that I had a collection—I'd never collected anything other than the knickknacks I'd collected as an eight-year-old. A collection provides a mission, a reason to visit new places, the excitement of the chase, a field of expertise (no matter how trivial), and, often, a bond with other people. It sounded like so much fun.

There are two kinds of collectors. The first kind seeks to have a complete set—of stamps, of coins, of Barbie dolls—and keeps a comprehensive and orderly kind of collection. The second kind of collector is driven by sheer desire, by the siren call of objects. My mother, of the second camp, has a tremendous knowledge and passion for objects and materials; she spends a lot of time visiting museums and walking through stores. Her collections of Japanese ikebana baskets, Tartanware, Royal Bayreuth porcelain tomatoes, and in particular her magnificent collection of Santa Clauses, give her great pleasure.

I wanted to start a collection—but what should I collect? I didn't have enough passion to justify an expensive collection, and I didn't want to collect junk. I decided to collect bluebirds, because bluebirds are a symbol of happiness. As far as I know, this connection arose from Maurice Maeterlinck's play *The Blue Bird*. A fairy tells two children, "The Blue Bird stands for happiness," and she orders them to set out to find the Blue Bird for her sick daughter. After many adventures, the children come home, unsuccessful—to find the Blue Bird waiting for them. "It's the Blue Bird we were looking for! We've been miles and miles and miles, and he was here all the time!" This unsubtle moral, of course, was quite fitting for my happiness project.

For no other reason except to keep my resolution to "Go off the path," one afternoon I stepped into an oddly comprehensive hardware store that's tucked into my neighborhood. It's small yet carries everything from light-bulbs to wooden puzzles to vacuum cleaners to fancy candles. I found myself staring up at an array of realistically carved, battery-operated "Breezy Singers" birds, which are outfitted with motion sensors so they move and twitter when anyone walks by. I wouldn't have considered buying one of the birds, except that I noticed that one of the birds was a bluebird. I stood transfixed. I could buy it for my *collection*. And so I did.

Another day, I went with a friend down to the Flower District. We wandered around looking at the fake and fresh flowers and the enticing cheap decorative gewgaws. I'm fascinated by bags of tiny plastic babies, fake zinnia heads, and butterflies made of gold sequins, and she's exactly the same way.

"Hey," I asked, "do you think any of these places would sell anything bluebird-related?" Having a collection transformed an aimless walk into a quest.

"Are you kidding?" she said. "There's a store that sells fake birds on this very corner." (How she knew this, I have no idea.) I bought a realistic bluebird for $2.71.

A year ago I wouldn't have allowed myself to make these purchases. I wouldn't have cluttered my office with bluebirds. I would've felt too guilty about taking time away from work to do "nothing." But my resolutions, like "Take time for projects" and "Go off the path," had changed my attitude. I saw that there was value in taking time to play, and along the same lines, I'd come to see the merit of treasuring a little clutter. I'd been relentlessly purging everything superfluous from our apartment when a friend said to me, "Remember to leave a little mess."

"Really?" I asked, surprised. "Why?"

"Every house needs a few junk drawers where you can find unexpected things. It's good to have a bit of chaos someplace, with some things that don't really belong anywhere but that you want to keep. You never know when stuff like that will come in handy, plus it's just nice to know it's there."

As soon as she said it, I knew she was right. Someplace I need an empty shelf, and someplace I need a junk drawer. Maybe my bluebirds do make for a bit of clutter—but that's fine. I want my office to house some playful elements that don't have to be useful.

As I wired my bluebird to the standing lamp next to my desk, I was glad that I'd gone off the path. It was fun. What's more, buoyed by this fun, I had the mental wherewithal to sit down and tackle something that I'd been postponing for a long time: figuring out how to post my own photographs onto my blog. So although I felt as though I'd been wasting time, in fact I'd been quite productive—just not in a typing-at-my-computer kind of way.

The work on Eliza's scrappy cap had given me an idea for another kind of collection. I started a "Happiness Box" in which I'd collect all sorts of little trinkets meant to trigger happy thoughts and memories.

I had the perfect box—a box I loved but that had never really been suitable for any purpose. My college roommate had given it to me. It was old, with a lid decorated with two panels painted with roses and two panels of cloudy mirror. It bothered me to have it sitting around, unappreciated; now I had a special plan for it. I put in an ancient, tiny Snoopy memo pad that reminded me of my sister when she was little. I added a miniature china teacup from my grandmother's teacup collection. I put in a figurine of Dorothy to remind me of home and Eliza's early love of ruby red slippers. ("Those ruby slippers have always had the power to take you back to Kansas," she'd croon as she'd reenact the climactic scene from *The Wizard of Oz*. "Just tap your heels together three times, Dorothy, and you'll be home in two seconds.") I put in my last pair of Coke-bottle glasses, made before they had the technology to make the lenses thin—they're hilarious, now that I don't have to wear them. A small cloth Little Red Riding Hood doll reminded me of all the times I'd read the story of "Little Red Hoodie" to Eleanor. A tiny Lego cone-shaped tree stood for all the Christmas trees of my childhood. I put in a New York Public Library bookmark—a reference to my favorite New York City institution. I put in an old, worn set of dice, to symbolize chance. I put in an American Girl miniature card featuring a bluebird.

The Happiness Box was as useful as the toy jars. I had lots of little objects lying around in odd corners that I'd kept for sentimental reasons. They were clutter when scattered around but extremely satisfying as a collection.

I asked blog readers about their collections. Did they find collecting fun? What did they collect?

My collections give me great joy. On the weekends and whenever I travel, I have an excuse to poke through little shops, flea markets, etc. It's not as much fun if I'm not looking for something. I collect glass snowglobes, Bakelite jewelry, light-up globes, and vintage Girl Scout stuff. It reminds me of my travels and good times with my friends, and also my apartment looks like "me" and (I think) stylish without me spending much money.

I love collecting vintage religious art books.

Yes, I have a few collections . . . vintage cake toppers, heart hankies, vintage bluebird "things" . . . and I think a few more. :) I used to collect hearts, but I started getting heart EVERYTHING from people as gifts. Then I felt obligated to display them. That took the fun out of it!

I think it's important to know that what you find fun can change. I've gotten rid of most of my doll collection because I don't enjoy them anymore. My mom says, "Save them for your daughter!" but I'm sure she'd have more fun making her own collection than inheriting 30–40 dolls that mean nothing to her. I'll just save a few.

As for collections, too much "stuff" displayed around the house makes me feel suffocated. I love to see how other people decorate their homes for the holidays, but to me it always seems like a chore—not fun. We tend to do simple, meaningful decorations for Christmas, and that's about it.

On the note of collections, I'm sure they're fun for others, but I simply don't want to store, clean, and maintain more things. I'd rather spend my time reading, decorating my house, or trying new recipes.

* * * * * * * * * * * * *

After having started both of my collections, I had to admit—I don't have a true collector's personality. Maybe one day I'll develop an interest in something that's intense enough to make a collection interesting—but I haven't found it yet. Turns out I can't just decide, "I'll start a collection!" and tap into the collector's high. Alas, that Secret of Adulthood is true: just because something is fun for *someone else* doesn't make it fun for *me*.

By the end of May, I'd figured out that "fun" falls into three categories: challenging fun, accommodating fun, and relaxing fun.

Challenging fun is the most rewarding but also the most demanding. It can create frustration, anxiety, and hard work. It often requires errands. It takes time and energy. In the end, however, it pays off with the most satisfying fun.

Usually less challenging, but still requiring a fair bit of effort, is *accommodating fun.* A family trip to the playground is accommodating fun. Yes, it's fun, but I'm really there because my children want to go. Was it Jerry

Seinfeld who said, "There's no such thing as 'Fun for the whole family'"? Going to a family holiday dinner, even going to dinner and a movie with friends, requires accommodation. It strengthens relationships, it builds memories, it's fun—but it takes a lot of effort, organization, coordination with other people, and, well, accommodation.

Relaxing fun is easy. I don't have to hone skills or take action. There's very little coordination with other people or preparation involved. Watching TV—the largest consumer of the world's time after sleeping and work—is relaxing fun.

Research shows that challenging fun and accommodating fun, over the long term, bring more happiness, because they're sources of the elements that make people happiest: strong personal bonds, mastery, an atmosphere of growth. Relaxing fun tends to be passive—by design. So if relaxing fun is the least fun kind of fun, why is watching TV so popular? Because although we get more *out* of challenging fun and accommodating fun, we must also put more *into* it. It takes energy and forethought.

The resolutions for this month were a bit of a struggle. I'd expected to find it fun to have fun, to go off the path, to start a collection, and it was fun, but only after I truly forced myself to do these things. I was a bit dismayed to realize how attached I was to my routine, how uninterested I was in trying new things, how much I disliked turning away from my self-assigned reading and writing. Was I really such a dull creature of habit?

Then I thought—wait. Novelty is stimulating, and it clearly was good for me, from time to time, to do something different. But my efforts had the unexpected benefit of making me realize how much I loved my habits and the familiar stops in my day. The pleasure of doing a thing in the same way, at the same time, every day, and savoring it, is worth noting. As Andy Warhol observed, "Either *once only,* or *every day.* If you do something once it's exciting, and if you do it every day it's exciting. But if you do it, say, twice or just almost every day, it's not good any more." I loved walking through the doors of the library that's just a block from my house and where I did most of my writing. I loved my three coffee shops where I worked when I wasn't in the library. I loved adding yet another volume to my tower of happiness-related books. I loved my workday. For me, that was fun.

As I finished up my month devoted to play, I was struck again by my good fortune in life; I didn't face an enormous obstacle to happiness. One of my main goals for my happiness project was to prepare myself for adversity, to develop the self-discipline and the habits to deal with a bad thing when it happened, but as I posted to my blog, I worried that people who faced a major happiness trial—such as a serious illness, job loss, divorce, addiction, depression—might be put off. Would they think, "Who is she to talk about happiness when everything in her life is fine?" I posted a few questions to ask readers their views:

. . . .

Are you more likely to think about happiness—and to take action to try to build happiness—when everything in your life is going well, or when you're facing a catastrophe?

If you're facing a catastrophe, does it help to think about taking little, ordinary steps to build happiness (having lunch with a friend, making your bed in the morning, going outside for a quick walk)? Or are modest efforts like that dwarfed by the magnitude of what you're facing?

My hope is that the ideas presented in the Happiness Project (book and blog) can help people trying to be happier within their ordinary life, and also help people trying to be happier in the context of a major happiness challenge. Do you think that following these kinds of strategies does help to build happiness?

Many readers responded. They seemed to agree that taking steps to be happy—whether in the context of ordinary life or catastrophe—was worth the effort.

* * *

I think it's important to recognize those happy moments when they are happening. As one who has struggled with chronic pain, I think it's a good day if I can get out and have that lunch with a friend or meet a deadline or notice the sunshine. Recognizing happy moments keeps me from being overwhelmed when the pain is too much.

I think you don't understand what happiness is until you are forced, through adversity, to look for it. I was divorced last year. The anger and sadness in both me and my children has been extreme, one child failed two semesters of school and finally started counseling for depression. Another one has been in trouble twice for alcohol-related problems. We handle things so differently: I work hard to find positive ways of dealing with my anger and sadness rather than just numb the pain . It's all about living in the moment and appreciating the smallest things. Surrounding yourself with things that inspire you and letting go of the obsessions that want to take over your mind. It is a daily struggle sometimes and hard work but I do understand happiness begins with my own attitude and how I look at the world . . .

I think adversity magnifies behavior. Tend to be a control freak? You'll become more controlling. Eat for comfort? You'll eat more. And on the positive, if you tend to focus on solutions and celebrate small successes, that's what you'll do in adversity. But with a correspondingly bigger success at the end.

I started what has amounted to my own happiness project about four years ago, by necessity rather than by choice. When my husband of 30 years died I realized that if I didn't make an active, conscious effort to figure out how to be happy, it wasn't going to happen. By this age, almost everyone has given at least some thought to happiness and how to go about achieving it. But in coming to terms with life as it is now, I realized that I wasn't even entirely certain what the hell happiness *was*.

I think a real life-shaking catastrophe can provide insights into happiness that you couldn't have any other way, but the more you know about what happiness really means for you before you come to that point, the better equipped you'll be to handle it. By all means, work on understanding happiness NOW.

I have had a difficult time these past few years and happiness was something I needed like water in a desert. I deliberately looked for EVERY LITTLE THING that might lift my mood, anything to get me through. One of the things I found was blogging. I practice yoga daily & meditate, which has provided great peace. I tend a vegetable garden, look after family & pets, cook and search for books I love to read. I make art and keep a journal. On sunny days, I think "great," a good day to be outdoors and on grey days I think "great," a good day to be indoors. It's all in your attitude. I choose to be happy, in spite of whatever drama that is going on in my life.

I was married a very long time and in all those years life revolved around my husband. Long story short, he dumped me, probably when things got too boring, dunno. I went into a depression for years. Why?? I had no life of my own, I didn't have the first clue as to who I was or what I wanted. It really never occurred to me in all those years of marriage that I needed to have a little tiny place for me to have my own things going on in life. Before the catastrophe, not after! After was too late. I was waiting to die, but I didn't die, God isn't ready for what little there is of me yet. Now, I see that it's like saving money, you can't save for when you get laid off, after you get laid off; rather, you have to save while you have a job and the money is still coming in. Life is like that, you have to DO while you are able to think of what you want, what you like, what needs it will fill, how it will enhance your life, how it will help you to maintain you, so that you have some reserves when crunch time comes.

For me, when things are going well, and I am happy, I don't think about happiness too much. It's when I start to become unhappy or depressed that I concentrate on it more and try to think of ways to improve it.

I have been through 2 serious bouts of depression in the last 4 years and because I have experienced this in the past I am very aware of the warning signs and try to catch it before it gets too bad. I find that keeping busy, especially seeing other people, is very helpful. It can be tough, as sometimes the last thing you want to do is see people or do ANYTHING at all, but if you can force yourself, you will usually end up having a good time and feeling better for it. The other strategy that certainly works for me although, it can be difficult to implement, is to become aware of your interior monologue and start arguing with it if it gets too negative. When I feel down, then I'll start thinking how useless I am; and pathetic and how nobody can really like me etc. etc. I find that determinedly interrupting these thoughts and forcing myself to think the opposite—or doing something that prevents thinking, like reading a book or watching a film, can really help avoid the downward spiral. (I admit mentally arguing with your thoughts can feel silly, but it does help!)

Remembering that joy exists is tough when you've been traumatized. Joy is a big concept and utterly unbelievable when we are in the depths of catastrophe. But happiness . . . happiness is more accessible. We can be miserable and then find ourselves laughing, even if just for a few seconds. It reaffirms the will to live, and from there we can branch out. Happiness, and the belief we have in it, is the foundation for survival. As a survivor of life-threatening trauma, it's been the small idea of happiness that propelled me toward the larger idea of joy that eventually freed me from complex-PTSD. And now here I am, happy daily and always striving for that joyful moment. It can be done! And your project—anyone's happiness project—can be a starting point for the long road to recovery.

I think you can "bank" happiness—that is to say, learn about yourself and what makes you happy while the sailing is smooth. When the waves swell up and get rough, you have the memories of the times you were happy. You've been there and done that so you know it's possible to do it again. It's a matter of weathering the storm and navigating to your happiness destination. It probably won't be the same path but it is achievable.

Reading these comments strengthened my conviction that happiness isn't something we should consider only when life is going well and also isn't something we should consider only when life is going badly. As Samuel Johnson said, "The business of the wise man is to be happy." In whatever condition life happens to offer.

6

JUNE

Make Time for Friends

- Remember birthdays.
- Be generous.
- Show up.
- Don't gossip.
- Make three new friends.

One conclusion was blatantly clear from my happiness research: everyone from contemporary scientists to ancient philosophers agrees that having strong social bonds is probably the *most* meaningful contributor to happiness.

The positive-psychology superstars Ed Diener and Martin Seligman cite studies demonstrating that "of 24 character strengths, those that best predict life satisfaction are the interpersonal ones." Epicurus agreed, albeit in slightly more poetic phraseology: "Of all the things that wisdom provides for living one's entire life in happiness, the greatest by far is the possession of friendship."

You need close long-term relationships, you need to be able to confide in others, you need to belong. Studies show that if you have five or more friends with whom to discuss an important matter, you're far more likely to describe yourself as "very happy." Some researchers argue that over the last twenty years, the number of confidants claimed by the average American has dropped. Perhaps because people move more frequently and work longer hours, they have less time for building friendships. (On the good side, family ties are strengthening.) In fact, if a midlife crisis hits, one of the most common complaints is the lack of true friends.

At the same time, no matter what they're doing, people tend to feel happier when they're with other people. One study showed that whether you are exercising, commuting, or doing housework, everything is more fun in company. This is true not just of extroverts but, perhaps surprisingly, of introverts as well. In fact, researchers reported that out of fifteen daily activities, they found only one during which people were happier alone rather than with other people—and that was praying. To my mind, that isn't an exception at all. The point of praying is that you're not talking to yourself.

Not only does having strong relationships make it far more likely that you take joy in life, but studies show that it also lengthens life (incredibly, even more than stopping smoking), boosts immunity, and cuts the risk of depression. To keep loneliness at bay, you need at least one close relationship with someone in whom you can confide (not just a pal with whom you talk about impersonal subjects, like sports, pop culture, or politics); you also need a relationship network, which helps provide a sense of identity and self-esteem and in which you can give and receive support.

For June, I focused on my relationships by strengthening old friendships, deepening existing friendships, and making new friends.

REMEMBER BIRTHDAYS.

All the happiness experts emphasized the importance of strengthening bonds with friends—but how exactly are you supposed to do that?

At a bare minimum, you can remember birthdays. I've never been good at remembering friends' birthdays—or, to be more accurate, I never remembered *any* friend's birthday (except one friend whose birthday falls the day after mine). Sending out birthday e-mails would ensure that I was in touch with my friends at least once a year. That sounded meager, but the fact is, it would be a vast improvement in many cases.

Many of my friends were on Facebook, which tracks birthdays, but many weren't, so I had to send out a bunch of e-mails to ask for birthdays. While I was at it, I decided to update my entire address book and copy the information onto my computer. For years, I'd been adding and crossing out entries in the pages of my Filofax, which were now practically illegible and dangerously irreplaceable.

Once I started getting replies, I found an Internet site, HappyBirthday .com, that sends out date reminders, and I started the long, tedious process of plugging birth dates into the Web site and typing address information into a Word document. Tackling this nagging task was dull work, but, as happiness theory would predict, completing it gave me a big boost of energy and satisfaction. Having the computerized address list didn't make me feel closer to anyone, but I think it will in the future, because it will be so much easier to stay close to people now that I have a legible, complete set of contact information.

When I told a friend about my resolution to send birthday e-mails, he said, "But you should *call!* A call is so much better." Along the same lines, when I started sending out "Happy birthday!" messages, I felt that I needed to send a long message if I hadn't been in contact with a friend for a long time. Then I remembered a Secret of Adulthood (courtesy of Voltaire): "Don't let the perfect be the enemy of the good." Fact is, I disliked talking on the phone and knew that I wouldn't call. Maybe I should, but I wouldn't. But I'd send an e-mail. And I decided that it was all right to send a very short e-mail. The important thing was to maintain the connection—and if I made the task too onerous, I might not stick with it.

I used HappyBirthday.com only for birthdays, but a friend told me that he also added significant dates from his children's lives. "That way I can be reminded of the first date the kids talked, waved bye-bye, or whatever. It's something nice to think about when I'm away at work." That struck me as a very happy idea.

Looking at my completed contacts list made me reflect sadly on some friendships that had faded. My address book held names of people who had once been close friends—but were no longer. In particular, I thought of a friend from high school. She'd been one grade ahead of me, and we were an archetypal case of the glamorous, hell-raising older girl and her studious, law-abiding, worshipful sidekick.

Without quite knowing how we'd fallen out of touch, I hadn't talked to her in more than a decade. I had her name on my list but no current information. I tried to get her phone number or e-mail address through our high school alumni office, but it didn't have anything. Of course not, that was so typical of her. She has a very common name, so I wasn't able to find her through an Internet search. After I'd finished my address list, though, I ran into a mutual friend from Kansas City who said that she might be living in New Orleans. That was all I needed finally to track her down. It was funny; after all these years, I still remembered that she was vain about her unusual middle name, and I found her by including the middle initial in my search terms. In these little ways, our childhood selves stay with us.

I called her at work. She sounded astounded to hear from me—but happy.

That night we talked for two hours. Hearing her voice brought back a lot of memories I'd forgotten; it reenergized some part of my brain that had been dormant.

Before we hung up, I remembered to ask, "What's your birthday?" This time, ten years won't go by without contact.

There wasn't really a way for us to become close friends again; we live too far apart, and too much time has passed. But for years, I'd been bothered by a sense of this dangling relationship; it gave me enormous pleasure to talk to her again. I made a note to pester her to come to Kansas City for the holidays.

BE GENEROUS.

Generous acts strengthen the bonds of friendship, and what's more, studies show that your happiness is often boosted more by providing support to other people than from receiving support yourself. I certainly get more satisfaction out of thinking about good deeds I've done for other people than I do from thinking about good deeds that others have done for me. It's a Secret of Adulthood: Do good, feel good.

For example, I felt great whenever I remembered how I'd helped a high school student. The organization Student Sponsor Partners had paired us as "sponsor" and "student" back when she was in ninth grade, and as a senior, she'd had trouble with her college applications. She'd been paralyzed by anxiety, and at first I'd had no idea how to help—but I asked around and managed to find a recommendation for a place to go, and one day we walked into the New Settlement Apartments College Center. We each breathed a sigh of relief when we saw the college posters, the bookshelves crammed with catalogues and test prep guides, and the sign asking "Need help writing your personal essay?" We'd found the right place. She got her applications in on time.

To do a better job of "Being generous," I had to reflect on the nature of generosity. Giving presents is one way to be generous, but taking a box of chocolates to a dinner party wasn't the answer for me. I don't begrudge spending money on friends, but I dislike shopping. I didn't want to create more errands for myself. So, okay. I don't like to shop or do errands, but what could I do, within the confines of my own nature, to be generous? I needed to cultivate generosity of spirit.

So I looked for other strategies. I hit on a few: "Help people think big," "Bring people together," "Contribute in my way," and "Cut people slack."

Help People Think Big.

One of the most generous acts, I've realized, is to help someone *think big*. Words of enthusiasm and confidence from a friend can inspire you to tackle an ambitious goal: "You should do that!" "You should start your own business!" "You should run for office!" "You should apply for that grant!"

I'd had a wonderful experience helping people think big myself. After Eliza started kindergarten, her nursery school arranged a reunion for all the children who had "graduated." While the children played with their former classmates, the nursery school directors, Nancy and Ellen, led a parent discussion about the kindergarten transition. As always, their insights were extremely helpful. When I stood up to leave, I thought, "These two should write a book." I was immediately convinced that this was the greatest idea ever. I suggested it to them on the spot.

"You know, we've thought about that," Ellen said, "but never very seriously."

That night I was so excited by the idea of their book project that I couldn't fall asleep. I didn't know these two women well, so I wasn't sure whether to press the issue. On the other hand, I felt positive that they could write a terrific book. I suspected that nothing more would happen unless I nudged them along, so I asked if they wanted to meet for coffee to discuss it. We met, and as we talked, they became increasingly enthusiastic. I put them in touch with my agent. They put some ideas down on paper. In a flash, they had a book contract, they wrote the book, and now Nancy Schulman and Ellen Birnbaum's *Practical Wisdom for Parents: Demystifying the Preschool Years* is on the shelves. Knowing that I played a small role in their achievement made me intensely happy.

As I was trying to stay alert for ways to "Help people think big," I had an enormous happiness breakthrough: my Second Splendid Truth. I'm not sure why it took me so long to see this plainly, because I'd understood the principles involved for a long time, but there was a circularity to these ideas that confused me. At last, one June morning, it came clear:

One of the best ways to make *yourself* happy is to make *other people* happy.

One of the best ways to make *other people* happy is to be happy *yourself*.

This was a major, major insight. Obvious, but major. The Second Splendid Truth clarified many things that had been mixed up in my mind.

For example, what is the relationship between altruism and happiness? Some people argue that because doing good deeds brings happiness, no act can be truly altruistic, because when we act for the benefit of others, we please ourselves.

The Second Splendid Truth (Part A) provides the answer: yes, of course, so what? All the better! That feeling of happiness doesn't minimize the "goodness" of the act. The fact is, the sight of someone performing a generous or kind act always makes me feel happy. *Especially* if it's *me!* The spectacle of virtue inspires the feeling of elevation—one of the most delicate pleasures that the world offers. As Simone Weil observed, "Imaginary evil is romantic and varied; real evil is gloomy, monotonous, barren, boring. Imaginary good is boring; real good is always new, marvelous, intoxicating." That's true no matter who is performing that real good.

Also, the Second Splendid Truth underscores the fact that striving to be happy isn't a selfish act. After all, one of the main reasons that I set out to become happier in the first place was that I figured I'd have an easier time behaving myself properly if I felt less anxious, irritated, resentful, and angry; when I reflected on the people I knew, the happier people were more kind, more generous, and more fun. By being happy myself, I'd help make other people happy. And vice versa. "Do good, feel good; feel good, do good."

Or to put it another way, suitable for a Snoopy poster: "There is an 'I' in 'happiness.'"

Bring People Together.

My children's literature reading group and my writers' strategy group showed me that another way to be generous was to "Bring people together." Studies show that extroverts and introverts alike get a charge out of connecting with others; also, because people are sources of information and resources for one another, if you help bring people together, you provide them with new sources of support.

I looked for ways to connect people. I helped organize a reunion of the Supreme Court clerks who clerked the same year that I did. (The justices organize reunions of their own clerks, but apparently, our group was the only one that held a reunion of all the clerks from a particular term.) I worked to start a group to support the children's rooms of the New York Public Library. I set up a friend on a blind date, which resulted in immediate, total love. I helped organize a barbecue taste-off: a bunch of people from barbecue-proud states brought their favorite home-state barbecue so we could debate the fine points of beef versus pork, tomato-based versus vinegar-based sauce, and whether popcorn, wilted greens, or baked beans were the most appropriate side dish. I introduced some friends who were moving to upstate New York to someone I knew up there, and they ended up being housemates. In each of these cases, bringing people together took some work from me: looking up e-mail addresses, coordinating schedules, and so on. But my resolutions kept ringing in my ears, so I stuck with it, and each time it was worth the effort.

I wanted some more ideas about how to "Bring people together," so I posted a question on my blog. Other people got the same charge from it that I did.

When team building for the churches I have worked with, we have a rule: FOOD, FOOD, FOOD, FOOD. I have found having really great finger foods are an excellent way to connect people. Particularly unusual foods that people have never tried. It allows you to spark up conversation between people about their interests.

The way I bring people together is by connecting them via whatever may be of interest to them. I know I am gifted at connecting the dots, and I use that skill in the relationships I build with others. I also have a tendency to collect and store what may seem like mundane information about people in my head. Inevitably, I will run into somebody who needs something, and because of the information I've collected I will have just the right person to introduce to them to help them achieve whatever they need. Ironically, I am not a social butterfly at all, but I always seem to be able to connect people at the right time.

I've found that whenever there's a get-together of friends, a simple "bring another friend!" prompt helps to make sure there are new people around. It's great for meeting new people or catching up with people you haven't met in ages that somebody happened to bump into and invite to the next get-together.

I get energy from meeting and aligning to new people but it wears my wife out. However, she is excellent at building and sustaining deep long-term relationships by "due dilligence," keeping on making appointments and maintaining correspondence. You have to find the aspect of connecting to others that works for you.

I use dinner parties as a way to connect people and to strengthen my relationship to all of them. The dinner parties are small—usually only 4–8 people—which allows for more in-depth conversation, and we put a lot of thought into matching all of the guests' interests to bring about a natural source of conversation [e.g., our last dinner party included couples who are animal lovers, another dinner party grouped world travelers, other occasions grouped knitters, Harry Potter fans, film buffs, tea lovers, etc.].

•   •   •   •   •   •   •   •   •   •   •   •   •   •

Contribute in My Way.

As I looked for other ways to "Be generous," it occurred to me that I should try to apply my First Commandment: "Be Gretchen." No, I didn't like to shop for gifts, but how could I be more generous?

Well, I reflected, I had the passion for clutter clearing that I'd developed back in January. Many of my friends felt oppressed by clutter, and I could help. I'd *love* to help. I started pressing my services on everyone I talked to. "Come on, let me come over!" I kept saying. "I need the buzz of clearing a closet! Believe me, you'll be happy you did it! You'll see, it's addictive!" My friends were intrigued but embarrassed. They didn't want me to see their messes. Once I managed to talk my way in, however, it was a hugely satisfying experience for both of us.

One night, for example, a friend and I worked on a single closet in her house for three hours. She hated her overstuffed closet so much that she never opened its door; rather than try to use it, she kept wearing the same clothes over and over again, and those she kept stacked on her bureau or draped over the side of the bathtub.

"What should I do before you come over?" she asked, the day before our meeting. "Should I buy any containers or special hangers or anything?"

"Do *not* buy one single organizing gadget," I said. "All you need is a few boxes of big garbage bags. Oh, one more thing—you need to figure out who's going to get all the stuff that you're going to give away."

"Can I decide that later?"

"No, it's better to know ahead of time. It's much easier to let go of things when you can imagine who'll benefit from receiving them."

"Okay, I can do that. Is that really all?"

"Well," I said, "maybe get some Diet Coke."

The next day, I showed up.

"I have no idea where to start," she said after the usual apologies for the disorder.

"Don't worry!" I said. "We'll go through it several times, and each time, we'll eliminate a new layer of clutter, until nothing's left except things you want to keep."

"Okay," she said dubiously.

"Let's just jump in." I knew from experience that I should start slow. "First, let's take out all the extra hangers."

As always, this initial step yielded a pile of unneeded hangers and cleared out a bunch of space. This was my flashy morale booster.

"Okay. Now we go through and look at each item. We're most suspicious of anything that still has tags or anything that was a gift or anything that doesn't fit you *now* or anything you associate with pregnancy."

We eliminated a layer. The giveaway pile was already large.

"Now we look for duplicates. If you have four pairs of black pants, are you really ever going to wear your least favorite pair? Nope." Good-bye to some khakis, some shirts, some turtleneck sweaters.

My friend clutched a T-shirt protectively. "I know you're going to tell me to get rid of this, but I can't. I never wear it, but it was my favorite shirt in college."

"No, keep it! Absolutely keep some clothes for sentimental value— just store them somewhere else. They don't need to be in your main clothes closet."

We started a box for keepsake clothes and slid it onto a high, unused shelf.

"Wow, it's looking great," she said as she surveyed our handiwork.

"We're not done yet," I cautioned. "Now we look for ways to make space. This closet is prime real estate. Let's put the heating pad and the duffel bag someplace else." She tucked those things into a hall closet. "Do you ever use these empty shoe boxes?"

"Nope! I have no idea why I kept those." She chucked them into the recycling pile. "What now?"

"Now you're warmed up. We'll go through the whole closet again, and you'll see, there's more you'll want to take out."

Slowly the back of the closet became visible. By the time she was done, her closet looked like something from a magazine. She had even achieved the ultimate luxury: an empty shelf. We both felt thrilled and triumphant. A few weeks later, I heard that when she'd had some friends over for dinner, she'd taken them all to view her closet.

I wasn't exaggerating when I said that I got a huge buzz from clearing her clutter. This kind of generosity was far easier for me to offer than giving a birthday present—and far more valuable to the recipient.

I looked for other opportunities to give. Last month, as part of my resolution to "Go off the path," I'd started carrying my camera everywhere, so I'd been taking more pictures. A friend was very pleased to get a photograph I had taken of her a few weeks before she gave birth; it was the only photo she had of herself pregnant with her second child. This was a tiny effort on my part, but it was significant to her.

Cut People Slack.

During this month of friendship, I happened to read two memoirs that reminded me of something that's easy to forget: people's lives are far more complicated than they appear from the outside. That's why, as part of my resolution to "Be generous," I meant to *cut people slack*.

The "fundamental attribution error" is a psychological phenomenon in which we tend to view other people's actions as reflections of their characters and to overlook the power of situation to influence their actions, whereas with ourselves, we recognize the pressures of circumstance. When other people's cell phones ring during a movie, it's because they're inconsiderate boors; if my cell phone rings during a movie, it's because I need to be able to take a call from the babysitter.

I tried to remember not to judge people harshly, especially on the first or second encounter. Their actions might not reveal their enduring character but instead reflect some situation they find themselves in. Forbearance is a form of generosity.

I reminded myself of this resolution when, as I stood calmly on a street corner with my arm outstretched for a taxi, a man came tearing up the street, flung out his arm, and jumped into the cab that, according to all New York City cab tradition, should have been mine. I started to get indignant about his unforgivable rudeness; then I thought of all the reasons that a person might be desperate to steal the first taxi he saw. Was he rushing to the hospital? Had he forgotten to pick up his child at school? I wasn't in any rush. I should cut the guy some slack.

In a letter to a friend, Flannery O'Connor put this precept another way: "From 15 to 18 is an age at which one is very sensitive to the sins of others, as I know from recollections of myself. At that age you don't look for what is hidden. It is a sign of maturity not to be scandalized and to try to find explanations in charity." "Find explanations in charity" is a more holy way of saying "cut people slack."

SHOW UP.

Just as Woody Allen said that "eighty percent of success is showing up," a big part of friendship is showing up. Unless you make consistent efforts, your friendships aren't going to survive.

I came to this realization during a conversation with a friend. I mentioned to her that I'd been procrastinating about making arrangements to visit some friends' new babies. I loved seeing the babies, but I often delayed because I felt that I should spend that time working.

"You should do it," she said. "That kind of thing really matters."

"You think so?" I asked. I'd been trying to convince myself that it didn't.

"Sure. Not that I hold it against anyone, but I remember who visited me after I had my baby. Don't you?"

Well, yes. These are the gestures that deepen casual friends into close friends, and confirm closeness between good friends. I immediately made dates to see the not-so-newborns. Around the same time, I made sure to stop by the opening day of a close friend's new clothing store. I came in about an hour after she opened, and I was the very first person to make a purchase. In each of these cases, I was very happy that I'd taken the trouble. It was fun, it made me feel closer to my friends, and it felt like the right thing to do (the First Splendid Truth in operation).

It was important not only to see close friends but also to see people I didn't know very well—say, by going to my husband's office party or showing up at parents' events at my daughter's school. Familiarity, it turns out, breeds affection. The "mere exposure effect" is the term for the fact that repeated exposure makes you like music, faces—even nonsense syllables—better. The more often you see a person, the more intelligent and attractive you'll find that person. I'd noticed this about myself. Even when I don't take an immediate liking to someone, I tend to like him or her better the more often we see each other. And at the same time, the more I show up, the more that person likes *me*. Of course, this doesn't always work. There are some people you just don't like, and seeing more of them would probably just lead to more aggravation. But in cases when you neither like nor dislike a person, mere exposure can work to warm your feelings.

DON'T GOSSIP.

Not infrequently, long-term happiness requires you to give up something that brings happiness in the short term. A good example? Gossip. When people gossip, they generally criticize other people, mostly for violating social and moral codes. Despite its bad reputation, gossip plays an important social role by reinforcing community values: it makes people feel closer to each other, it unifies people who play by the rules, it helps people get a sense of the values of their community, and it exposes the misbehavior of those who cheat on their spouses, don't return phone calls, or take credit for others' work. Interesting tidbit: both men and women prefer to gossip to women, because women are more satisfying listeners.

But although gossip may serve an important social function and it's certainly *fun,* it's not a very nice thing to do—and I always felt bad after a gossipy conversation, even though I enjoyed it at the time. I wanted to stop telling unkind stories, making unkind observations (even if factually accurate), or being too inquisitive about sensitive subjects. Even expressions of concern can be tricked-up forms of gossip: "I'm really worried about her, she seems down, do you think she's having trouble at work?" That's gossip. Even harder, I wanted to stop *listening* to gossip.

I was at a meeting when someone mentioned of mutual acquaintances, "I heard that their marriage was in trouble."

"I hadn't heard that," someone replied. *So fill us in!* was the implication of her tone.

"Oh, I don't think that's true," I said dismissively. *Let's not talk about that* was the implication of my tone. I'm embarrassed to admit how hard it was for me to resist this conversation. I *love* a rousing analysis of the dynamics of other people's marriages.

It wasn't until I tried to stop gossiping that I realized how much

I did, in fact, gossip. I don't consider myself mean-spirited, and it was sobering to realize how often I said something I shouldn't. Jamie and I went to a dinner party, and I sat next to someone whom I found insufferable. (The mere exposure effect definitely would not have worked its magic in this relationship.) I did a fairly good job of being friendly during dinner, but when we got home and Jamie said, "Jim's a nice guy, isn't he?" I answered, "You didn't spend any time with him. I think he's insufferable, and I could barely stand talking to him." I immediately felt terrible for saying something mean about someone who seemed like a nice enough guy (even though insufferable). Also, if Jamie liked someone, I shouldn't poison his mind with criticisms. I tried to convince myself that there was a spousal privilege for gossip that would permit me to gossip freely with Jamie, but I concluded that though it's *better* to gossip only to Jamie, it's still best to avoid gossiping altogether.

I learned another reason not to say critical things about other people: "spontaneous trait transference." Studies show that because of this psychological phenomenon, people unintentionally transfer to me the traits I ascribe to other people. So if I tell Jean that Pat is arrogant, unconsciously Jean associates that quality with me. On the other hand, if I say that Pat is brilliant or hilarious, I'm linked to those qualities. What I say about *other people* sticks to *me*—even when I talk to someone who already knows me. So I do well to say only good things.

MAKE THREE NEW FRIENDS.

It's easy to say to yourself, "I don't have time to meet new people or make new friends," but usually that's not true, and if you can find the time, making a new friend is tremendously energizing, not enervating. New friends expand your world by providing an entrance to new interests, opportunities, and activities and can be an invaluable source of support and information—and, just as happiness-inducing, you can play the same role for them.

One strategy I adopted for making more friends sounds a bit cold-blooded and calculating, but it really worked. I set myself a target goal. When I entered a situation where I was meeting new people, I set myself the goal of making three new friends—among the parents of Eliza's class, say. Starting a new job, taking a class, or moving to a new neighborhood, for example, are obvious opportunities to make new friends. Having a numerical goal seemed artificial at first, but it changed my attitude from "Do I like you? Do I have time to get to know you?" to "Are you someone who will be one of my three friends?" Somehow this shift made me behave differently: it made me more open to people; it prompted me to make the effort to say more than a perfunctory hello. Of course, "being friends" means different things in different stages of life. In college, I spent hours each day with my friends; these days I don't spend nearly that much time with Jamie. I have several friends whose spouses I've never met. That's okay.

As I was trying to meet my friend quota, I often had to push myself to act friendlier than I felt. Once again, though, I saw the value of my Third Commandment: "Act the way I want to feel." By *acting* more friendly, I made myself *feel* more friendly. Also, research shows that acting in an outgoing, talkative, adventurous, or assertive way makes people—even introverts—feel happier. That surprised me, because I thought introverts were happier in solitude and quiet. In fact, when introverts push themselves to act more outgoing, they usually enjoy it and find it cheering. Connecting with other people lifts people's moods.

Trying to make friends focused my attention on the challenge of making a good first impression—that is, how to act so that others would be interested in befriending *me*. First impressions are important, because when people evaluate others, they weigh initial information much more heavily than later information. Within ten minutes of meeting a new person, in fact, people decide what kind of relationship they want. I made a checklist for myself for my first encounters.

Smile more frequently.

Studies show that you tend to like people who you think like you; and that the amount of time you smile during a conversation has a direct effect on how friendly you're perceived to be. (In fact, people who can't smile due to facial paralysis have trouble with relationships.)

Actively invite others to join a conversation.

This is polite and appreciated by everyone. A person outside the conversation is relieved to be inside, and a person already in the conversation feels good that the kind gesture has been made.

Create a positive mood.

Don't focus attention on something negative, such as the long line at a bar or a bad experience on the subway. As Samuel Johnson said, "To hear complaints is wearisome alike to the wretched and the happy." Another reason why this is important: Jamie and I were standing in the hall outside the main room of a large function. A guy we knew slightly came up to us and said, "Why don't you go on in?"

I answered, "The room is freezing, and the music is too loud." Guess what? He was one of the chief organizers for the night.

Open a conversation.

Talk about the immediate circumstances: the reason for the event, the decor of the room, or even that old chestnut, the weather. A friend checks Google News right before he goes into any social situation to find a piece of news to use as a conversational hook: "Did you see that . . . ?"

Try to look accessible and warm.

Nod and say "Uh-huh," lean forward to show interest, try to catch every word, have good eye contact, use an energetic and enthusiastic tone, try to match the speed of the other person's speech. You want to try *not* to glance around the room, sit with your legs extended, or turn your body away from your interlocutor—these postures show a lack of engagement.

Show a vulnerable side and laugh at yourself.

Show a readiness to be pleased.

Most people would prefer to make people laugh than to laugh themselves; to educate rather than to be educated. It's important to allow yourself to be amused and to be interested. After all, one of the most delightful of pleasures is to please another person.

Follow others' conversational leads.

I often feel a perverse desire to thwart a person who is trying to drive a conversation in a particular way. I remember chatting with a guy who clearly wanted to talk about the fact that he had once lived in Vietnam, because he mentioned it a couple of times, casually and extremely tangentially. I should cooperate when I can tell that someone wants to talk about a certain issue.

Ask questions.

It's a way to show interest and engagement, and most people love to talk about themselves.

My research drew my attention to a phenomenon that I'd noticed in my own experience: when making friends, you'll find it easier to befriend someone who is already the friend of a friend. "Triadic closure" helps explain why I enjoy my kidlit book group and my writers' groups so much. Friendship thrives on interconnection, and it's both energizing and comforting to feel that you're building not just friendships but a social network.

The end of June marked the halfway point in my happiness project year, and I took some time to ponder my progress beyond my usual end-of-month assessment. I'm a big believer in using milestone moments as cues for evaluation and reflection. As I'd seen in my own life, and as many blog readers noted in various comments, a milestone such as a major birthday, marriage, the death of a parent, the birth of a child, the loss of a job, an important reunion, or the accomplishment of a career marker such as getting tenure or making partner (or not) often acts as a catalyst for positive change.

Evaluating myself at the six-month milestone for my happiness project, I confirmed that yes, I was feeling happier. When I asked myself what resolutions had contributed most to my happiness, I realized again that, far more than any particular resolution, my Resolutions Chart was the key element of my happiness project. Constantly reviewing my resolutions kept them fresh in my mind, so that as I went through my days, the words of my resolutions flickered constantly in my mind. I'd see my messy desk and think, "Tackle a nagging task." I'd be tempted to leave my camera at home and I'd think, "Be a treasure house of happy memories."

Keeping a Resolutions Chart was an idea that lots of people found appealing, as I discovered after I added this note at the bottom of my daily blog posts:

Interested in starting your own Happiness Project? If you'd like to take a look at my personal Resolutions Chart, for inspiration, just email me.

Over the next several months, hundreds of readers requested a copy.

I'm a college freshman and I think your charts will help me be happier and maybe also stay more on top of my work.

In addition to wanting to try something like this myself, my husband and I are going to create a month of resolutions together about Focusing on Our Marriage.

Please would you send me your resolutions list. I am a probation officer in London and I need to nail it to my wall, paste it gently on the ceiling in my head, and be mindful of there being ANOTHER WAY!

When asking for a copy of my charts, many people noted that they were starting their own happiness projects, and several sent me their own versions of my Twelve Commandments. These lists of personal commandments fascinated me, because they gave such a rich sense of the diversity of people's experiences:

Forget the past.
Do stuff.
Talk to strangers.
Stay in touch.
Stop the venting and complaining.
Go outside.
Spread joy.
Never bother with people you hate.
Don't expect it to last forever. Everything ends and that's okay.
Stop buying useless crap.
Make mistakes.
Give thanks: for the ordinary and the extraordinary.
Create something that wasn't there before.
Notice the color purple.

Make footprints: "I was here."

Be silly. Be light.

Be the kind of woman I want my daughters to be.

Shit happens—count on it.

Friends are more important than sex.

Choose not to take things personally.

Be loving and love will find you.

Soak it in.

This too shall pass.

"Be still, and know that I am God."

Remember, everyone's doing their best all the time.

Get a hold of yourself, Meredith!

Imagine the eulogy: how do I want to be remembered?

Expect a miracle.

I am already enough.

Let it go, man.

Light a candle or STFU.

Recognize my ghosts.

What do I really, really, really want?

Help is everywhere.

What would I do if I weren't scared?

If you can't get out of it, get into it.

Keep it simple.

Give without limits, give without expectations.

React to the situation.

Feel the danger (many dangers—saturated fat, drunk driving, not making deadlines, law school—don't feel dangerous).

Start where you are.

People give what they have to give.

Be specific about my needs.

Let go, let God.

If you're not now here, you're nowhere.

Play the hand I'm dealt.

Own less, love more.

One is too many; a hundred aren't enough.

Nothing too much.

Only connect.

Be a haven.

It was amusing to see that some people's commandments directly contradicted other people's commandments, but I could envision how different people would benefit from opposing advice:

Just say yes.
Just say no.
Do it now.
Wait.
One thing at a time.
Do everything all at once.
Always strive to do your best.
Remember the 80/20 rule.

As for me, six months into the project, I could say that although, as I'd realized in April, my basic temperament hadn't changed, each day I felt more joy and less guilt; I had more fun, less anxiety. My life was pleasanter with cleaner closets and a cleaner conscience.

One thing that had surprised me as my project progressed was the importance of my physical state. It really mattered whether I got enough sleep, got regular exercise, didn't let myself get too hungry, and kept myself warm. I'd learned to be more attentive to keeping myself feeling energetic and comfortable. On the other hand, one thing that didn't surprise me was that the most direct boosts to my happiness came from the steps I devoted to social bonds. Jamie, Eliza, and Eleanor, my family, my friends—it was my efforts to strengthen those relationships that yielded the most gratifying results. What's more, I noticed that my happiness made it easier for me to be patient, cheerful, kind, generous, and all the other qualities I was trying to cultivate. I found it easier to keep my resolutions, laugh off my annoyances, have enough energy for fun.

But the areas that had been toughest for me when I started were still the toughest. When I looked back on my Resolutions Charts, I could see definite patterns. The checks and X marks revealed that I was continuing to struggle to keep my temper, to go off the path, and to be generous, among many other things. In some ways, in fact, I'd made myself less happy; I'd made myself far more aware of my faults, and I felt more disappointed with myself when I slipped up. My shortcomings stared up at me reproachfully from the page. One of my Secrets of Adulthood is "Happiness doesn't always make you feel happy," and a heightened awareness of my failings, though salutary, wasn't bringing me happiness in the short term—but in the long term, I was sure, I'd be happier as a consequence of behaving better. I was comforted by the words of my model Benjamin Franklin, who reflected of his own chart: "On the whole, though I never arrived at the perfection I had been so ambitious of obtaining, but fell far short of it, yet as I was, by the endeavor, a better and a happier man than I otherwise should have been had I not attempted it."

Ironically, too, I suspected that I had lost some of my playtime to the happiness project. My resolutions were making me happier and I was having more fun, true, but it did feel as though I had less pure leisure time. Observing the evening tidy-up, remembering friends' birthdays, showing up, making time for projects, and all the rest meant that I had less time to reread *David Copperfield* in bed. Though of course I could make a resolution to cover that activity, too.

7

JULY

Buy Some Happiness

MONEY

- Indulge in a modest splurge.
- Buy needful things.
- Spend out.
- Give something up.

The relationship between money and happiness was one of the most interesting, most complicated, and most sensitive questions in my study of happiness. People, including the experts, seemed very confused.

As I did my research, Gertrude Stein's observation frequently floated through my mind: "Everyone has to make up their mind if money is money or money isn't money and sooner or later they always do decide that money is money." Money satisfies basic material needs. It's a means and an end. It's a way to keep score, win security, exercise generosity, and earn recognition. It can foster mastery or dilettantism. It symbolizes status and success.

It buys time—which can be spent on aimless drifting or purposeful action. It creates power in relationships and in the world. It often stands for the things that we feel are lacking: if only we had the money, we'd be adventurous or thin or cultured or respected or generous.

Before I could figure out my resolutions for the month, I had to clarify my thinking about money. I was skeptical of much of what I read. In particular, I kept seeing the argument "Money can't buy happiness," but it certainly seemed that people appear fairly well convinced about the significance of money to their happiness. Money is not without its benefits, and the opposite case, though frequently made, has never proved widely persuasive. And in fact, studies show that people in wealthier countries *do* report being happier than people in poorer countries, and within a particular country, people with more money *do* tend to be happier than those with less. Also, as countries become richer, their citizens become less focused on physical and economic security and more concerned with goals such as happiness and self-realization. Prosperity allows us to turn our attention to more transcendent matters—to yearn for lives not just of material comfort but of meaning, balance, and joy.

Within the United States, according to a 2006 Pew Research Center study, 49 percent of people with an annual family income of more than $100,000 said they were "very happy," in contrast to 24 percent of those with an annual family income of less than $30,000. And the percentages of reported happiness increased as income rose: 24 percent for those earning under $30,000; 33 percent for $30,000 to under $75,000; 38 percent for $75,000 to under $100,000; and 49 percent for more than $100,000. (Now, it's also true that there may be some reverse correlation: happy people become rich faster because they're more appealing to other people and their happiness helps them succeed.)

Also, it turns out that while the *absolute level* of wealth matters, *relative ranking* matters as well. One important way that people evaluate their circumstances is to compare themselves with the people around them and with their own previous experiences. For instance, people measure themselves against their age peers, and making more money than others in their age group tends to make people happier. Along the same lines, research shows that people who live in a neighborhood with richer people tend to be less happy than those in a neighborhood where their neighbors make about as much money as they do. A study of workers in various industries showed that their job satisfaction was less tied to their salaries than to how their salaries compared to their coworkers' salaries. People understand the significance of this principle: in one study, a majority of people chose to earn $50,000 where others earned $25,000, rather than earn $100,000 where others earned $250,000. My mother grew up feeling quite well-to-do in my parents' little hometown of North Platte, Nebraska, because her father had a highly coveted union job as an engineer on the Union Pacific Railroad. By contrast, a friend told me that he had felt poor growing up in New York City because he lived on Fifth Avenue above 96th Street—the less fashionable section of a very fashionable street.

The proponents of the "Money can't buy happiness" argument point to studies showing that people in the United States don't rate their quality of life much more highly than do people living in poverty in Calcutta—even though, of course, they live in vastly more comfortable circumstances. Most people, the world over, rate themselves as mildly happy.

It's admirable that people can find happiness in circumstances of poverty as well as in circumstances of plenty. That's the resilience of the human spirit. But I don't think that a particular individual would be indifferent to the disparities between the streets of Calcutta and the ranch houses of Atlanta. The fact is, people aren't made deliriously happy by the luxuries of salt and cinnamon (once so precious) or electricity or air-conditioning or cell phones or the Internet, because they come to accept these once-luxury goods as part of ordinary existence. That doesn't mean, however, that because people have learned to take clean water for granted, it no longer matters to their quality of life. Indeed, if that were true, would it mean it would be pointless to bother to try to improve the material circumstances of those folks in Calcutta?

But as I went deeper into the mystery of money, I was pulled toward research and analysis suitable for an entirely different book, away from my most pressing interest. Sure, I wanted to "Go off the path" to a point, and maybe one day I would devote an entire book to the topic, but for the moment, I didn't have to solve the enigma of money. I just needed to figure out how happiness and money fit together.

So was I arguing that "Money *can* buy happiness"? The answer: no. That was clear. Money alone can't buy happiness.

But, as a follow-up, I asked myself, "Can money *help* buy happiness?" The answer: yes, used wisely, it can. Whether rich or poor, people make choices about how they spend money, and those choices can boost happiness or undermine it. It's a mistake to assume that money will affect everyone the same way. No statistical average could say how a particular, *individual* would be affected by money—depending on that individual's circumstances and temperament. After a lot of thinking, I identified three factors that shape the significance of money to individuals:

It depends on what kind of person you are.

Money has a different value to different people. You might love to collect modern art, or you might love to rent old movies. You might have six children and ailing, dependent parents, or you might have no children and robust parents. You might love to travel, or you might prefer to putter around the house. You might care about eating organic, or you might be satisfied with the cheapest choices at the grocery store.

It depends on how you spend your money.

Some purchases are more likely to contribute to your happiness than others. You might buy cocaine, or you might buy a dog. You might splurge on a big-screen TV, or you might splurge on a new bike.

It depends on how much money you have relative to the people around you
and relative to your own experience.

One person's fortune is another person's misfortune.

Developing and applying a three-factor test brought back pleasant memories of being a law student, and it was a helpful framework, but it was complex. I wanted a more cogent way to convey the relationship between money and happiness.

As I was mulling this over, one afternoon I picked up Eleanor the wrong way as I leaned over her crib, and the next morning, I woke up with agonizing back pain. For almost a month, I couldn't sit for long, I found it hard to type, I had trouble sleeping, and of course I couldn't stop picking up Eleanor, so I kept reaggravating the injury.

"You should go see my physical therapist," urged my father-in-law, who had suffered from back problems for years. "There's a lot they can do."

"I'm sure it will get better on its own," I kept insisting.

One night as I struggled to turn over in bed, I thought, "Ask for help! Bob says that physical therapy works; why am I resisting?"

I called Bob at work, got the information, made an appointment at the physical therapist's office, and two visits later, I was 100 percent better. It felt like a miracle. And one day after my pain was gone, I took my health for granted once again—and I had the Epiphany of the Back Spasm. *Money* doesn't buy happiness the way *good health* doesn't buy happiness.

When money or health is a problem, you think of little else; when it's not a problem, you don't think much about it. Both money and health contribute to happiness mostly in the negative; the lack of them brings much more unhappiness than possessing them brings happiness.

Being healthy doesn't guarantee happiness. Lots of healthy people are very unhappy. Many of them squander their health or take it for granted. In fact, some people might even be better off with some physical limitation that would prevent them from making destructive choices. (I once went on vacation with a group that included the most wild and reckless guy I'd ever met, and I was quite relieved when he broke his foot during an early escapade, because the mishap prevented him from getting up to much more mischief.) Ditto, money. But the fact that good health doesn't *guarantee* happiness doesn't mean that good health doesn't *matter* to happiness. Similarly, money. Used wisely, each can contribute greatly to happiness.

The First Splendid Truth holds that to think about happiness, we should think about *feeling good, feeling bad, and feeling right, in an atmosphere of growth*. Money is most important for happiness in the "feeling bad" category. People's biggest worries include financial anxiety, health concerns, job insecurity, and having to do tiring and boring chores. Spent correctly, money can go a long way to solving these problems. I was extremely fortunate to be in a position where money wasn't a source of *feeling bad*. We had plenty of money to do what we wanted—even enough to feel secure, the toughest and most precious thing for money to buy. I resolved to do a better job of spending money in ways that could boost my happiness by supporting the other three elements of happiness.

INDULGE IN A MODEST SPLURGE.

I didn't spend enough time thinking about how money could buy me happiness.

I'd always had a vague sense that spending money was self-indulgent and that I should avoid spending money whenever possible. I once spent six very satisfying months living in San Francisco on $5 a day (except when I had to use the Laundromat). Now, however, I decided to find ways to spend to further my happiness goals. Studies show that people's basic psychological needs include the need to feel secure, to feel good at what they do, to be loved, to feel connected to others, and to have a strong sense of control. Money doesn't *automatically* fill these requirements, but it sure can help. People at every level of income can choose to direct their spending in ways that take them closer to happiness—or not.

I wanted to spend money to stay in closer contact with my family and friends; to promote my energy and health; to create a more serene environment in my apartment; to work more efficiently; to eliminate sources of boredom, irritation, and marital conflict; to support causes that I thought important; and to have experiences that would enlarge me. So, category by category, I looked for ways to spend money to support my happiness goals—within reason, of course.

For health and energy: in January, I'd already found a way to spend money to get better exercise. My strength-training workouts were expensive, but I was happy to know that I was doing something important for my long-term health. I also started spending more for food when I had to grab lunch outside our apartment. I'd always congratulated myself when I ducked into a deli to buy a bagel, because it was such a cheap and quick meal, but I stopped that. Instead, I gave myself a mental gold star for getting a big salad or soup and fruit, even though those choices were much more expensive.

For relationships: I'd give a party for my sister's wedding. It would be a major expenditure but also a major source of happiness. My relationship with my sister—and now with her fiancé—were among the most important in my life, but the fact that they lived in Los Angeles was a challenge. Hosting a party would be a way to make my own contribution to the wedding weekend.

For work: I bought some pens. Normally, I used makeshift pens, the kind of unsatisfactory implements that somehow materialized in my bag or in a drawer. But one day, when I was standing in line to buy envelopes, I caught sight of a box of my favorite kind of pen: the Deluxe Uniball Micro.

"Two ninety-nine for one pen!" I thought. "That's ridiculous." But after a fairly lengthy internal debate, I bought four.

It's such a joy to write with a good pen instead of making do with an underinked pharmaceutical promotional pen picked up from a doctor's office. My new pens weren't cheap, but when I think of all the time I spend using pens and how much I appreciate a good pen, I realize it was money well spent. Finely made tools help make work a pleasure.

For others: I wrote a check to the New York Public Library's Library Cubs program. I was already donating my time and energy to helping form this group, which supports the children's rooms in library branches. Time and energy helped the library; money was also useful.

For happy memories: I bought those file boxes in April—an excellent modest splurge. Also, I've never forgotten an older friend's observation: "One of my regrets about my children's childhoods is that I didn't have more professional photographs taken." As luck would have it, I know a terrific photographer. I arranged to have pictures taken of our children, and I was thrilled with the results. These photographs were far better than any snapshot I could take, and I bought several for us and for the grandparents, too. Remembering happy times gives a big boost to happiness, and looking at photographs of happy times helps make those memories more vivid. The money I spent on the photographs will strengthen family bonds, enhance happy memories, and capture fleeting moments of childhood. That's a pretty good return on the happiness investment.

I pushed a friend to "Buy some happiness" when I stopped by her apartment to admire her new baby (in keeping with my June resolution to "Show up").

"One thing is really bothering me," she said. "As a child, I was close to my grandparents, but my in-laws, who live nearby, aren't very interested in the baby. They already have seven grandchildren. My mother would love to see the baby all the time, but she lives in Cleveland and only comes to New York once a year."

"Well," I suggested, "at least until your son is in school, why don't you go to Cleveland every few months?"

She laughed. "That's way too expensive."

"It's a lot of money, but it's important to you. Could you afford it?" I knew she could.

"Well, yes, I guess," she admitted, "but it would be such a hassle to fly with a baby."

"You could tell your mother you'll buy her plane tickets if she'll come to New York more often. Would she come?"

"You know . . . I bet she would!" my friend said. This solution shows both the importance of thinking about how money can buy happiness and also the importance of my Eighth Commandment: "Identify the problem." What was the problem? Finding a way for grandmother and grandson to spend time together.

Money, spent wisely, can support happiness goals of strengthening relationships, promoting health, having fun, and all the rest. At the same time, the emotions generated by sheer buying, by acquisition, are also powerful. Happiness theory suggests that if I move to a new apartment or buy a new pair of boots, I'll soon become accustomed to my new possession and be no happier than I was before. Nevertheless, many people make purchases for the fleeting jolt of happiness they get from the very act of gain.

Now, you might say—that's not true happiness; true happiness comes from doing good for others, being with friends and family, finding flow, meditating, and so on. But when I look around, I certainly see many people who look and act happy as they do their buying. The fact that the happiness boost that hits at the cash register isn't particularly admirable doesn't mean that it's not real—or that it doesn't shape people's behavior. Research and everyday experience show that receiving an unexpected present or being surprised by a windfall gives people a real boost; in one study, in fact, when researchers wanted to induce a good mood in their subjects to study the effects, the way they accomplished this good mood was to arrange for those subjects to find coins in a telephone booth or to be given bags of chocolates. For some people, the rush of happiness that accompanies gain is so seductive that they spend more money than they can afford and are hit by remorse and anxiety once they get their bags home. The quick fix of happiness turns into a longer-lasting unhappiness.

The happiness that people get from buying stuff isn't attributable only to consumerist indulgence. Any kind of gain creates at least a momentary atmosphere of growth, and there are a lot of reasons why people love to make a purchase: to keep their home in good repair, attractive, and well stocked; to provide for loved ones or strangers; to master something new (such as the latest gadget); to possess an admired object; to teach their children; to live as their peers live; to live differently from their peers; to beautify themselves; to maintain a collection; to keep up with fashion; to defy fashion; to support a hobby or expertise; to benefit others; to justify the enjoyment of shopping as an activity; to offer and return hospitality; to give gifts and support; to win or maintain status; to establish dominance and control; to express personality; to celebrate; to maintain traditions; to break traditions; to make life more convenient, healthier, or safer; to make life more challenging, adventurous, or risky.

I myself rarely feel cash register happiness. Quite the opposite. I'm usually hit by buyer's remorse when I spend, a feeling that I call "shop shock." Perhaps that's why I really notice other people's enthusiasm. Nevertheless, even for me, indulging in a modest splurge could bring a lot of happiness, if I made my purchases wisely.

When I posted on my blog about my resolution to "Indulge in a modest splurge," and people posted examples of their own modest splurges, I was struck by the extraordinary variety in people's tastes.

* * *

For years I had cheap crappy cutlery in my kitchen. But last year I "spent out" on a few good knives. I paid $200 for three knives (a santoku, paring knife and a bread knife) and they were soooo worth the money and will last me forever.

I hate to say it but I hired a personal organizer to deal with our basement. There was an ad on the bulletin board in the grocery store. My wife had been after me since we moved to deal with the junk down there, which was three years ago. I have never been so happy to write a check in my life. It wasn't even that expensive especially because we ended up selling some stuff we had in storage in the basement.

My Christmas present to myself this year was a few pillows :-). I knew I didn't like mine, but the chain reaction of how they affect my comfort level -> hours and quality of sleep -> my mood the next day -> my productivity in work was pretty enlightening.

I got a dog. Having a pet turned out to be more expensive than I expected (food, shots, paying a neighbor to take care of her when I travel, and so forth) but it has also been a lot more fun than I expected. I live by myself and having a dog has brought me a huge amount of happiness.

* * * * * * * * * * * * *

For that matter, one of my own favorite "modest splurges" was something that wouldn't appeal to most people—but for me meant getting my hands on something I'd coveted for years. I called Books of Wonder, a famous children's bookstore in Manhattan, and ordered the "Wizard's Super Special," the complete set of the fifteen Oz books by L. Frank Baum. Two weeks later, I got a huge thrill when I opened the large box. The hardback set had a unified design, with matching spines, gorgeous covers, and the original color illustrations.

Now, positive psychologists might argue that I'd adapt to my purchase. Soon I'd be accustomed to owning these books, they'd sit on a shelf and gather dust, and I'd be no better off than I was before. I disagree. Because I have a real passion for children's literature, I knew these books would give me a boost every time I saw them. After all, I keep a big stack of the old, beat-up *Cricket* magazines I had as a child, and just seeing them on the shelf makes me happy.

As always, the secret was to "Be Gretchen" and to choose wisely. What makes me happy is to spend money on the things *I* value—and it takes self-knowledge and discipline to discover what *I* really want, instead of parroting the desires of other people. One of the purchases that made my father happiest was a pinball machine. He'd played hours of pinball as a boy, and one of his childhood dreams was to have his own so he could play whenever he wanted, for free. This isn't a purchase that would have made everyone happy, but it made him extremely happy.

While I was thinking hard about the relationship between money and happiness, I struck up a conversation with a fellow guest at a bridal shower. I told her that I was trying to figure out ways to "Buy some happiness." (As I explained the issue, it began to dawn on me, dimly, that I might be becoming a happiness bore.)

She became quite indignant at my suggestion. "That's so wrong!" she said. "Money can't buy happiness!"

"You don't think so?"

"I'm the perfect example. I don't make much money. A few years back, I took my savings and bought a horse. My mother and everyone told me I was crazy. But that horse makes me incredibly happy—even though I end up spending all my extra money on him."

"But," I said, confused, "money *did* make you happy. It makes you so happy to have a horse!"

"But I don't have any money," she answered. "I spent it all."

"Right, because you used it to *buy a horse.*"

She shook her head and gave up on me.

In some cases, though, when I tried to "Buy some happiness," it didn't work. I'd call this the "expensive-gym-membership effect," after the futile tendency to pay a lot for a gym membership with the thought, "Gosh, this costs so much, I'll feel like I have to go to the gym!"

I see the expensive-gym-membership effect when I pay money for something as a way to encourage myself to make time for something fun. For example, I went to three stores to hunt down the combination glue/sealer/finish Mod Podge, because I wanted to experiment with découpage. I really want to do it. But I bought that Mod Podge ages ago, and I've never used it. I want to take time for creative projects, but merely spending money on an art supply won't make it a priority. I have to decide to make time—and apparently I haven't. (Using Mod Podge can be another resolution for Happiness Project II.) Along the same lines, a workaholic friend of mine bought a fancy new tennis racquet because he wants to play more tennis, but he still hasn't used it. The tennis racquet is an expression of his desire to change something in his life, but just making a purchase won't accomplish that. He should have concentrated on fixing his calendar, not on finding the right racquet.

"Buy some happiness," of course, has its limits. I knew I'd better not overlook the effects of the hedonic treadmill, which quickly transforms delightful luxuries into dull necessities. Indulging in a modest splurge would give me a happiness jolt only if I did it rarely. Take room service. Until my honeymoon, I'd never had room service in my life—and it was a thrill. But if I traveled for business and got room service frequently, it wouldn't be a treat anymore.

Because money permits a constant stream of luxuries and indulgences, it can take away their savor, and by permitting instant gratification, money shortcuts the happiness of anticipation. Scrimping, saving, imagining, planning, hoping—these stages enlarge the happiness we feel.

Even a modest pleasure can be a luxury if it's scarce enough—ordering coffee at a restaurant, buying a book, or watching TV—which is why deprivation is one of the most effective, although unenjoyable, cures for the hedonic treadmill. A friend told me that when she lived in Russia in the 1990s, the hot water would periodically stop working for weeks at a time. She said that very few experiences in her life have matched the happiness she felt on the days when the hot water started working again. But now that she's back in the United States, where her hot water has never failed, she never thinks about it.

The hedonic treadmill means that spending often isn't a satisfying path to happiness, but nevertheless, money can help. My father still talks about the day he realized that he could afford to pay someone to mow the lawn. Some of the best things in life aren't free.

Another way to think about money's effect is in terms of the First Splendid Truth, as part of the "atmosphere of growth" that's so important to happiness. We need an atmosphere of *spiritual* growth, and as much as some people deny it, *material* growth is also very satisfying.

We're very sensitive to change. We measure our present against our past, and we're made happy when we see change for the better. In one study, people were asked whether they'd rather have a job that paid $30,000 in year one, $40,000 in year two, and $50,000 in year three or a job that paid $60,000, then $50,000 then $40,000. In general, people preferred the first option, with its raises—despite the fact that at the end of the three years, they would have earned only $120,000 instead of $150,000. Their decision might seem irrational, but in fact, the people who chose the first option understood the importance of *growth* to happiness. People are very sensitive to relative changes in their condition, for better or worse.

A sense of growth is so important to happiness that it's often preferable to be progressing to the summit rather than to be at the summit. Neither a scientist nor a philosopher but a novelist, Lisa Grunwald, came up with the most brilliant summation of this happiness principle: "Best is good, better is best."

One challenge of parenthood that I hadn't tackled in April, though perhaps I should have, was setting limits on buying treats for my children. For example, as a surprise, I bought Eliza a big book of optical illusions. As I expected, she loved the book—pored over it, looked at it with her friends, kept it out on her bedside table. I was so pleased with myself for choosing it for her. One day, not long after, I was in a drugstore that had a rack of cheap children's books. I spotted a book of optical illusions and almost bought it for Eliza; she'd enjoyed the other book so much. Then I stopped myself. She already had a book with three hundred illusions; this book probably didn't have much new. But even beyond that, I wondered if having two books of optical illusions might, in fact, dim Eliza's pleasure in the first book. It wouldn't seem as magical and definitive.

The head of Eliza's school told a story about a four-year-old who had a blue toy car he loved. He took it everywhere, played with it constantly. Then when his grandmother came to visit, she bought him ten toy cars, and he stopped playing with the cars altogether. "Why don't you play with your cars?" she asked. "You loved your blue car so much." "I can't love lots of cars," he answered.

It's easy to make the mistake of thinking that if you have something you love or there's something you want, you'll be happier with more.

BUY NEEDFUL THINGS.

When I began to pay attention to people's relationship to money, I recognized two different approaches to buying: "underbuying" and "overbuying." I'm an underbuyer.

As an underbuyer, I delay making purchases or buy as little as possible. I buy saline solution, which I use twice a day, one little bottle at a time. I scramble to buy items like a winter coat or a bathing suit after the point at which I need them. I'm suspicious of buying things with very specific uses—suit bags, hand cream, hair conditioner, rain boots, Kleenex (why not just use toilet paper to blow your nose?). I often consider buying an item, then decide, "I'll get this some other time" or "Maybe we don't really need this." As an underbuyer, I often feel stressed because I don't have the things I need. I make a lot of late-night runs to the drugstore. I'm surrounded with things that are shabby, don't really work, or aren't exactly suitable.

I gaze in wonder at the antics of my overbuyer friends. Overbuyers often lay in huge supplies of slow-use items like shampoo or cough medicine. They buy things like tools or high-tech gadgets with the thought "This will probably come in handy someday." They make a lot of purchases before they go on a trip or celebrate a holiday. They throw things away—

milk, medicine, even cans of soup—because they've hit their expiration date. They buy items with the thought "This will make a great gift!" without having a recipient in mind. Like me, overbuyers feel stressed. They're oppressed by the number of errands they feel obliged to do and by the clutter and waste often created by their overbuying.

After I posted about these two approaches, many underbuyers and overbuyers posted comments. People had no trouble recognizing themselves in my descriptions.

* * *

I tend to be an overbuyer because underbuying makes me feel stressed and disorganized. I like it when my girls have more than enough pairs of tights, when we have a two-week supply of paper towels on hand, when I have a full bottle of shampoo at the ready should I run out. Running out of tissues or milk or diapers makes me feel like a poor excuse for a mother. I love that feeling of coming home from Costco and putting everything away and feeling fully stocked.

I'm an underbuyer, and those 15-year-old L.L. Bean pajamas were just fine until the day all of the elastic fell out, all at once. . .

I'm a huge underbuyer and used to feel very proud of myself because of it. That was until I realized it was more of an obsession than a choice. I rarely have backup supplies like toothpaste or soap. I usually leave buying the backups until just hours before I'm about to run out. I used to be a performer so I think that's where I got my frugal training. But now it's hard to break this pattern. However, I'm happy to say that I recently let myself buy 6 rolls of paper towels instead of the 2 pack I usually get and also 3 new facecloths. And all of a sudden I felt incredibly wealthy. I was surprised at how giddy I became with such simple things.

* * *

I knew that I'd be happier if I made a mindful effort to thwart my underbuying impulse and instead worked to buy what I needed. For instance, I ended my just-in-time policy for restocking toilet paper. One of my Secrets of Adulthood is "Keep a roll of toilet paper tucked away someplace," so we never actually ran out, but we teetered on the dreary brink.

I mentioned this problem to Jamie. "We're like Walmart," he said. "We keep all our capital working for us instead of sitting on a lot of inventory."

"Well," I said, "now we're going to invest in some redundant supply." Moderation is pleasant to the wise, but toilet paper was something I wanted to keep on hand. This kind of little annoyance puts a surprisingly big drag on happiness. As Samuel Johnson remarked, "To live in perpetual want of little things is a state, not indeed of torture, but of constant vexation."

Another thing that I really needed was white T-shirts, because I wear them practically every day. I enjoy shopping only when I'm with my mother, so I waited to buy my T-shirts until my mother was visiting from Kansas City. I wanted T-shirts that were soft, stretchy, not too thin, V-necked, and long-sleeved, and to me, tracking down and buying such shirts seemed like an overwhelming challenge. My mother was undaunted. "We'll go to Bloomingdale's," she decided.

Though I felt dazed the minute I entered the store, my mother walked purposefully from one area to the next. As she began her systematic inspection, I trailed along behind her and carried the shirts she'd pulled out. After she'd considered every white shirt on the floor, I tried on—conservative estimate—twenty shirts. I bought eight.

My mother had joined with zeal my quest for the perfect white T-shirt, but when she saw the stack of monochrome cotton at the cash register, she asked, "Are you sure you don't want any other colors or styles? This is a lot of white shirts."

"Well . . ." I hesitated. Did I really want this many white shirts? Then I remembered a study showing that people think they like variety more than they do. When asked to pick a menu of snacks for the upcoming weeks, they picked a variety, but if they chose week to week what to eat, they picked their favorite snack over and over.

In the store, it seemed like a good idea to have a variety of colors. But I knew from experience that when I stood in front of my closet, I always wanted to pull out the same things: white V-neck T-shirt; black yoga pants or jeans; and running shoes.

Buy needful things. "Yes, I just want white," I said firmly.

Inspired by my shirt success, I replaced our leaky blender. I bought a personalized return-address stamp. I'd realized that the paradoxical consequence of being an underbuyer was that I had to shop *more often,* while buying extras meant fewer trips to the cash register. I bought batteries, Band-Aids, lightbulbs, diapers—things I knew we would need eventually. I finally ordered business cards, which I'd been putting off for years. I was inspired when, at a meeting, someone handed me the best-looking business card I'd ever seen. I got all the information so I could order a copycat version for myself.

My decision-making process for ordering a business card showed me that not only was I an "underbuyer," I was also a "satisficer"—as opposed to a "maximizer." *Satisficers* (yes, satisficers) are those who make a decision or take action once their criteria are met. That doesn't mean they'll settle for mediocrity; their criteria can be very high, but as soon as they find the hotel, the pasta sauce, or the business card that has the qualities they want, they're satisfied. *Maximizers* want to make the optimal decision. Even if they see a bicycle or a backpack that meets their requirements, they can't make a decision until after they've examined every option, so they can make the best possible choice.

Studies suggest that satisficers tend to be happier than maximizers. Maximizers spend a lot more time and energy to reach a decision, and they're often anxious about whether they did in fact make the best choice. As a shopper, my mother is a good example of what I'd call a "happy limited maximizer." In certain distinct categories, she's a maximizer, and she loves the very process of investigating every possibility. Now that Eliza and Eleanor were going to be flower girls in my sister's wedding, I knew my mother would love nothing more than to examine every possible dress, just for the fun of it. But too often maximizers find the research process exhausting yet can't let themselves settle for anything but the best. The difference between the two approaches may be one reason some people find a big city like New York disheartening. If you're a maximizer in New York City, you could spend months surveying your options for bedroom furniture or even wooden hangers. In Kansas City, even the most zealous maximizer can size up the available options pretty quickly.

Most people are a mix of both. In almost every category, I was a satisficer, and in fact, I often felt guilty about not doing more research before making decisions. In law school, one friend interviewed with fifty law firms before she decided where she wanted to go as a summer associate; I think I interviewed with six. We ended up at the same firm. Once I learned to call myself a "satisficer," I felt more satisfied with my approach to decision making; instead of feeling lazy and unconscientious, I could call myself prudent. A great example of reframing.

SPEND OUT.

I tend to cling to things—to stuff, to ideas. I reuse razor blades until they're dull, I keep my toothbrushes until they're yellowed and frayed. There is a preppy wabi-sabi to soft, faded khakis and cotton shirts, but it's not nice to be surrounded by things that are worn out or stained or used up. I often found myself saving things, even when it made no sense. Like those white T-shirts I bought. I'd surmounted the challenge of buying them; then came the challenge of *wearing* them. When I took them out of the shopping bag and laid them on my shelf—perfectly folded by the salesclerk as I've never learned to do—I could feel myself wanting to "save" them in their pristine glory. But not wearing clothes is as wasteful as throwing them away.

As part of my happiness project I wanted to stop hoarding, to trust in abundance, so that I could use things up, give things away, throw things away. Not only that—I wanted to stop worrying so much about keeping score and profit and loss. I wanted to *spend out*.

A few years ago, my sister gave me a box of beautiful stationery for my birthday. I loved it, but I'd never used it. When I was mailing some photos to the grandparents, I hesitated to use the new stationery because I was "saving" it; but to what better use could it be put? Of course I should use those notes. Spend out.

I looked through my apartment for ways to spend out. The toughest choices I made concerned things that sort of worked: the camera that had lost its zoom function, the label maker that didn't print properly. I hate waste, but it would probably have cost me as much money (and far more time) to repair these items as to replace them—and using them in their crippled states weighed me down. I replaced them.

My goal wasn't limited to my treatment of my possessions; it also involved my ideas. For example, when I thought of a great subject for a blog post, I often found myself thinking "That's a good idea, save it for another day." Why? Why delay? I needed to trust that there would be more, that I would have great ideas in the future and so should use my best stuff *now*. Pouring out ideas is better for creativity than doling them out by the teaspoon.

"Spending out" also meant not being rigidly efficient. The other night, Jamie and I rented *Junebug*—an extraordinary movie, all about the nature of love and happiness. I was tempted to watch a few of my favorite scenes again after we saw it the first time, but I decided that would be a "waste" of time. Then I remembered my resolution, which included spending out my time. After all, I know that sometimes the things I do when I'm wasting time turn out to be quite worthwhile. I went to "Scene Selection" to rewatch the scene at the church social.

The most important meaning of "Spend out," however, is not to be a scorekeeper, not to stint on love and generosity. This was related to my February resolution, "Don't expect praise or appreciation." I wanted to stop constantly demanding praise or insisting on getting paid back. Saint Thérèse of Lisieux wrote, "When one loves, one does not calculate." I'm a big calculator, always looking for a return, especially with Jamie.

"I gave Eleanor a bath last night, so you . . ."

"I let you take a nap, so you . . ."

"I had to make the plane reservations, so you . . ."

No! Spend out. Don't think about the return. "It is by spending oneself," the actress Sarah Bernhardt remarked, "that one becomes rich." What's more, one intriguing study showed that Sarah Bernhardt's pronouncement is *literally* true: people who give money to charity end up wealthier than those who don't give to charity. After doing complex number crunching to control for different variables, a researcher concluded that charitable giving isn't just correlated with higher income; it actually *causes* higher income. Some explanations for this surprising effect include the brain stimulation caused by charitable activity and also the fact that those who are seen behaving charitably are likely to be elevated to leadership positions.

It's certainly true in my household that spending out creates a wealth of love and tenderness, while calculation and scorekeeping build resentment.

To keep this important yet elusive resolution uppermost in my mind, I maintained a relic. In one of my last visits to my grandmother before she died, I picked up the My Sin perfume that had been sitting on her bureau for as long as I could remember. The bottle was still in its box, and when I opened it, I saw that it was still full to the top. I didn't ask her about it, but I'm sure someone, many years ago, gave her that bottle of perfume and she was "saving it." For what? After she died, I took the box home with me, and I keep it in my office to remind me to "Spend out."

I posted on my blog about that bottle of perfume, and several readers responded with their own experiences of "spending out."

Your story reminds me of some pretty linen napkins that I found in my mother's house after she died. I lived in that house for a LONG time and never even SAW those napkins. She was apparently "saving" them. For what, I have no idea. But she never did get to use them. Now they're mine and I'm sure as heck gonna use them the next time I have someone over for dinner, which come to think of it, is tomorrow night!

Life is too short to save your good china or your good lingerie or your good ANYTHING for later because truly, later may never come.

I can't believe that there is someone else out there that does this, too! I have struggled with this for years. I realized it WAS contributing to my mental dismalness! I thought I should be keeping some of my new, better stuff just in case of (so pessimistic, here!) "bad days ahead." Sadly, I found that I have even pushed it over on my own daughter (i.e., don't use up all the battery power in your toys!). I think that's when I realized it. Now, I am on the track to using it all up today . . . 'cause who knows about tomorrow!

I learned this lesson painfully. When I was a child, my grandparents gave me a very elaborate box of art supplies for Hanukkah—really beautiful paints, brushes, chalks, paper, etc. I kept "saving it," planning to use it only once I was a better artist, because I didn't want to waste any of these treasures. (As a kid, you really do see yourself getting more skillful, so this wasn't totally crazy.) One day, I happened to look for the box, and couldn't find it. My mother said, "Oh, you never touched that art set, so I figured you weren't interested." She'd taken it to the thrift shop! I was crushed. But I've never forgotten it. Sometimes "later" becomes "never."

GIVE SOMETHING UP.

Sometimes something that makes you happy also makes you unhappy, like smoking cigarettes, having one more cupcake, staying up until

3:00 A.M. to watch *The Godfather* for the fifth time, and—surely one of the most popular happy/unhappy activities—shopping. Many people get a big kick out of buying things, but once they're home, cash register happiness changes to remorse and guilt.

Although I'm generally an underbuyer, every once in a while I do switch to a "Buy" setting; a friend once described this as my "drive-by shopping mode." This happened when we moved to our current apartment. For the first time, I had my own little home office, and I went nuts outfitting it. I bought a complicated desk chair, a wooden desktop organizer, special boxes to hold my supplies, all kinds of mailing envelopes and elaborate notebooks and sticky pads, fancy rubber bands printed with patterns, a headset for my phone, an extra battery for my laptop, anything I could think of.

It was after I bought a magnetic paper clip holder shaped like a little chirping bird that I started to feel guilty about the amount of stuff I was accumulating. I resolved to "Give something up." I had everything I really needed, and I made a rule for myself: no more purchases for the office. I cut that category of spending out altogether—and it felt good to say no to myself and to stop buying. Enough.

When I wrote a blog post about my experience of resolving to "Give something up," someone wrote to say, "It's better to focus on the positive. Instead of telling yourself 'no' or 'never' or 'don't,' focus on what you want, and be moderate. Otherwise you're just setting yourself up to backslide and fail."

That's a good point to keep in mind, but I don't agree that it's always true. First of all, when I'm trying to give something up, I find it easier to give it up entirely than to try to indulge moderately. Also, sometimes it feels *good* to say, "I'm going to stop!" "No more!" "Maybe tomorrow, but not today." Happiness experts point out that merely making and sticking to a decision is a source of happiness, because it gives you a feeling of control, of efficacy, of responsibility. At times of financial stress in particular, taking control of your finances—even symbolically—can boost your mood because you're taking steps to control and improve your situation. At a time when I was feeling anxious about the expenditures related to our new apartment, it was comforting to refuse to spend any more in one particular area. (This wasn't really economically rational, because buying one kitchen chair dwarfed my savings on a stapler, but it was psychologically effective, nevertheless.)

I asked blog readers if anyone had ever boosted his or her happiness by giving up a category of purchases entirely, and many people posted about their own forfeits: "grabbing a Cinnabon in airports—so expensive and so unhealthy," "owning a car," "lottery tickets," "printed periodicals—now I read newspapers and magazines on-line only," and "trading up to get the latest cell phone."

* * *

When I moved into my current place, about a year and a half ago, I didn't subscribe to cable TV. Which meant I had no broadcast TV at all. Since then, TV watching has been "Netflix or nothing."

It was a choice based on frugality that had a philosophical savor to it. When that level of frugality is no longer necessary to reach my financial goals, I'll re-evaluate—but dollars to donuts, even if I resubscribe to cable I'll still watch less than I did before.

-bottled water
-no sugar-based snacks at work
-eating out at any time other than Friday/Saturday nights
As a result, the wife and I are losing weight and saving money.

No more buying things on eBay. At first it was fun but then it started to get out of hand. I was ending up with things I didn't really need or want, because I loved looking around and making discoveries. It was showing up in my wallet however. One day I clicked on the site and said to myself, "No more!" It has really been a relief. Plus I hadn't realized what an amount of time it was using.

Readers also mentioned that they'd been happy to give up things unrelated to spending, such as "sleeping until noon on the weekends," "checking TMZ.com," "eating cereal," and "sunbathing."

I have a story to tell about feeling happier as a result of giving up something.

About five years ago, I got a job at a local animal shelter. At the time I began my job, I was a big-time carnivore. However, the longer I worked at the shelter, the more I became uncomfortable with the fact that I was eating SOME animals at the same time that I was saving OTHERS. I was being irrational. More importantly, I was also being inhumane.

A few of my coworkers were vegans, and I soon joined them. I don't eat meat, dairy products, or eggs. I don't buy clothing made from fur, leather, or wool. I've read Gary Taubes's book (*Good Calories, Bad Calories*), so I'm not certain whether my diet produces any dramatic benefits in my health. But I do know that my behavior is now more consistent with my moral code. I also know that no matter what kind of a day I had, at the very least I can go to bed knowing that I did not contribute to the exploitation of sentient creatures.

I gave up processed sugar. This has been difficult, but not exactly for the reasons I thought it would be. I am a candy addict. I thought I would miss my Skittles and Starbursts and Life Savers and Twizzlers and Rainblo gum balls like crazy! But because I really went cold turkey—and TOLD PEOPLE about my plan—it has not been so tough. No negotiations, no little bits here and there—just, NO. I am still getting used to taking my coffee black, though. Such a change from 5–7 Splendas! 34 days later, is it worth it? YES! This is my one and only life.

Obviously, people's choices will be different. Just because I'm happier when I don't buy office equipment doesn't mean that other people should stop buying highlighters. But although the resolution to "Give something up" may sound severe and spartan, it can feel good to choose to forgo something.

Samuel Butler wrote, "Happiness and misery consist in a progression towards better or worse; it does not matter how high up or low down you are, it depends not on this, but on the direction in which you are tending." This seems the key to understanding the relationship between money and happiness.

However, because people differ wildly from one another in how they respond to money and the things it can purchase, it's practically impossible to make generalizations. Take my blender. When I replaced our leaky blender, I splurged and bought a very expensive, very powerful blender. For me, because I make smoothies every day, this blender is a daily joy. For a person who never cooks, a fancy blender would be nothing but a means of conspicuous consumption; he'd never give it another thought after buying it, and it wouldn't add to his happiness. If money is to enhance your happiness, it must be used to support aspects of life that themselves bring happiness to *you*.

Money. It's a good servant but a bad master.

It was during this month, in the midst of trying to understand the mysteries of money, that I had a bout of happiness project despair.

It had been a horrible Saturday morning. We were all in bad moods. Jamie had let me sleep late, which was nice, but my morning went downhill from the moment I emerged from the bedroom. After I'd had a cup of coffee, he asked if he could go to the gym, and I said yes—but I was simmering with resentment. Once he left, Eliza and Eleanor played nicely together for about five minutes, then started poking, teasing, and yelling.

At the nadir, Eleanor was throwing a tantrum—lying on the floor, kicking her feet, beating her fists against the floor, and shrieking. Why?

"Eliza looked at me!" Eliza joined in, sobbing, "It's not my fault! I hate it when she cries!"

All my happiness project resolutions started flashing through my mind, but I didn't want to "Sing in the morning" or "Take time to be silly" or "Give proofs of love." I wanted someone to worry about making *me* feel better. I'd been trying so hard to keep my resolutions, but was it working? No. Nothing about me had changed. But if I abandoned my resolutions, what were my options? I could sit on the floor and start howling. I could walk away from the girls, get into bed, and read a book. But would I be happier if I did? No.

Minutes passed, and none of us seemed able to move. I was furious at Jamie for being at the gym. Eleanor kept crying, Eliza kept crying, I stood in the doorway.

"This is ridiculous!" I yelled. "Both of you, stop it! You're crying about nothing!" Eleanor cried harder, Eliza cried harder. I fought back the urge to smack each of them.

"Don't yell at me!" Eliza wailed. "It's not my fault!" Eleanor rotated her body on the floor so she could start kicking the walls instead.

I had to do something. It took every ounce of moral strength that I possessed to say, "Crying makes a person thirsty. I'm going to get you each a glass of water." (Both girls love to drink water.)

I went to the kitchen. First I opened a can of Diet Coke for myself; then I poured two glasses of water. I took a deep breath and tried to sound cheerful. "Who's thirsty? Does anyone want some almonds?" I crossed my fingers.

Eliza and Eleanor straggled into the kitchen, sniffling melodramatically. They each took a drink of water and a few almonds. Then they sat down and drank more water and ate more almonds. Suddenly the mood lightened a bit.

"Hey," I said to Eliza, "did you eat much breakfast?"

"No," she said. "We started playing with the My Little Ponies."

"Note to self," I said, "don't let you two get too hungry." I started laughing hysterically, and the girls stared at me as they munched away.

That bad moment passed, but the rest of the day was hardly better. Eliza and Eleanor kept squabbling, Jamie and I kept bickering. Everybody was getting on my nerves.

That afternoon, while I was trying to prod the girls into tidying up the dozens of crayons that they'd scattered over the kitchen floor, I suddenly noticed that Jamie had vanished. "Jamie!" I yelled a few times, then went to hunt him down. I was enraged to find him fast asleep in the flying-Superman position on our bed. My scorekeeping kept running through my head: I got to sleep late, he got to go the gym, why did he get to take a nap, too? What was I going to get in return? "Remember," my conscience whispered, "no calculation." I ignored it.

My happiness project was making me feel worse, not better. I was acutely aware of all the mistakes I was making and the steps I *could* be taking—but I just couldn't. I wouldn't. To hell with the resolutions. Why was I even bothering with the resolutions? Many of them were actually directed at making other people happier, and no one appreciated my efforts, no one even noticed. I was particularly mad at Jamie. Did he ask me about my research? Did he utter one word of gratitude for the clean closets, the sweet e-mails, the decline in nagging? Nope.

I could hear the girls in the next room. "Mine!" "No, mine!" "Well, I was playing with it!" "Don't push!" "You hurt my arm!" And so on.

I stormed into Jamie. "Get up! Are you just going to listen to that? Do you enjoy hearing that shrieking and hitting?"

Jamie rolled over and rubbed his eyes. He fixed me with a look that I interpreted to mean "I'm waiting for you to get yourself under control."

"Don't just lie there, this is *your* problem, too," I snapped at him.

"What is?"

"Listen to Eliza and Eleanor! They've been like this all day. You fix it!"

"I'm sorry I'm not being helpful," he said. "I just don't know exactly what to do."

"So you figured you'd wait for *me* to deal with it."

"Of course," he said, smiling. He held out his arms to me. (I knew from my February research that this was a "repair attempt.")

"Are you giving me a gold star?" I lay down next to him on the bed.

"Yes," he said. The yelling from the girls got louder, then ominously quiet. "Ah, the happy sounds of home." We both started laughing.

"Are we in harmony?" he asked. "Even if I am a slacker napping husband?"

"I guess," I said. I put my head against his chest.

"I'll tell you what, let's go to the park. We need to get outdoors." He sat up and yelled, "Put your shoes on, you two! We're going to the park."

This announcement was greeted with wails of indignation: "Don't wanna put on shoes!" "I don't want to go the park!"

"Well, you're going to. I'll help you both get ready."

It was one of those days—and there would be others. A happiness project was no magic charm. But that night I did manage to keep one resolution, "Go to sleep earlier," and in the morning, things looked a little better. Although it took several days before my bad mood lifted completely, at least I was ready to tackle my resolutions again.

8

AUGUST

Contemplate the Heavens

ETERNITY

- Read memoirs of catastrophe.
- Keep a gratitude notebook.
- Imitate a spiritual master.

I'd become firmly convinced that money could help buy happiness. Still, there was something unappealing about thinking about money too much; it made me feel grasping and small-minded. By the end of July, I was relieved to turn from the worldly subject of money to the spiritual realm.

I figured August was a particularly good time to focus on eternal things, because we'd be taking our family vacation. Stepping out of my usual routine would allow me to see more clearly the transcendent values that underlay everyday life. First, however, I had to figure out exactly what I wanted to achieve in my contemplation of eternity.

My upbringing wasn't religious. As a child, I went to Sunday school when I visited my grandparents in Nebraska, and we celebrated Christmas and Easter with lots of decorations, but that was the extent of it. Then I married Jamie, who is Jewish. His upbringing had been about as religious as mine, and since we now had a "mixed" household, we had even less religion at home. We celebrated Christian holidays with my parents and Jewish holidays with his parents (which made both sets of parents very happy, because they never had to switch off) and observed all holiday traditions in a very secular, Hallmark-y way.

Nevertheless, I've always been interested in learning about religion and in the experiences of devout people. I'd describe myself as a reverent agnostic. I'm attracted to belief, and through my reading, I enter into the spirit of belief. Also, although I'd never thought of myself as particularly spiritual, I'd come to see that spiritual states—such as elevation, awe, gratitude, mindfulness, and contemplation of death—are essential to happiness.

When I mentioned to Jamie that my focus for August was "Eternity," he asked suspiciously, "You're not going to engage in a lot of morbid activities, are you?"

That actually sounded intriguing.

"I don't think so," I answered. "Like what?"

"I have no idea," he said. "But contemplating eternity sounds like something that might get tiresome for the rest of the family."

"No," I assured him. "No skulls on the coffee table, I promise."

But I had to find some way to steer my mind toward the transcendent and the timeless, away from the immediate and the shallow. I wanted to cultivate a contented and thankful spirit. I wanted to appreciate the glories of the present moment and my ordinary life. I wanted to put the happiness of others before my own happiness. Too often, these eternal values got lost in the hubbub of everyday routines and selfish concerns.

Will focusing on spiritual matters make you happier? According to the research, yes. Studies show that spiritual people are relatively happier;

they're more mentally and physically healthy, deal better with stress, have better marriages, and live longer.

READ MEMOIRS OF CATASTROPHE.

In AD 524, while in prison awaiting execution, the philosopher Boethius wrote, "Contemplate the extent and stability of the heavens, and then at last cease to admire worthless things." The challenges to my serenity were insignificant compared to execution, of course, but I wanted to cultivate the same sense of perspective so I could remain unruffled by petty annoyances and setbacks. I wanted to strengthen myself so I'd have the fortitude to face the worst, if (i.e., when) I had to. To achieve this, the great religious and philosophic minds urge us to think about death. As the Buddha counseled, "Of all mindfulness meditations, that on death is supreme."

But I wasn't sure how to go about meditating on death.

Medieval monks kept images of skeletons in their cells as memento mori. Sixteenth-century *vanitas* artists painted still lifes that included symbols of the brevity of life and the certainty of death, like guttering candles, hourglasses, rotten fruit, and bubbles. What could I do to achieve the heightened awareness that death and catastrophe bring—without putting that skull on the coffee table?

I hit on a memento mori that suited me: I'd read memoirs by people facing death.

I went to the library and checked out an enormous stack of books. I started by collecting accounts by people grappling with serious illness and death, but then I broadened my search to include any kind of catastrophe: divorce, paralysis, addiction, and all the rest. I hoped that it would be possible for me to benefit from the knowledge that these people had won with so much pain, without undergoing the same ordeals. There are some kinds of profound wisdom that I hope never to gain from my own experience.

August was a month of sunshine and vacation, which, because it made such a stark contrast to the dark confidences of these books, was probably the best backdrop. The reassurance of being with my family made it easier to experience vicariously so much unhappiness and loss.

As we were packing for a trip to the beach, Jamie glanced at a few of the books I'd stuffed into our battered duffel bag.

"Is this really what you want to be reading while we're away?" he said doubtfully as he scanned the book jackets. "Stan Mack on cancer, Gene O'Kelly on brain tumors, and Martha Beck on having a baby with Down syndrome?"

"I know, it seems like it would be incredibly depressing to read these books, but it's not. It's sad, but it's also—well, I hate to say 'uplifting,' but they are uplifting."

"Okay," he shrugged, "whatever. I'm taking *A Bright Shining Lie* and *Middlemarch*."

By the end of our trip, I'd finished every book I'd packed. I didn't agree with Tolstoy's observation that "Happy families are all alike," but perhaps it was true that "every unhappy family is unhappy in its own way." Although many of these memoirs described a similar circumstance— grappling with a life-threatening condition—each was memorable for its story of unique suffering.

As a consequence of reading these accounts, I found myself with a greatly heightened appreciation for my ordinary existence. Everyday life seems so permanent and unshakable—but, as I was reminded by these writers, it can be destroyed by a single phone call. One memoir after another started with a recitation of the specific moment when a person's familiar life ended forever. Gilda Radner wrote, "On October 21, 1986, I was diagnosed with ovarian cancer." "The call comes at 7:00 P.M. The tumor is malignant and inoperable." Cornelius Ryan recalled July 23, 1970: "On this soft morning I think I must begin to acknowledge the distinct possibility that I am dying. . . . The diagnosis changes everything."

Reading these accounts also gave me a new and intense appreciation for my obedient body—for the simple ability to eat or walk or even pee in the usual fashion. Being on vacation pulled me off my usual eating routine, and I found myself indulging in potato chips, milk shakes, grilled cheese sandwiches, and other treats that I wouldn't ordinarily eat. One morning I felt dejected because I'd gained a few pounds. But having just finished an account by a prostate cancer survivor made me feel far more kindly to my own body. Instead of feeling perpetually dissatisfied with my weight, I should delight in feeling vital, healthy, pain-free, fear-free.

A common theme in religion and philosophy, as well as in catastrophe memoirs, is the admonition to live fully and thankfully *in the present*. So often, it's only after some calamity strikes that we appreciate what we had. "There are times in the lives of most of us," observed William Edward Hartpole Lecky, "when we would have given all the world to be as we were but yesterday, though that yesterday had passed over us unappreciated and unenjoyed."

As I became more aware of the preciousness of ordinary life, I was overwhelmed by the desire to capture the floods of moments that passed practically unnoticed. I never used to think much about the past, but having children has made me much more wistful about the passage of time. Today I'm pushing Eleanor in a stroller; one day she'll be pushing me in a wheelchair. Will I then remember my present life? I couldn't get a line from Horace out of my head: "The years as they pass plunder us of one thing after another."

I decided to start a one-sentence journal. I knew I couldn't write lyrical prose for forty-five minutes each morning in a beautiful notebook (and my handwriting is so bad that I wouldn't be able to read it afterward if I did), but I could manage to type one or two sentences into my computer each night.

This journal became a place to record the fleeting moments that make life sweet but that so easily vanish from memory. It also helped me amplify the effect of happy experiences by giving me an opportunity to observe the third and fourth prongs of the Four Stages of Happiness, by expressing and recalling my feelings. Even after this summer had faded into the past,

I'd have a way to remind myself of unmemorable but lovely moments—the night Jamie invented a new kind of pie or Eliza's first trip alone to the grocery store. I can't imagine forgetting the time when Eleanor pointed to her spaghetti and said politely, "Mo' pajamas, please," when she meant "Parmesan," but I will.

On our last day at the beach, when we were packed up and ready to leave, Jamie and I sat reading the newspaper as we all waited for the ferry. Eleanor wandered off to practice her stair climbing on a short set of three stairs, so I went to help her climb up and down, up and down. I considered going to get a section of the paper to read as I stood with her—and then I realized, *this is it.*

This was my precious, fleeting time with Eleanor as a little girl, so adorable and cheery and persistent, as she went up and down those wooden stairs. The sun was shining, the flowers were blooming, she looked so darling in her pink summer dress; why would I want to distract myself from the moment by reading the paper? She'd already grown so much; we'd never have a tiny baby again.

I'd had this thought before—but suddenly I grasped that *this* was my Third Splendid Truth: *The days are long, but the years are short.* It sounds like something from a fortune cookie, but it's true. Each day, each phase of life seems long, but the years pass so quickly; I wanted to appreciate the present time, the seasons, this time of life. With Eliza, so much had already passed away—the Wiggles, *Pat the Bunny,* the make-believe games we used to play. One day—and that day wasn't too far away—I'd think back on Eleanor's babyhood with longing. This moment of preemptive nostalgia was intense and bittersweet; from that moment of illumination, I've had a heightened awareness of the inevitability of loss and death that has never left me.

I made a note of this moment in my one-sentence journal, and now I can hang on to it forever. "All packed up to go home—waiting for the ferry—Eleanor had as much fun climbing the beach stairs as anything we did all summer: up and down, up and down. Heartbreakingly adorable in her white hat that Jamie bought. Clutching her favorite toothbrush of

200 / THE HAPPINESS PROJECT

course. But everything changes, everything passes." (Sometimes I do cheat and write more than one sentence.)

When I introduced the idea of the one-sentence journal on my blog, I was surprised by the enthusiastic response. Clearly, a lot of people suffer from the same thwarted journal-keeping impulse that I do; like me, they find the prospect of "keeping a journal" enticing but intimidating. The idea of keeping a limited journal, to enjoy the satisfaction of keeping a record of experiences or thoughts but without the guilt or burden of writing at length, struck a chord.

Several people shared their own versions of a one-sentence journal. One reader kept a journal that he planned to give to his three children; he travels a lot for work, so he keeps a small notebook in his briefcase, and every time he gets on a plane—and only while passengers are boarding—he fills a few pages about the latest goings-on in their family. I think this is a particularly brilliant solution because it transforms wasted time (boarding time) into an enjoyable, creative, and productive period. Another reader wrote to say that, after seeing an interview with the writer Elizabeth Gilbert on *Oprah,* she'd been inspired to imitate Gilbert's practice of keeping a happiness journal in which she writes down the happiest moment of every day. Another reader, an entrepreneur, keeps a work journal, in which he notes any important work-related events, problems, or discoveries. He reported that it was an invaluable resource, because whenever he wants to remember how he handled a particular situation, his journal prompts his memory of how he handled it and what he learned: "I work alone, and if I didn't have a work journal, I'd probably keep making the same stupid mistakes over and over. Also it gives me a feeling of progress by reminding me how far I've come since I started my company."

Along with keeping the one-sentence journal, the catastrophe memoirs spurred me to take another, less pleasant kind of action. I realized that Jamie and I needed to get our affairs in order. All the memoirs emphasized how horrible it was to deal with cold logistics at a time of shock and grief.

"You know," I said to Jamie, "we really need to update our wills."

"Okay, let's do it," he answered.

"We've been saying that we should for *years,* and we really need to."

"Okay."

"We're never going to feel like doing it, so we just have to decide to *do* it." .

"Yes, you're right!" he said. "I'm agreeing with you. Let's get something on the calendar."

And we did. Zoikes, there's nothing like seeing the words LAST WILL AND TESTAMENT in lawyerly, old-fashioned typewriter-style Courier font to act as a memento mori. And although it sounds supremely unromantic, rarely have I felt such love for Jamie as I did in that lawyer's office. I was so grateful for the fact that he was alive and strong and that the wills seemed like play documents that would never matter.

With our wedding anniversary approaching on September 4, it occurred to me that a (slightly grim) way to mark the occasion would be to use our anniversary as an annual prompt to review our situation. Were our wills up-to-date? Did Jamie and I both have access to the financial information that the other person routinely handled? I knew offhand that Jamie had no idea where I kept our tax or insurance information or the girls' birth certificates. I should probably mention that to him. Repeating this "Be Prepared Day" review annually on our anniversary would keep it from seeming morbid—instead, it would be an ordinary expression of family responsibility.

Along the same lines, one night, as I lay reading in bed after Jamie had fallen asleep, I finished Joan Didion's *The Year of Magical Thinking,* about the first year after her husband's death. As I closed the book, I was overwhelmed with thankfulness at the fact that Jamie, snoozing gently beside me, was safe for now. Why did I get so irritated when he waited for me to change Eleanor's diaper? Why did I keep complaining about his failure to return my e-mails? Let it go!

I felt a bit guilty about my reaction to these memoirs of catastrophe. Was it wrong to feel reassured by reading about these sorrowful events? Viewed one way, there was a ghoulish quality to this downward comparison—a schadenfreude-ish exploitation, however benign, of other people's anguish. But the feeling of happy relief that came from recognizing my good fortune (for the moment) was something most of these writers had sought to create. Over and over, they emphasized the importance of cherishing health and appreciating ordinary life. (Other themes: keep up with your doctor's appointments, don't ignore big changes in your body, make sure you have health insurance.)

That said, I don't think these memoirs would cheer me if I'd had more brushes with serious illness; I don't think I'd be able to *stand* reading them. Jamie, for one, would never read these books. He's had too many unpleasant experiences in hospitals to want to visit voluntarily, even through the lives of other people.

KEEP A GRATITUDE NOTEBOOK.

Reading catastrophe memoirs made me extremely grateful for the fact that I wasn't experiencing a catastrophe. Research shows that because we measure ourselves relative to others, our happiness is influenced by whether we compare ourselves to people who are better or worse off. In one study, people's sense of life satisfaction changed dramatically depending on whether they completed sentences starting "I'm glad I'm not . . ." or instead, "I wish I was . . ." In the days after September 11, 2001, the emotion people most commonly experienced—after compassion—was gratitude.

Gratitude is important to happiness. Studies show that consistently grateful people are happier and more satisfied with their lives; they even feel more physically healthy and spend more time exercising. Gratitude brings freedom from envy, because when you're grateful for what you have, you're not consumed with wanting something different or something more. That, in turn, makes it easier to live within your means and also to be generous to others. Gratitude fosters forbearance—it's harder to feel disappointed with someone when you're feeling grateful toward him or her.

Gratitude also connects you to the natural world, because one of the easiest things to feel grateful for is the beauty of nature.

But I find it hard to stay in a grateful frame of mind—I take things for granted, I forget what other people have done for me, I have high expectations. To cure this, following the advice repeated by many happiness experts, I started a gratitude notebook. Each day, I noted three things for which I was grateful. Usually I logged my gratitude entries at the same time that I made my daily notes in my one-sentence journal. (These various tasks were making me happier, but they were also keeping me busier.)

After keeping the notebook for a week, I noticed something: I never thought to mention some of the most important bases of my happiness. I took for granted that I lived in a stable, democratic society; that I could always count on my parents' love, support, and general lack of craziness; the fact that I loved my work; the health of my children; the convenience of living right around the corner from my in-laws—not to mention the fact that I loved living right around the corner from my in-laws, a situation that many people might consider undesirable. I loved living in an apartment instead of a house: no yard work, no shoveling snow, no going outside to get the newspaper in the morning, no carrying out the trash. I was grateful that I would never again have to study for an exam or a standardized test. I tried to push myself to appreciate better the fundamental elements of my life, as well as the problems that I *didn't* have.

For example, one morning after Jamie had one of his regular appointments with his liver doctor, he still hadn't called me by lunchtime. Finally I called him. "So what did the doctor say?"

"No change," he said absentmindedly.

"What does that mean, 'No change'?"

"Well, nothing has changed."

Usually I wouldn't have given this report much thought, but pondering gratitude and reading catastrophe memoirs made me realize—what a happy day. No news is *fantastic* news. It got a starred entry in my gratitude notebook. I was mindful of being grateful, too, for all the bad fortune that had narrowly passed me by: the near miss on a bridge on an icy road, the time Eliza dreamily walked out into busy traffic before I could stop her.

Blog readers recounted their experiences with their own versions of a happiness notebook:

* * * * * * * * * * * *

I started a journal of my own a few months ago, in the form of a private blog on my own computer. I've spent a lot of time writing in it the things that have bothered me, or things in my life that I feel I have botched, but far less time writing down what I have to be grateful for.

From my experience, a gratitude journal is a great thing—and it doesn't really need to be a written journal. I tried a written journal for a couple of weeks, but it always felt artificial. Now, every day as part of my evening meditation I take some time to really become conscious of the things I am grateful for—and I intensify the emotion. Switching from writing down what I am grateful for to feeling gratefulness with my heart is a great thing. I learned a lot of that in Thailand, where many people have the habit of visiting temples and making merit. The first couple of times I went with them, I always asked them what to do and how to behave, and they answered you shall just pray with your heart, make gratitude for everything you experience a real heartfelt emotion. And this really made a big difference for me, from "a fake make-up gratitude" to a real, enriching experience.

I went through a terrible period when everything, and I mean everything, in my life went wrong. I had no self-esteem, no confidence in myself. So I started keeping a gratitude journal of things that I was grateful for about MYSELF. I was grateful that I had the discipline to keep exercising, even when I didn't feel like it. I was grateful that I'd given up smoking two years ago. I was grateful that I managed to organize a birthday party for my father. Maybe this makes me sound conceited, but keeping that journal helped me not be paralyzed by self-loathing.

* * * * * * * * * * * *

But after two weeks of keeping a gratitude notebook, I realized that although gratitude boosts happiness, my gratitude notebook wasn't having that effect anymore. It had started to feel forced and affected, and instead of putting me in a grateful frame of mind, it made me annoyed. Later, I read a study that suggested I might have had better luck with my gratitude notebook if I had kept it twice a week instead of every day; expressing gratitude less often seemed to keep it more meaningful. But by then I'd soured on the task. I gave it up.

Because my gratitude notebook didn't work, I had to find other ways to cultivate gratitude. I tied the action of typing my password into my computer to a moment of gratitude; while I waited for my computer to wake up from its slumber, I thought grateful thoughts. This gratitude meditation had the same effect as a gratitude notebook, but somehow it didn't bug me. (Speaking of "gratitude meditation," I noticed that if I put the word "meditation" after any activity, it suddenly seemed much more high-minded and spiritual: when waiting for the bus, I'd tell myself I was doing "bus-waiting meditation"; in the slow line at the drugstore, I was doing "waiting-in-line meditation.") I worked harder to appreciate my ordinary day. This thought arose most naturally when I put the girls to bed. I give Eleanor her sippy cup of milk, then cuddle her in my lap as I rock her to sleep. With Eliza, after Jamie has read to her from Harry Potter for half an hour, I go snuggle with her for fifteen minutes or so. We lie together on her bed, her head on my shoulder, and talk. I tried to appreciate the seasons more, too—to notice, in the midst of concrete and cabs, the color of the sky, the quality of light, the flowers in window boxes. "There is, indeed," wrote Samuel Johnson, "something inexpressibly pleasing in the annual renovation of the world, and the new display of the treasures of nature."

When I was feeling a distinct *lack* of gratitude, I tried to cure it by applying my Third Commandment to "Act the way I want to feel." Could I turn complaints into thankfulness? When I felt annoyed at having to take

Eleanor for her pediatrician's checkup, I told myself, "I feel grateful for taking Eleanor to the doctor." The crazy thing is—it worked! How disappointed I'd be if someone else took her. One sleepless morning, I was wide awake at 3:00 A.M., and at 4:00, instead of continuing to toss and fume, I told myself, "I feel grateful for being awake at 4:00." I got up, made myself some tea, and headed to my dark, quiet office. I lit my orange-blossom-scented candle and settled in—knowing that I'd have no interruptions for at least two hours. Instead of starting my day feeling frustrated or groggy, I started my day with a feeling of tranquility and accomplishment. Voilà! A complaint turned into thankfulness.

I'd been spending a lot of time thinking about trying to be more grateful. Then one hot Sunday afternoon, when we were at the pool with Jamie's parents, Eliza said to me, "You know what I was just thinking? 'I'm in the pool, it's summer, I'm seven years old, I'm wearing a very cute bathing suit, and my grandmother is asking me if I want anything to eat or drink.'" By which she meant: Life doesn't get better than this.

"I know exactly what you mean," I replied.

IMITATE A SPIRITUAL MASTER.

One of the most universal spiritual practices is the imitation of a spiritual master as a way to gain understanding and discipline. Christians, for example, study Thomas à Kempis's *Imitation of Christ* and ask, "What would Jesus do?" In the secular world, I believe, people often read biographies for spiritual reasons: they want to study and learn from the example of great lives, whether those of Winston Churchill, Abraham Lincoln, Oprah Winfrey, or Warren Buffett. That desire had certainly been one of the reasons why I'd wanted to write biographies myself. Now I decided to study and imitate a new spiritual master—but whom? I asked blog readers what spiritual masters they followed.

greatly admire & have learned a lot from 2 Zen teachers (although that's not a tradition I practice). Norman Fischer is a person of wisdom, patience & common sense. My favorite Jewish Zen grandmother (not mine), a woman of great wisdom, eloquence and candor, is Sylvia Boorstein. And lastly, from my own tradition, Rabbi Charles Kroloff.

Vincent Van Gogh. I know, I know, how could someone whose legacy involves cutting off his ear be a spiritual mentor? (Well, first of all, he didn't really cut off his ear . . .) All you have to do is read his collected letters, DEAR THEO, to see how spiritual Van Gogh was, and also, to gain inspiration from the life, thoughts, ideas, philosophies, and perseverance of this incredibly talented man, both in the art of painting, and also in the art of transcendence, self-empowerment, and self-belief.

Charles Darwin. Fantastically dedicated to finding out why the natural world looked the way it does; he didn't teach, he showed. His insights were down to long deep thought and lots and lots of hard work. There are several very good biographies that tell of his unexceptional childhood, his voyage on the *Beagle,* and how he deliberately chose to earn scientific respectability before he published his world-shaking ideas, backed by huge amounts of examples. It turns out that he was a fairly nice gentle man too. Anyone that looks that clearly at the world merits profound respect.

Anne Lamott because she is so honest and Rabbi Wayne Dosick even though I'm not Jewish.

Two that come to mind: Dr. Andrew Weil, an integrative medicine practitioner and author of many books on the subject. He discusses how people can feel better mentally, physically, and spiritually and his advice always resonates with me. Another is Natalie Goldberg, author of the popular writing book, *Writing Down the Bones.* It's a zen approach to writing, but as she points out, her advice can really apply to many things. To me, what's central to her ideas is self-forgiveness.

Actually, I would name the natural world as a spiritual teacher (I don't like the term "master"). Western culture assumes that only a human can teach spirituality, but in Indigenous worldview, any creature, any natural element can be a teacher. We can learn a lot if we learn to listen to and observe the natural world.

Viktor Frankl.

I'm not sure I've found a spiritual master, though the poetry and passion of Saint Paul have captivated me. My husband finds inspiration in the life of George Orwell.

The Dalai Lama. Just seeing a photo of him makes me happy. I never considered imitating him, though. Food for thought.

I've picked one and plan to learn more about his fascinating life. He's none other than one of our founding fathers—Ben Franklin. I just read the Wikipedia on him and it states—"A noted polymath, Franklin was a leading author and printer, satirist, political theorist, politician, scientist, inventor, civic activist, statesman and diplomat." I do remember reading that he did all these things but to this day I still can't figure out how. I have to do more research here.

Lama Norlha Rinpoche (www.kagyu.com if you're curious to know about him. Tibetan Buddhist like the Dalai Lama!). He's been my meditation teacher for over 25 years. The way he teaches is, in a way, the opposite of emulation, though he is very inspiring himself (funny, I first wrote that as "inspiriting"). It's more like he's trying to free me to be myself, in a deep down positive way.

I know this is weird, but I'm going with Dan Savage (the sex advice columnist). He's not so much a spiritual master as an ethical one. And yes, he's a self-admitted potty-mouth, but he also advocates honesty, love, and respect. And he's just so quotable, i.e., "it's a relationship, not a deposition." As you always say, we don't choose what we like to do, only what we do . . . and I might not have chosen to elevate Dan to that level, but it's how I genuinely feel about him.

Henry David Thoreau sprang immediately to mind. Also, Nature. This quote from Saint Bernard says it well: "You will find something more in woods than in books. Trees and stones will teach you that which you can never learn from masters." Perhaps I should research Saint Bernard . . .

Hermann Hesse. While I never thought about him as a spiritual guide I suppose he is, as I have a collection of all his books, memoirs and poetry. A quote from him I think you'd find interesting is "Happiness is a how; not a what. A talent, not an object."

Mother Teresa and Gloria Steinem!

St Francis of Assisi has taught me so much about accepting things that might appear as my enemy. Instead of hating, I can reframe a situation. For example, instead of hating mosquitoes, I remind myself how they feed the birds and they too have a purpose. I still dislike them, but I don't hate them like I used to. I love many things about St Francis and try to emulate him.

I work with people who—among other things—are seeking happiness. However, rather than encouraging them to model themselves on some-one—a spiritual someone—I ask them to consider several persons of their own gender whom they admire. It could be a figure from history, literature, the cinema, or someone they personally know, a figure from politics, a mentor, a family member, a celebrity. It really makes no difference who it is, as long as these two or three persons are individuals that they admire.

Once they have named those people, I ask them to identify specifically those characteristics that they admire (not their looks, please!).

Then I tell them this (very Jungian, but very useful to know): whatever it is that they admire in these individuals (and generally the characteristics tend to coincide for all the people they have mentioned) is something that is nascent in themselves, but that they have not yet brought into being.

That—the fact that it is still in the nascent and unrecognized stage in themselves—is the real reason why they admire it in the others. Once they have begun to bring these characteristics forth in themselves, they will begin to admire something different in others, in order to continue the cycle of growth into inner freedom and happiness.

Knowing what you admire in others is a wonderful mirror into your deepest, as yet unborn, self.

These suggestions were intriguing, and I was reading stacks of books about various figures, but I didn't feel a particular affinity for anyone until I came across Saint Thérèse of Lisieux. I'd become interested in Saint Thérèse after I saw her praised in Thomas Merton's memoir *The Seven Storey Mountain*. I'd been so surprised to see the cranky, monkish Merton write reverently about the sappily named "Little Flower" that I was curious to read her spiritual memoir, *Story of a Soul*. That book fascinated me so much that, without quite realizing it, I developed a mini-obsession with Saint Thérèse. I bought one book about her, and then another, and then another. I reread *Story of a Soul* several times.

One day, as he saw me trying to cram my latest Saint Thérèse biography onto the shelf (between *The Hidden Face of St. Thérèse* and *Two Portraits of St. Thérèse*), Jamie asked with a note of disbelief in his voice, "How many books about Saint Thérèse are you going to buy?" There are few topics that would interest Jamie less than the life of a Catholic saint.

I looked with surprise at the shelf and counted the biographies, histories, and analyses of Saint Thérèse. I'd bought *seventeen,* and I'd read every single one. I also had a videotape and a used book that was nothing but Saint Thérèse photographs—for which I'd paid $75 ("Indulge in a modest splurge"). Light dawned. I *had* a spiritual master. *Saint Thérèse* was my spiritual master. But why was I attracted to this Catholic saint, a French woman who had died at the age of twenty-four after having spent nine years cloistered with some twenty nuns—Saint Thérèse, the "Little Flower," known for her "Little Way"?

After I thought about it for five seconds, it became perfectly obvious.

I'd started my happiness project to test my hypothesis that I could become happier by making small changes in my ordinary day. I didn't want to reject the natural order of my life—by moving to Walden Pond or Antarctica, say, or taking a sabbatical from my husband. I wasn't going to give up toilet paper or shopping or experiment with hallucinogens. I'd already switched careers. Surely, I'd hoped, I could change my life without changing my life, by finding more happiness in my own kitchen.

Everyone's happiness project is different. Some people might feel the urge to make a radical transformation. I was vicariously exhilarated by these dramatic adventures, but I knew they weren't the path to happiness for me. I wanted to take little steps to be happier as I lived my ordinary life, and that was very much in the spirit of Saint Thérèse.

Thérèse Martin was born in Alençon, France, in 1873. Before her parents' marriage, her father had tried to become a monk and her mother a nun, but both had been rejected by religious orders; her five sisters who survived childhood all became nuns, and Thérèse became a saint. Thérèse tried to enter a Carmelite convent at Lisieux at age fifteen (two of her sisters were already there), but the bishop wouldn't permit it because she was too young. She traveled to Rome to ask Pope Leo XIII's permission personally, but the pope stood by the bishop's decision. Then the bishop changed his mind. When Thérèse was in the convent, her "Mother" was her older sister Pauline, who instructed Thérèse to write the story of her childhood, which became the basis of *Story of a Soul*. In 1897, at the age of twenty-four, Thérèse died an agonizing death from tuberculosis.

While she lived, no one outside her family and convent had heard of Thérèse. After she died, an edited version of her memoir was sent to Carmelite convents and Church officials as an obituary notice. Just two thousand copies were printed initially, but the popularity of this "Springtime Story of a Little White Flower," as she'd characteristically titled it, spread with astonishing rapidity; just two years after her death, her grave had to be placed under guard to protect it from pilgrims seeking relics. (It's hard to understand how such a short, modest account of childhood and youth could have such spiritual power—yet of course I feel it myself.)

Accordingly, in a suspension of the ordinary requirements, Thérèse got a fast-track canonization in 1925 and became "Saint Thérèse" just twenty-eight years after her death. To mark the centenary of her death, in 1997 Pope John Paul II made her a Doctor of the Church, the elite category of thirty-three supersaints that includes Saint Augustine and Saint Thomas Aquinas.

To me, the fascinating aspect of her story was Thérèse's achievement of sainthood through the perfection of small, ordinary acts. That was her "Little Way"—holiness achieved in a little way by little souls rather than by great deeds performed by great souls. "Love proves itself by deeds, so how am I to show my love? Great deeds are forbidden me. The only way I can prove my love is by . . . every little sacrifice, every glance and word, and the doing of the least actions for love."

There was nothing outwardly striking about Thérèse's life or her death. She lived an obscure existence, much of it without stepping foot outside her convent, and though she was born just one year before Churchill (while she was dying in the convent infirmary, he was fighting as part of the Malakand Field Force in British India), she seems like a figure from the distant, quaint past. Thérèse didn't overcome a dysfunctional family or monumental difficulties; she had loving parents and a tender, indulgent upbringing in prosperous circumstances. Although Thérèse confided in *Story of a Soul* that "I want to be a warrior, a priest, an apostle, a doctor of the Church, a martyr . . . I should like to die on the battlefields in defence of the Church," she didn't perform outstanding feats or undertake daring adventures; indeed, except for her trip to petition the pope, she stayed in her neighborhood and with her immediate family for her whole life. She wanted to suffer and to spill her blood for Jesus, and she did, but in a *little* way—not in a glorious confrontation in war or at the stake but by dying in agony, spitting up blood, as a pitiful tuberculosis victim.

As Pope Pius XI emphasized in the Bull of Canonization, Thérèse achieved heroic virtue "without going beyond the common order of things." (Reading about Thérèse taught me a lot about Bulls of Canonization and all the mechanics of saint making.) I couldn't aspire to Thérèse's saintliness, but I could follow her by aspiring to perfection within the common order of my day. We expect heroic virtue to look flashy—moving to Uganda to work with AIDS victims, perhaps, or documenting the plight of homeless people in Detroit. Thérèse's example shows that ordinary life, too, is full of opportunities for worthy, if inconspicuous, virtue.

One of my favorite examples: Thérèse intensely disliked one of her fellow nuns, Teresa of Saint Augustine, whom Thérèse described, without identifying her, as "a Sister who has the faculty of displeasing me in everything, in her ways, her words, her character." Instead of avoiding her, Thérèse sought out this nun at every turn and treated her "as if I loved her best of all"—so successfully that this sister once asked Thérèse, "Would you tell me . . . what attracts you so much toward me; every time you look at me, I see your smile?"

After Thérèse's death, when this disagreeable nun gave her testimony during the process of Thérèse's beatification, she said smugly, "At least I can say this much for myself: during her life I made her really happy." Teresa of Saint Augustine never knew that *she* was the unlikable sister mentioned in *Story of a Soul* until thirty years later, when the chaplain, in a fit of exasperation, told her the truth. It's a little thing, of course, but anyone who has ever suffered from a whiny coworker, a narcissistic roommate, or interfering in-laws can appreciate the heavenly virtue that befriending such a person would require.

Because of my happiness research, one of the passages in *Story of a Soul* that most struck me was Thérèse's observation that "for the love of God and my Sisters (so charitable toward me) I take care to appear happy and especially *to be so.*" Thérèse succeeded so well at seeming effortlessly happy, and her laughter came so easily, that many of her fellow nuns didn't recognize her virtue. One sister said, "Sister Thérèse gets no merit for practicing virtue; she has never had to struggle for it." Near the end of Thérèse's life, another sister observed that Thérèse made visitors to the infirmary laugh so much that "I believe she will die laughing, she is so happy"—at a time when Thérèse was in both secret spiritual torment and excruciating physical pain.

Buddhists talk about "skillful" and "unskillful" emotions, and this has the right connotation of effort and competence. People assume that a person who *acts* happy must *feel* happy, but although it's in the very nature of happiness to seem effortless and spontaneous, it often takes great skill.

I set out to imitate Thérèse by doing a better job of acting happy when I knew that my happiness would make someone else happy. I didn't want to be fake, but I could make an effort to be less critical. I could look for ways to be honestly enthusiastic—about foods that weren't necessarily my favorite things to eat, activities that weren't my first choice, or movies, books, and performances with which I could find fault. Usually I could find something to praise.

Also, I saw that I needed to make a bigger show of my happiness. For example, when my Kennedy biography came out, various family members asked questions that, in retrospect, I realize were meant to elicit responses from me such as "I'm so thrilled! It's so exciting to see it on the shelves! Everything is going great! I'm so happy!" But I have a perfectionist, dissatisfied, fretful, worrying nature, and I'm not easily thrilled. Looking back, I realize that the loving thing to do would have been to act happy not only for myself but also *for them.* I know how happy I am when one of them is very happy. How happy I was to hear Eliza say excitedly to my mother, as they were setting up an elaborate tea party, "Bunny, this is *so fun!*" and to hear my mother say, "Yes, it *is!*"

As often happened with the happiness project, it was only once I vowed to stop criticizing and carping that I realized the strength of my instinct to criticize and carp. But for the love of my family and friends, so loving toward me, I tried to appear happy and especially *to be so.*

A worthy model closer to home than Thérèse was my father. Nicknamed "Smilin' Jack Craft" by my sister's friends, one of his most lovable traits is that he is—or, I should say, he *acts*—unflaggingly cheerful and enthusiastic, and this makes a tremendous difference to everyone else's happiness. One day not too long ago, when we were visiting Kansas City, my father came home from work and my mother told him, "We're having pizza for dinner." My father answered, "Wonderful! Wonderful! Do you want me to go pick it up?" I knew my father well enough to know that he'd answer that way even if he didn't want pizza for dinner and even if the last thing he felt like doing was heading back out the door. This kind of unswerving enthusiasm looks easy, but when I tried to adopt that attitude myself, I realized how difficult it is. *It is easy to be heavy: hard to be light.*

Acting happy and, even more, *being* happy is challenging. Furthermore—and it took me a long time to accept this perverse fact—many people don't want to be happy or at least don't want to seem happy (and if they act as if they're not happy, they're not going to feel happy). I'm not including depressed people in this category. Depression is a serious condition outside the happy/unhappy continuum. Whether in response to a particular situation, such as a job loss or the death of a spouse, or an imbalance of chemicals in the brain, or some other cause, depression is its own beast. But many nondepressed people are unhappy, and some seem to want to be that way.

Why? It turns out there are a lot of reasons.

Happiness, some people think, isn't a worthy goal; it's a trivial, American preoccupation, the product of too much money and too much television. They think that being happy shows a lack of values, and that being unhappy is a sign of depth.

At a party, a guy said to me, "Everyone's too worried about being fulfilled, they're so self-indulgent. It's there in the Declaration of Independence, and people think they should be *happy*. Happiness isn't the point."

"Well," I said, "now that our country has achieved a certain standard of prosperity, people set their goals on higher things. Isn't it admirable that people want to be happy? If happiness isn't the point, what is?"

"Working for goals like social justice, peace, or the environment is more important than happiness."

"But," I ventured, "you think it's important to help other people, to work for the benefit of others, and of course it is—but why? Why worry about children living in poverty or malaria in Africa unless, at bottom, it's because you want people to be healthy, safe, and prosperous—and therefore happy? If their happiness matters, doesn't yours? Anyway," I added, "studies show that happier people are more likely to help other people. They're more interested in social problems. They do more volunteer work and contribute more to charity. Plus, as you'd expect, they're less preoccupied with their personal problems. So being happy actually makes you more likely to work for the environment or whatever."

He laughed derisively, and I decided that the proper happiness project response was to change the subject rather than get in an argument. Nevertheless, he'd raised the most serious criticism of happiness: it's not right to be happy when there is so much suffering in the world.

Refusing to be happy because someone else is unhappy, though, is a bit like cleaning your plate because babies are starving in India. Your unhappiness isn't making anyone else happier—in fact, quite the opposite, given the fact that happier people are more likely to act altruistically. That's the circle of the Second Splendid Truth:

> One of the best ways to make *yourself* happy is to make *other people* happy.
> One of the best ways to make *other people* happy is to be happy *yourself.*

Some people associate happiness with a lack of intellectual rigor, like the man who said to Samuel Johnson, "You are a philosopher, Dr. Johnson. I have tried too in my time to be a philosopher; but, I don't know how, cheerfulness was always breaking in." Creativity, authenticity, or discernment, some folks argue, is incompatible with the bourgeois complacency of happiness. But although somber, pessimistic people might *seem* smarter, research shows that happiness and intelligence are essentially unrelated.

Of course, it's *cooler* not to be too happy. There's a goofiness to happiness, an innocence, a readiness to be pleased. Zest and enthusiasm take energy, humility, and engagement; taking refuge in irony, exercising destructive criticism, or assuming an air of philosophical ennui is less taxing. Also, irony and world-weariness allow people a level of detachment from their choices: fast food, a country club membership, a gas-guzzling SUV, reality TV. I met someone who couldn't stop talking about the stupidity of celebrities and people who read celebrity gossip, but her disdainful remarks revealed that she herself followed it very closely. I had to bite my tongue not to quote Samuel Johnson's observation of Alexander Pope: "Pope's scorn of the Great is too often repeated to be real; no man thinks much of that which he despises." Ironic commentary was her strategy both to embrace and to disavow celebrity gossip.

Other people cultivate unhappiness as a way to control others. They cling to unhappiness because without it they'd forgo the special consideration that unhappiness secures: the claim to pity and attention. I know I've pled unhappiness to get points for something. For example, if Jamie asks me to go to a business dinner with him and I honestly tell him, "I don't want to go, I *really* don't want to go, but I will if you want me to," I feel as if I get more gold stars from him for going than if I fibbed, "I'm happy to go, I'm really looking forward to it." If I didn't complain, if I didn't express my unhappiness, Jamie might take my complaisance for granted.

Some people exploit unhappiness for decades. "My mother always made a big point that she'd sacrificed completing her Ph.D. program to stay home with me and my brother," a friend told me. "She was frustrated and angry, and she brought it up all the time. She used her unhappiness to control us and my father. We all felt guilty."

The belief that unhappiness is selfless and happiness is selfish is misguided. It's more selfless to act happy. It takes energy, generosity, and discipline to be unfailingly lighthearted, yet everyone takes the happy person for granted. No one is careful of his feelings or tries to keep his spirits high. He seems self-sufficient; he becomes a cushion for others. And because happiness seems unforced, that person usually gets no credit. Thérèse didn't get credit, even from her fellow nuns, for her tremendous efforts. Because she seemed so happy, they assumed that her behavior was effortless. I know a fortunate few people—such as my father—who seem naturally sunny-tempered. Now I wonder how effortless this really is.

There's yet another group of people who have a superstitious dread of admitting to happiness, for fear of tempting fate. Apparently, this is practically a universal human instinct and seen in nearly all cultures—the dread of invoking cosmic anger by calling attention to good fortune. This feeling haunted me as I worked on my happiness project. By directing attention at my happiness, was I somehow putting it at risk?

There's the related superstition that if you anticipate trouble and tragedy, you'll somehow forestall it. Fear and worry can be useful, because thinking about unpleasant consequences can prompt prudent actions, such as wearing a seat belt or exercising. But for many people, fear of what *might* happen is a source of great unhappiness—yet they feel there's a propitiatory virtue in fretting. For example, on some level, I feel guilty about not worrying more about Jamie's hepatitis C. I keep track of every piece of information we get, I go to many of Jamie's appointments, I've learned a lot about hepatitis C. But when it isn't an active issue in our lives, I don't think much about it, and sometimes my detachment seems . . . irresponsible. Shouldn't I be more concerned? But my worry won't change the reality of Jamie's liver. Whipping myself up into a frenzy of fear, however, would make both Jamie and me unhappy. (On the other hand, some believe that if you allow yourself to be *unhappy,* terrible things will happen—most likely cancer. This kind of thinking isn't new. During the Great Plague of London in 1665, for example, people believed that staying cheerful would ward off infection.)

Last, some people are unhappy because they won't take the trouble to be happy. Happiness takes energy and discipline. It is easy to be heavy, etc. People who are stuck in an unhappy state are pitiable; surely they feel trapped, with no sense of having a choice in how they feel. Although their unhappiness is a drag on those around them—emotional contagion, unfortunately, operates more powerfully for negative emotions than for positive emotions—they suffer, too.

Philosophers, scientists, saints, and charlatans all give instruction on how to be happy, but this doesn't matter to a person who doesn't *want* to be happy. If you don't believe you're happy, you're not. As Publilius Syrus observed, "No man is happy who does not think himself so." If you think you're happy, you are. That's why Thérèse said, "I take care to appear happy and especially *to be so*."

One of the key underlying purposes of this month's resolutions and my entire happiness project was to be able to bear up courageously when the phone rang with bad news—as inevitably, it would.

Well, bad news did come, right at the end of the month.

My mother called. "Have you talked to Elizabeth?" she asked.

"No, not for about a week," I answered. "What's up?"

"Well, she has diabetes."

"Diabetes?"

"Yes. Type 2, they think, but they're not sure. It's lucky they diagnosed her when they did—her blood sugar level was dangerously high."

"How did she figure it out? What happens now? Why did she get it?" Every random thing I knew about diabetes began zipping through my mind: the responsiveness of type 2 to changes in diet and behavior; the tensions that had arisen in the diabetes community between advocates for type 1 and type 2 over allocation of research money; memories from sixth grade, when I watched my friend injecting herself in her stomach with insulin. My mother told me what she knew. Then I called my sister to hear her tell the story over again.

Over the next several weeks, the news kept changing. At first the doctors thought Elizabeth had type 2, even though she doesn't fit the usual profile—she's young, thin, fit. That diagnosis was a blow, but two things cushioned it. First, she'd been feeling lousy, and getting her blood sugar under control made her feel much better. Also, we were relieved that she didn't have type 1, which requires daily insulin and can't be alleviated by diet and exercise. Well—it turned out she *did* have type 1.

When people are faced with serious setbacks, a psychological mechanism kicks in to help them see positive aspects in the situation, and I could feel myself starting to search for opportunities for "posttraumatic growth." With various resolutions ringing in my ears, I tried to keep perspective and feel gratitude. "It's so lucky they caught it when they did," I told Elizabeth. "You'll be eating well and exercising regularly. You'll get this under control, you'll get used to it, and you'll do great."

Elizabeth deployed the downward-comparison strategy.

"Yes," she said. "And think about all the other things it *could* have been. The diagnosis could have been so much worse. Diabetes really is manageable." What she didn't say, and I didn't say, was that sure, it could have been a lot worse—but it also could have been *nothing at all.*

After college, my roommate was in a bad car accident, and I flew out to Hawaii to see her. She was wearing a halo brace with bolts drilled into her skull.

"Do you feel lucky to be alive?" I asked.

"Well, actually," she said, "I feel like I really wish I hadn't been in a damn car crash."

It's not easy to stay focused on the positive. But I think that my resolutions did help me cope with this news. What if I'd been the one diagnosed with diabetes? I think they would have helped even more. A common eighteenth-century epitaph reads:

> *Remember, friends, as you pass by,*
> *As you are now so once was I.*
> *As I am now, so you must be.*
> *Prepare yourself to follow me.*

A true happiness project sentiment. *Now,* I kept reminding myself, is the time to keep my resolutions. Because the telephone is going to ring again.

9

SEPTEMBER

Pursue a Passion

BOOKS

- Write a novel.
- Make time.
- Forget about results.
- Master a new technology.

Returning from vacation made me appreciate my beloved library anew. This library, just one block from my apartment, is perfect: a beautiful building, open stacks, Internet access, a terrific children's section, and a quiet study room in which to do my writing—and boy, is that room quiet. I still remember the glares I got one morning when I forgot to mute the start-up tones on my laptop. It was easy to take the library for granted—I'd been going there several times a week for seven years—but my brief absence reminded me how much I loved it (thus proving the advice of happiness experts, who advocate periods of deprivation to sharpen pleasures).

Given my happiness to be back at the library—and also September's association with the beginning of the school year—it was appropriate that this month revolve around books. My chief resolution for the month was to "Pursue a passion," which in my case meant everything related to books. I love reading and writing, and my work centers on reading and writing, yet these activities still get crowded out of my time.

Long ago, I read the writer Dorothea Brande's warning that writers are too inclined to spend their time on wordy occupations like reading, talking, and watching TV, movies, and plays. Instead, she suggested, writers should recharge themselves with language-free occupations like listening to music, visiting museums, playing solitaire, or taking long walks alone. That made sense to me, and I'd sporadically tried to follow that advice. But during the period when I was preparing for my happiness project, while browsing in a bookstore, I had a glaringly obvious realization: for better or worse, what I loved to do was to read, to write, and to make books—really, if I was honest, to the exclusion of practically any other activity.

A while back, a friend with three children mentioned to me, "On the weekends, I like a day when we all spend at least two hours in the morning and two hours in the afternoon playing outside."

"On the weekends," I answered, "I like a day when we all lie around reading in our pajamas until after lunch." True—but I felt bad about it. Why? Why did I think her inclinations were superior? Why do I feel guilty for lying around, "just reading"? Probably because that's what comes most naturally to me. I *wish* I were different, that I had a wider range of interests. But I don't. Now, though, it was time to be more thoughtful about pursuing my passion for reading and writing. To me, that sounded like a lot more fun than playing outside. (Of course, until Eleanor was older, mornings spent reading would be pure fantasy, but we'd had them before, and we'd have them again.)

To keep this month's resolution to "Pursue a passion," I first had to recognize my passion. Done. My next step was to make time for it, to find ways to integrate my passion into my ordinary days, and to stop measuring myself against some irrelevant standard of efficiency. I also wanted to learn to master some of the new technology that makes bookmaking easy.

Not everyone shares my particular passion, of course; instead of books, it might be college football, or community theater, or politics, or garage sales. But whatever your passion might be, happiness research predicts that making time for a passion and treating it as a real priority instead of an "extra" to be fitted in at a free moment (which many people practically never have) will bring a tremendous happiness boost.

One thing I learned from my blog, however, was that some people feel overwhelmed by the question "What's your passion?" It seems so large and unanswerable that they feel paralyzed. If so, a useful clue to finding a passion to pursue, whether for work or play, is to *"Do* what you *do."* What you enjoyed doing as a ten-year-old, or choose to do on a free Saturday afternoon, is a strong indication of your passion. (One blog reader pointed to an even more basic indicator: "Actually very similar to advice from a physics professor of mine, who said, 'What do you think about when you're sitting on the toilet? Because that's what you *want* to think about.'") "Do what you do" is helpful because it points you to examining your behavior rather than your self-conception and therefore may be a clearer guide to your preferences.

WRITE A NOVEL.

My most ambitious project for the month was to write a novel. In thirty days. I'd never had the urge to run marathons or climb mountains, but the thought of completing a novel in a month filled me with the same kind of lust for the thrill of exertion. I wanted to find out whether I could do it.

A while back, when I'd run into an acquaintance on the street, she'd mentioned that she was writing a novel in a month.

"You are?" I asked, immediately intrigued. "How?"

"I got this book, *No Plot? No Problem!* by Chris Baty. You start without any preparation, you don't edit yourself, and by writing 1,667 words a day, you write a fifty-thousand-word novel in thirty days."

"Fifty thousand words?" I asked. "Is that long enough to be a real novel?"

"That's as long as *The Catcher in the Rye* or *The Great Gatsby*."

"Really? You know," I said slowly, "I might try it, too."

"He also started National Novel Writing Month. That's in November. Lots of people all over the country do it."

We were standing on a street corner one block from the Barnes & Noble at Union Square. "I'm going to buy the book right now," I said, making up my mind. "I really am going to think about it."

I bought the book, and I came up with an idea: two people having an affair in Manhattan. I'd been reading Laurie Colwin, Roxana Robinson, and other novelists writing about the problems of middle marriage, and I wanted to think about the happiness and unhappiness consequences of a middle-marriage crisis like an affair. Also, I thought it would be fun to try to think through the logistics of how two people in the same social circle would keep their affair a secret and to write about New York City.

On the first day of September, I typed HAPPINESS on the title page and wrote my first sentence: "When she thought about it later, Emily realized that she knew exactly when her affair with Michael Harmon had its start: about 8:00 p.m. on the night of September 18, at a cocktail party at Lisa and Andrew Kessel's apartment." And so on, for 1,667 words.

Writing the novel was a lot of work, but I had less trouble squeezing the writing into my day than I'd expected. Of course I had it easier than most people, since I was already a full-time writer, but even so, I had to scrimp on time otherwise spent reading newspaper and magazines, meeting people for coffee, reading for fun, or generally puttering around. My blog posts became noticeably shorter.

After the first ten days, I ran into a problem: I'd reached the end of my plot. I hadn't thought of much action—Emily and Michael have lunch, they start an affair, they end their affair—and I'd already written most of that story before I'd hit even 25,000 words. Baty's book promised that I wouldn't have trouble coming up with more story, and somehow I kept going. And going. Each day, one way or another, I managed to eke out the minimum word requirement, until on September 30, I typed the sentence, "She'd do her shopping at a different drugstore. THE END." I calculated the word count: 50,163 words. I'd finished a novel that was long enough to be a real book—as long as some of my favorite novels, like Flannery O'Connor's *Wise Blood* and Chuck Palahniuk's *Fight Club*.

It was a huge amount of work, plunked on top of everything else I needed to accomplish in my days. Did it make me happy? It sure did. Writing *Happiness* took a lot of time and energy, it's true, but it gave me a substantial boost in happiness. Tackling such a big project and carrying it through to the end in a single month contributed hugely to the atmosphere of growth in my life. It was thrilling to see what I could accomplish in a short time if I put my mind to it. Also, because I was always searching for material that could enrich the story, the world came alive to me in a new way. On my way home from the library one afternoon, I saw a large crowd milling around in front of the famous Frank E. Campbell Funeral Chapel. "This would make a great scene for my novel," I thought.

But perhaps the most acute source of happiness from writing was the happiness of expressing a very complicated idea—the kind of idea that takes hundreds of pages to capture. I remember the precise moment when the idea struck me. I'd been at a dinner party with several couples who lived in my neighborhood. I'd seen two of my friends engaged in an intense, surely innocent conversation, and I'd thought, "What if they were having an affair? How could they pull it off? What would happen?" Always before, it had taken me years to write books that I'd envisioned. This novel might not be very good, but I'd completed it in one month.

As I'd seen in February with Extreme Nice, the boot-camp approach has many advantages. The brilliant Scott McCloud suggests a similar exercise, "The 24-Hour Comic," in his book *Making Comics:* "Draw an entire 24-page comic book in a single 24-hour period. No script. No preparation. . . . Great shock therapy for the creatively blocked." The boot-camp approach also gave me a sense of creative freedom, because I realized that when I had the uncontrollable urge to write a novel—a little-discussed but widespread occupational hazard that affects many writers—I could just sit down and *do* it.

And, to my surprise, writing *Happiness* was fun. Usually when I'm writing, I constantly question my work. With novel-writing month, I couldn't take the time, and it was a relief to be free from my inner critic. As one friend told me, "Face it, your novel is probably terrible—but that's okay!" This project helped me to keep my March resolution to "Enjoy the fun of failure." After I'd written the 50,163rd word, I was immediately itching to go back and edit it—but I resisted. I didn't even reread it. At some point, I will.

Writing a novel provided the "atmosphere of growth" that, I was becoming more and more convinced, was essential to happiness; I'd included this element in my First Splendid Truth, but it was even more significant than I'd initially understood. The satisfaction gained from the achievement of a large undertaking is one of the most substantial that life affords. When I asked blog readers if tackling a big goal had ever brought them happiness, many people wrote to share their own experiences:

•   •   •   •   •   •   •   •   •   •   •   •   •

I took on a big commitment and surprised myself by completing it. I joined a youtube group called the 100 day reality challenge. I made a video blog every day for 100 days. I'd never made videos for youtube before but I had a camera that took movies. I set up the commitment to make me focus on something positive and share it every day. Doing a video every day was probably easier than just once a week just because it was a daily habit. Although the challenge was really about something called "the law of attraction" (which I didn't myself manage to attract), I did find myself happier from having fun making the videos to making new friends though all the comments.

I decided this would be the year I would train to do a sprint triathlon. I joined a team, worked out nearly every day for eight weeks, and after I completed the triathlon, I signed up to do a second one. I am typically a person who lies in bed and reads, but I always thought it would be good to do a tri before I turn 40 (two years away). It was terrific training, and I'd highly recommend doing a sprint triathlon if it's something anyone's ever thought about doing.

I am learning Italian in less than 7 months. I was given the opportunity to do so, and I took it. I knew absolutely no Italian when I began the course, and just under 7 months from the start date, I will be fluent. I am only partway through, and I can already have conversations with native speakers. It's a huge undertaking, and I have almost quit many times, but it is wonderful and fun, too.

After coming out of depression I built my own wooden dinghy in about six weeks. I did it both as a symbol of victory and as part of the process. It made me very happy to finish, and the few times I had it on the water were all memorable experiences. In addition, owning the dinghy made me join a sailing club, which gives me access to a beautiful and peaceful site and brings me into contact with interesting people. All of this increases my happiness.

I am writing a memoir. I started working part-time as a nurse so I could focus more on the writing, and I am very happy doing this. I would say I am about half way through the manuscript. What galvanized me into doing this was a life-altering illness that I went through. I spent months on crutches not knowing if I would ever walk again. Permanent disability was a real possibility. After you go through something like that, through a quagmire of despair, you let go of a lot. And you realize, experientially, that life is way too short NOT to follow your passion. So, that's what I do these days.

As I'm growing up, I'm learning how important doing what you love is to your happiness. My BIG goal is to find a way to make money doing what I love. I'm 22 and two years into the corporate world, but my passion is designing and making jewelry. I'm starting small making custom jewelry for family and friends, and I just launched an online shop at etsy.com. I've loved designing jewelry for a while, but only recently have I gotten the courage to truly chase after my passion. Although I'm nowhere near having a viable business, I hope to eventually! Sometimes it gets frustrating to see that my goal is just a tiny seed right now; but having a vision of what I want it to become keeps me motivated to just go for it without giving up! Working hard for something that you are passionate about is SO satisfying and adds so much genuine happiness to life.

●　　●　　●　　●　　●　　●　　●　　●　　●　　●　　●　　●　　●

You might experiment with new recipes, go camping in your fifteenth state park, plan a sixtieth birthday party, or watch your favorite team progress to the Super Bowl. I liked writing a novel.

MAKE TIME.

Although reading was one of my most important priorities and certainly one of my greatest pleasures, I never really gave it much thought. I wanted to make more time to read—more books, with more enjoyment. To do so, I gave myself permission to read at whim. Samuel Johnson observed, "If we read without inclination, half the mind is employed in fixing the attention; so there is but one half to be employed on what we read." Science backs this up. When researchers tried to figure out what helped third- and fourth-graders remember what they read, they found that the students' interest in a passage was far more important than the "readability" of the passage—*thirty times* more important.

So between the books I read for happiness research, such as Jonathan Haidt's *The Happiness Hypothesis,* Anne Lamott's *Plan B,* and some biographies of Tolstoy, I threw in Lesley Lewis's *The Private Life of a Country House 1912–1939.* Along the same lines, I let myself reread William Makepeace Thackeray's *Vanity Fair,* Charlotte Yonge's *The Heir of Redclyffe,* and Laura Ingalls Wilder whenever I had the urge, instead of steering myself to read something new. I've always thought that the best reading is rereading. I pushed myself to keep reading lists. I asked people for recommendations (as a side benefit, this turned out to be a relationship booster; people responded warmly when I wrote down their suggestions). On the advice of a fellow member of the children's literature book group, I subscribed to *Slightly Foxed,* a charming British quarterly that publishes people's essays about their favorite books, and I noted suggestions from the magazine *The Week*'s "The Book List" section.

But the main hurdle keeping me from reading more wasn't the problem of figuring out *what* to read but rather having enough *time* to read. No matter how much time I spent reading, I wanted more. Of course, whenever anyone complains of not having enough time, the first suggestion is always "Watch less TV." Which makes sense—the average American spends between four and five hours watching TV each day.

"Do you think we watch too much TV?" I asked Jamie.

"We hardly watch any TV," he said.

"Well, we do watch some. What do you think, five or six hours a week? But we only watch what we've TiVo'd or from a DVD."

"I don't think we should give up all TV," he said. "TV is great—if you're not watching in a stupid way."

He was right. It was fun to watch a show once the girls were asleep. Watching TV seemed more companionable than reading in the same room; I suppose the fact that we were sharing the same experience made it seem cozier.

I did, however, vow to stop reading books that I didn't enjoy. I used to pride myself on finishing every book I started—no longer. And just as I used to make myself finish every book, I used to keep every book I bought, and we had messy stacks on every surface of our house. I culled ruthlessly, and we dropped off several heavy bags of books at a thrift store. I also accepted my idiosyncratic reluctance to read any book (or see any play or movie) that centers on the theme of unjust accusation. I was never going to be able to force myself to read *Oliver Twist, Othello, To Kill a Mockingbird,*

Atonement, A Passage to India, Burmese Days, Crime and Punishment, or *Arthur and George* if I could avoid it—and that was okay.

FORGET ABOUT RESULTS.

As I read, I love to take notes—often for no apparent reason. I'm always marking up books, making odd lists, gathering examples in strange categories, copying passages. For some reason, I like working on some permanent, undefined research project. I feel compelled to make lists of foreign words that describe concepts that English can't convey (*flâneur, darshan, eudaimonia, Ruinensehnsucht, amae, nostalgie de la boue*), explanations of concepts that I find queerly charged with significance (the Fisher King, the westerly road, Croatoan, Eleusinian Mysteries, offering of first-fruits, the hunting of the wren, the Corn-Spirit, *sparagmos,* the Lord of Misrule, cargo cult, Greek *herm,* potlatch, the Golden Ratio), and hundreds of other topics.

Note taking takes a lot of time and energy, and I used to discourage this impulse in myself. It seemed pointless and self-indulgent. But following this month's resolutions and my First Commandment to "Be Gretchen," I allowed myself to "Forget about results" and take notes guilt-free.

Perversely, it was only once I said to myself, "Okay, Gretchen, take all the notes you want, it doesn't matter why," that it occurred to me how *useful* these notes had been. My first book, *Power Money Fame Sex,* grew out of a huge body of notes. When I had a chance to write my book *Profane Waste,* about the question of why people would choose to destroy their possessions, I was able to pack the book with startling, apt examples because I'd been taking notes (for no discernible reason) for years. Because note taking didn't look like "real work" to me, it didn't register as valuable— even though it was.

One thing that makes a passion enjoyable is that you don't have to worry about results. You can strive for triumph, or you can potter around, tinker, explore, without worrying about efficiency or outcomes. Other people may wonder why you've been happy to work on the same old car for years, even though it's still not running, but that doesn't matter to you. An atmosphere of growth brings great happiness, but at the same time, happiness sometimes also comes when you're free from the pressure to see much growth. That's not surprising; often, the opposite of a great truth is also true.

MASTER A NEW TECHNOLOGY.

To me, making books sounded like fun. As a child, I'd spent countless hours working on my Blank Books. I'd written two horrible novels before I became a professional writer. Throughout my life, I'd made minibook projects as gifts for my family and friends. When I thought about the projects that I'd loved doing with Eliza, they all involved making books.

For example, she and I made a book using some of her bright, elaborate drawings. She dictated a caption for each picture while I typed; then we cut out the captions, taped them on the pictures, made color copies, and had the copies spiral-bound into a book. It was a fun project to work on, made a wonderful keepsake, supplied a Christmas/Hanukkah gift for the grandparents, captured a moment in Eliza's development, *and* allowed me to throw away the enormous stacks of pictures without a smidgen of guilt. (However, I will admit that when I wrote about this project on my blog, one reader was shocked: "I can't believe you actually threw out the originals of your daughter's drawings. I would have made the copies, as you did, but bound the originals into a scrapbook of sorts. The originals can NEVER be duplicated. I must confess to actually gasping when I read this.")

Recently I'd been intrigued to read about a self-publishing site, Lulu .com. According to the Web site, I could print a proper hardback book, complete with dust jacket, for less than thirty dollars. I mentioned this to Jamie, and he snorted, "What would anyone use that for?"

"You mean, who has book-length documents lying around that they'd like to print in book form?" I asked.

"Right."

"Are you kidding? *Me!*" I said. "If this works, I'll print up a dozen." At last, something to do with all those notes I'd been taking without a purpose. For the trial run, I made a book out of the journal I'd kept for the first eighteen months of Eliza's life (another book I'd written without really noticing it). I sat down at the computer, preparing to "put myself in jail" to cope with my frustration and my desire to rush. Instead, the whole process took about twenty minutes.

When my self-published book arrived a few weeks later, it exceeded my wildest expectations. There was my baby journal! As a *real book!* What next? I did a book of my favorite quotations about the nature of biography, I did a book of my favorite uncategorized quotations, and I fantasized about future books. When I finished my research on happiness, I'd print out a book of my favorite happiness quotations; maybe I could even include photo illustrations. I'd make a book of my blog posts. I'd print out my novel, *Happiness*. I'd print up my one-sentence journal—I could even make copies for the girls! Plus I had so many ideas for great happiness-related books. If I couldn't publish them with a real publisher, I would publish them myself.

I also learned that through Shutterfly, an online photo service site, I could print a hardback photo album. Figuring out how to do this turned out to be challenging, but eventually I mastered it, and once I was done, I ordered a copy for us and the grandparents, and everyone received a neat, organized book, stuffed with photos. Although it was expensive, I reminded myself that not only was I keeping my resolution to "Master a new technology," I was also keeping my resolutions to "Make purchases that will further my goals," "Indulge in a modest splurge," and "Be a treasure house of happy memories."

And once I got through the painful learning curve, it was fun. The novelty and challenge of mastering the technology—though I was maddened with frustration at times—did give me enormous satisfaction, and it gave me a new way to pursue my passion for books.

Of all the months so far, September's resolutions had been the most pleasant and easiest to maintain. This showed me, once again, that I was happier when I accepted my own real likes and dislikes, instead of trying to decide what I *ought* to like; I was happier when I stopped squelching the inclinations toward note taking and bookmaking that I'd had since childhood and instead embraced them. As Michel de Montaigne observed, "The least strained and most natural ways of the soul are the most beautiful; the best occupations are the least forced."

I needed to accept my own nature—yet I needed to push myself as well. This seemed contradictory, but in my heart, I knew the difference between lack of interest and fear of failure. I'd seen this in March with my blog. Although I'd been nervous about launching a blog, I did recognize that running a blog is the kind of thing I would like to do. In fact, I realized, my work on my childhood Blank Books, where I had pulled together interesting information, copied quotations, and matched text with striking images, sounded an awful lot like . . . posting to my blog. Sheesh. In fact, once I realized that, I decided to give up working on my new Blank Book. I'd had fun working on it since May, and I'd gotten a nostalgic kick from resuming an activity that had given me so much pleasure in childhood, but I'd grown tired of it. My blog had taken its place as an outlet to record the odds and ends I felt compelled to gather.

On the very last day of the month, I had an important realization: my Fourth Splendid Truth. Jamie and I were having dinner with a guy we knew slightly. He asked me what I was working on, and after I described the happiness project, he said, in polite disagreement, that he himself subscribed to John Stuart Mill's view—and he gave the precise quotation from Mill, I was impressed—"Ask yourself whether you are happy, and you cease to be so."

One of the problems of thinking about happiness all the time is that I've developed rather decided views. I wanted to pound the table and yell, "No, no, NO!" Instead, I managed to nod and say in a mild voice, "Yes, a lot of people take that view. I can't say that I agree."

I could see it in the guy's face: *John Stuart Mill v. Gretchen Rubin.* Hmmm . . . who's more likely to be right? But, in my experience at least, thinking about happiness had made me far happier than I was before I gave happiness much consideration. Now, Mill may have been referring to the state of "flow" identified by the researcher Mihaly Csikszentmihalyi. In flow, it's true, people are completely absorbed, so focused on their tasks that they forget themselves at the perfect balance of challenge and skill. But I think that Mill meant, or people generally believe, that thinking about your happiness makes you self-absorbed; you're not thinking about other people, work, or anything other than your own satisfaction. Or perhaps Mill meant that happiness comes as a consequence of pursuing other goals, such as love and work, and shouldn't be a goal in itself.

Of course it's not enough to sit around wanting to be happy; you must make the effort to take steps toward happiness by acting with more love, finding work you enjoy, and all the rest. But for me, asking myself whether I was happy had been a crucial step toward cultivating my happiness more wisely through my actions. Also, only through *recognizing* my happiness did I really *appreciate* it. Happiness depends partly on external circumstances, and it also depends on how you view those circumstances.

I'd thought about this question many times during the course of the year, but finally it hit me that *this* was my Fourth Splendid Truth: *You're not happy unless you think you're happy.* Then it struck me that the Fourth Splendid Truth has a corollary: *You're happy if you think you're happy.*

And that means thinking about happiness, no matter what John Stuart Mill said.

10

OCTOBER

Pay Attention

MINDFULNESS

- Meditate on koans.
- Examine True Rules.
- Stimulate the mind in new ways.
- Keep a food diary.

When I told people I was working on a book about happiness, the single most common response was "You should spend some time studying Buddhism." (A close second was "So are you drinking a bottle of wine every night?") The Dalai Lama's *The Art of Happiness* was the book most often recommended to me.

I'd always been intrigued by Buddhism, so I was eager to learn more about both the religion and the life of the Buddha. But although I admired many of its teachings, I didn't feel much deep connection to Buddhism, which, at its heart, urges detachment as a way to alleviate suffering. Although there is a place for love and commitment, these bonds are considered fetters that bind us to lives of sorrow—which of course they do. Instead, I'm an adherent of the Western tradition of cultivating deep passions and profound attachments; I didn't want to detach, I wanted to embrace; I didn't want to loosen, I wanted to deepen. Also, the Western tradition emphasizes the expression and the perfection of each unique, individual soul; not so in the Eastern tradition.

Nevertheless, studying Buddhism made me realize the significance of some concepts that I'd overlooked. The most important was mindfulness—the cultivation of conscious, nonjudgmental awareness.

I have several tendencies that run counter to mindfulness. I constantly multitask in ways that pull me away from my present experience. I often run on automatic pilot—arriving home with no recollection of having gone from point A to point B. (This sometimes terrifies me when I'm driving; I have no recollection of watching the road.) I tend to dwell on anxieties or hopes for the future, instead of staying fully aware in the present moment. I often break or spill things because I'm not paying attention. When I'm introduced to someone in a social situation, I often forget the person's name as soon as I hear it. I finish eating before I've even registered the taste of my food.

In September a jarring experience had reminded me of the importance of mindfulness. After a pleasant family weekend, spent mostly going to children's birthday parties (three in two days), I was walking down the hallway after putting both girls to bed. All of a sudden, as I headed to my desk to check my e-mails, I had the sensation that I was zooming back into my body. It was as if I had just returned from a two-week trip away from myself. The very hallway in which I stood seemed unfamiliar, yet I'd been living my ordinary life the whole time. It was very, very unnerving. If I was just getting back home—where had I been? I needed to do a better job of staying in the moment.

Mindfulness brings many benefits: scientists point out that it calms the mind and elevates brain function, it gives clarity and vividness to present experience, it may help people break unhealthy habits, and it can soothe troubled spirits and lift people's moods. It reduces stress and chronic pain. It makes people happier, less defensive, and more engaged with others.

One highly effective way to practice mindfulness is through meditation, which is recommended by Buddhists as a spiritual exercise and also by happiness experts of all sorts. Nevertheless, I just couldn't bring myself to try meditation. (I took yoga twice a week, but my class didn't emphasize the mental aspect of yoga.)

"I just can't believe you're not practicing meditation," a friend chided me. "If you're studying happiness, you really *have* to try it." She herself was a veteran of a ten-day silent meditation retreat. "The fact that you don't want to try meditation means that you need it desperately."

"You're probably right." I sighed. "But I just can't bring myself to do it. It holds no appeal for me."

Everyone's happiness project is unique. I enjoyed posting to my blog six days a week—a task that some people wouldn't dream of undertaking— but sit in silence for fifteen minutes each day, as my friend urged? I couldn't bring myself to do that. Another friend made an eloquent case for why I should spend more time in nature. Both arguments left me cold. When I'd started planning my happiness project, I told myself that I would try everything, but I'd quickly realized that this goal was neither possible nor desirable. Perhaps I'd try meditation in Happiness Project II, but for now I would seek happiness in the ways that seemed most natural to me.

There were other ways to harness the power of mindfulness, however, apart from meditation. I was already using my Resolutions Chart, a practice that led me to act more mindfully through the purposeful review of my actions and my thoughts. I filled in my chart at the end of the day, at a quiet time when I was undistracted and alone—though, given the nature of my personality, this period of self-examination felt more like conversation with Jiminy Cricket than communion with the universe. This month, I sought to find other strategies that would help me pay attention and stay in the moment. I also hoped to stimulate my brain to think in new ways—to jolt myself out of automatic behavior and to awaken sleepy parts of my mind.

MEDITATE ON KOANS.

Although I didn't take up meditation, I did find certain aspects of Buddhism fascinating. I was struck by the symbolism of Buddhism, the way the Buddha was sometimes portrayed by an empty seat, a pair of footprints, a tree, or a pillar of fire to signify that he'd passed beyond form. I loved the numbered lists that pop up throughout Buddhism: the Triple Refuge; the Noble Eightfold Path; the Four Noble Truths; the eight auspicious symbols: parasol, golden fish, treasure vase, lotus, conch shell, endless knot, victory banner, and dharma wheel.

The aspect that intrigued me most, however, was the study of Zen koans (rhymes with Ben Cohen's). A koan is a question or a statement that can't be understood logically. Zen Buddhist monks meditate on koans as a way to abandon dependence on reason in their pursuit of enlightenment. The most famous koan is "Two hands clap and there is a sound. What is the sound of one hand?" Another is "If you meet the Buddha, kill him." Or "What was your face before your parents were born?" A koan can't be grasped by reason or explained in words; meditating on koans promotes mindful thinking because it's not possible to comprehend their meaning with familiar, conventional logic.

After I learned about koans, I realized that I already had my own list of personal koans—I just hadn't thought of them that way. For years, in another example of seemingly pointless note taking, I'd been keeping a list of enigmatic lines, and in odd moments, I'd think about them. I was surprised to see how many I'd collected. My favorites:

Robert Frost: The best way out is always through.

J. M. Barrie: We set out to be wrecked.

Saint Thérèse of Lisieux: I choose all.

Francis Bacon/Heraclitus: Dry light is ever the best.

Mark 4:25: For he that hath, to him shall be given: and he that hath not, from him shall be taken even that which he hath.

Gertrude Stein: I like a room with a view but I like to sit with my back turned to it.

Elias Canetti: Kant Catches Fire.

T. S. Eliot: Oh, do not ask, "What is it?"/Let us go and make our visit.

Virginia Woolf: She always had the feeling that it was very, very dangerous to live even one day.

These fragments haunted me. They floated through my mind at odd times—when I was waiting on a subway platform or staring at my computer screen—and they seemed strangely relevant in many circumstances.

The personal koan I reflected on most often was a Spanish proverb quoted by Samuel Johnson in Boswell's *Life of Johnson:* "He, who would bring home the wealth of the Indies, must carry the wealth of the Indies with him." I'd read that line years ago, and I often found myself turning it over in my mind. Much later, I'd discovered a reference in Henry David Thoreau's *Journal* in which he echoed Johnson: "It is in vain to dream of a wildness distant from ourselves. . . . I shall never find in the wilds of Labrador any greater wildness than in some recess of Concord, i.e. than I import into it."

With time, I think I began to grasp the meaning of these two koans, which had profound implications for a happiness project. I was trudging up the stairs of the library when I thought, "She who would find the happiness of the Indies must carry the happiness of the Indies with her." I couldn't look outside myself for happiness. The secret wasn't in the Indies or in Labrador but under my own roof; if I wanted to find happiness, I had to carry happiness with me.

Ruminating on my koans didn't bring me any closer to satori, the lasting enlightenment promised by Zen (at least not as far as I could tell), but it did ignite my imagination. Because koans forced me to challenge the usual, straightforward boxes of meaning, they pushed me to *think* about *thinking*. That in turn brought me the delicious intellectual happiness that comes from grappling with an expansive, difficult question.

EXAMINE TRUE RULES.

Part of the challenge of mindfulness was to keep myself from falling into mechanical thoughts and actions. Instead of walking through life on autopilot, I wanted to question the assumptions I made without noticing.

My research into cognitive science led me to the concept of heuristics. Heuristics are mental rules of thumb, the quick, commonsense principles you apply to solve a problem or make a decision. For example, the recognition heuristic holds that if you're faced with two objects and you recognize one and don't recognize the other, you assume that the recognized one is of higher value. So if you've heard of Munich but you haven't heard of Minden, you assume that Munich is the larger German city; if you've heard of Rice Krispies cereal but you haven't heard of Wild Oats cereal, you assume that Rice Krispies is the more popular brand.

Usually heuristics are helpful, but in some situations our cognitive instincts mislead us. Take the availability heuristic: people predict the likelihood of an event based on how easily they can come up with an example. This is often useful (is a tornado likely to hit Manhattan?), but sometimes a person's judgment is skewed because the vividness of examples makes an event seem more likely than it actually is. A friend of mine, for example, is hypervigilant about not eating anything that might contain raw eggs. She practically went into hysterics when she found out that her mother-in-law had allowed her kids to eat raw cookie batter. Why? Because her aunt got salmonella twenty-five years ago. This same friend, by the way, never wears a seat belt.

Although they might not fit precisely into the definition of "heuristics," I had my own idiosyncratic collection of principles—which I called "True Rules"—for making decisions and setting priorities. My father often talks about "True Rules." For example, when I started working after college, he said, "Remember, it's one of the True Rules—if you're willing to take the blame, people will give you responsibility." I've applied my own True Rules to help me make decisions, mostly without quite realizing that I was using them. They flicker through my brain so quickly that I have to make a real effort to detect them, but I identified a handful of rules that I frequently use:

My children are my most important priority.
Get some exercise every day.
Jamie is my top priority, in matters big or small.
"Yes" comes right away; "no" never comes.
Get some work done *every* day.
Whenever possible, choose vegetables.
I know as much as most people.
I'm in a hurry.
Try to attend any party or event to which I'm invited.
My parents are almost always right.
Ubiquity is the new exclusivity.
If I'm not sure whether to include some text, cut it out.
Never eat hors d'oeuvres, and never eat anything at a children's
    party.
When making a choice about what to do, choose work.

Looking at my True Rules showed me something. Several of them were difficult to balance. How could my kids, Jamie, and work *all* be top priorities? Also, I was pretty sure that Jamie operated under the rule of "Try to skip as many social events as possible." That explained certain ongoing marital debates.

242 / THE HAPPINESS PROJECT

Some of my True Rules were very helpful, such as one I learned from my mother: "The things that go wrong often make the best memories." This is very comforting and very true. For example, my mother put a tremendous amount of work into planning Jamie's and my wedding—right down to the wedding-weekend informational letter decorated with cows and ruby slippers to symbolize Kansas City—and our wedding was gorgeous and perfect in every way, except for one single, tiny detail: the misspelling of the composer Haydn's name as "Hayden" in the order of services. And sure enough, now I love remembering that superfluous "e." Somehow it reminds me of all the time my mother and I spent together planning the wedding (she did most of the work); the one flaw throws the loveliness of the whole wedding into focus. I remember reading that the Shakers deliberately introduced a mistake into the things they made, to show that man shouldn't aspire to the perfection of God. Flawed can be more perfect than perfection.

On the other hand, some of my True Rules were unhelpful. "I'm in a hurry" ran through my head dozens of times each day—not always a constructive thought. I worked to change that rule to "I have plenty of time for the things that are important to me." By questioning my True Rules instead of applying them unthinkingly, I could make sure I applied them only when they'd guide me to decisions that reflected my true priorities.

Was I the only one who thought this way? When I asked my friends if they had True Rules, they understood exactly what I was talking about, and they had their own examples:

Always say hello.
What would my mother do?
Don't get up in the 5:00's or go to sleep in the 8:00's (A.M. or
   P.M.).
Down with boredom.
Change is good.
First things first (example: eat before a job interview).

Choose the bigger life.

Buy anything you want at the grocery store; cooking is always
cheaper than eating out.

Things have a way of turning out for the best.

Use it up, wear it out, make it do, or do without.

I picked up a very helpful True Rule from my sister. Elizabeth told me,
"People succeed in groups."

As a TV writer in Los Angeles, she works in a notoriously competitive, jealous industry. Jamie and I had coined a phrase, "the funny
feeling," to describe the uncomfortable mixture of competitiveness and
self-doubt that we feel when a peer scores a major success. When a friend
of Elizabeth's cowrote the screenplay of a movie that was a box-office hit,
I asked her, "Does it give you the funny feeling that your pal had such a
huge success?"

She answered, "Well, maybe a bit, but I remind myself that 'People
succeed in groups.' It's great for him to have a big success, and his success
is also likely to help me to be successful."

By contrast, I have a friend who described her brother as having a zero-
sum attitude toward good fortune: if something good happens to someone
else, he feels as if something good is less likely to happen to him. As a
result, he's never happy for anyone else.

Now, it's debatable whether it's *true* that people succeed in groups. I
happen to think it is true—but whether or not it's objectively true, it's a
True Rule that makes a person much happier. Of course, pure magna-
nimity would be more admirable, but telling yourself that "People succeed
in groups" helps when you're feeling small-minded.

Jamie has a very helpful True Rule: he says, "The first thing isn't the
right thing." So when a friend doesn't get the job he wanted or wasn't able
to buy the apartment she bid on, Jamie says, "The first thing isn't the right
thing—wait and see, you'll be glad in the end that this didn't work out."
Again, the point isn't whether this True Rule is factually true (I recognize

that his precept has the "Why do you always find a lost object in the very last place you look?" kind of logical flaw), but that it's a way of thinking that boosts happiness.

Gathering True Rules was a fun exercise, and it was useful, because as I questioned my True Rules, I became far more aware when I applied them. By mindfully deciding how to act in line with my values instead of mindlessly applying my rules, I was better able to make the decisions that supported my happiness.

STIMULATE THE MIND IN NEW WAYS.

As I looked for ways to become more mindful, I realized that using my brain in unfamiliar ways would enhance my experience of the present moment and my awareness of myself. I came up with several strategies.

First, I posted sticky notes around the apartment to remind me of the frame of mind I wished to cultivate. The note on my laptop reads, "Focused and observant." The bedroom note reads, "Quiet mind." After I put a note in the master bathroom that read, "Tender and lighthearted," Jamie crossed it out and wrote, "Light and flaky"—I had to laugh. The note in my office reads, "Enthusiastic and creative." I also switched on the "Breezy Singer" bluebird that I'd bought in May so that the goofy birdsong would make me mindful of thoughts of gratitude. A blog reader adopted a similar strategy to stay mindful.

•   •   •   •   •   •   •   •   •   •   •   •   •   •

Every day, I type passwords into programs and computers too many times to count. I don't save my passwords on the computer but am a compulsive email-checker. So a multitude of times a day, I type the same thing over and over and over.

And one day, I realize that what I use for my password gets ingrained in me, due to constant repetition. Like a mantra. Let's say my password is "tennis" (I play tennis, by the way), and although I do not think about tennis on purpose all the time, I eventually realized that it's my favourite activity, it's what I put a lot of time and effort on, it's what I do most outside of work.

I later changed my passwords to a goal I've been working on, or an achievement I want. They become a constant reminder of my goals, my dreams, of what I want to achieve. It's basically the same idea as surrounding yourself with reminders of your aims, your dreams. Or repeating positive thoughts in your mind.

. . . .

Next I decided to try hypnosis as a different route to cultivate my mind. A friend is "super-suggestible," and her crazy stories about what she'd done under hypnosis had piqued my interest. My first act for October was to take a train to Old Greenwich, Connecticut, to meet Peter, my yoga instructor's cousin and a hypnotist.

I wasn't sure what I thought about hypnotism. Proponents argue that the hypnotic state, with its concentration, boosted relaxation, and increased suggestibility, brings heightened focus and responsiveness to instructions, so hypnosis helps people break bad habits and imprint new patterns on their minds. Or it might be, I speculated, that posthypnotic change was due to the "Hawthorne effect" I'd experienced in January (studying a behavior can lead to its alteration) or the "placebo effect" (treatment works because it's expected to work). Nevertheless, whatever the particular mechanism involved, hypnosis sounded worth a try.

As I got into Peter's car in Old Greenwich, I realized that I hadn't done much research on him. It felt a bit odd to be off in some small town in Connecticut, getting into a stranger's car, and being driven to his office in a small apartment in a residential building. Fortunately for me, Peter was legitimate.

First he led me through a series of relaxation exercises; then we talked about the list of aims he'd asked me to bring. I'd included goals small and large—everything from eliminating nighttime snacking to expressing daily gratitude. Then came the actual "hypnosis." First Peter asked me to imagine myself gradually becoming heavier, tracing numbers with my eyes, visualizing my left hand rising into the air (my hand didn't move an inch). Then he slowly instructed me on the behavior that I would change.

When I feel myself feeling snappish, I'll remind myself to lighten up. I can make my points more effectively with humor and tenderness than with irritation.

When I feel myself getting annoyed because someone is giving me bad service—a pharmacist, a nurse, a clerk, etc.—I'll establish a friendly, cooperative tone. I'll remember to cut people slack.

As I turn to my computer or sit down to eat or walk down the street, I'll feel happy and grateful for my health, for loving my work so much, for having such a great family, for having such a comfortable life—and from this derive a feeling of lightheartedness, enthusiasm, and tenderness.

When I'm listening to other people speak, I will *listen* intently, so that I follow up their comments, laugh at their jokes, engage deeply. No more interrupting or waiting impatiently for my turn.

I'll stop overusing the phrases "you know" and "like" and slang. When I hear myself talking that way, I'll take a deep breath, slow down my speech, and choose my words more carefully.

After dinner, I'll turn out the lights in the kitchen and not return. No snacking, no picking at one thing or another. When I'm hungry, I will reach for fresh fruit and vegetables.

He counted backward and suggested that I'd wake up feeling "refreshed." The whole instruction took about twenty minutes, and Peter had recorded it on an old-fashioned cassette tape. "Listen to this tape each day," he instructed. "You should be relaxed, attentive, and not sleepy—before bed is the *worst* time to do it."

"Does it really work?" I couldn't resist asking.

"I've seen extraordinary results," he assured me.

I dug out my old Walkman and bought an extra pair of AA batteries. I listened to the tape each day, and, as instructed, each time I heard it, I imagined myself acting according to the goals I'd set.

Jamie enjoyed making fun of me; he thought the entire exercise was ridiculous. He made a lot of jokes of the "What's going to happen if I tell you to quack like a duck?" variety. It was easy to laugh off his teasing, but I got a bit discouraged. I'd hoped to find hypnosis an easy, passive shortcut to self-improvement, but it was a struggle to concentrate on the tape.

But I did my best, and I do think it helped. For example, one day I felt enraged because after I had spent about five hours putting together an online photo book on Shutterfly, when I logged into my account to complete the finishing touches, it was *gone*. All I found was "Empty Folder." I was ready to yell, but as I dialed customer service, I heard a soft voice in my ear: "I'll establish a friendly, cooperative tone." And I did. (Of course, it helped that the file popped back into existence before too long.) I also stopped eating brown sugar out of the jar. Gross, but something that I did do quite frequently. To me, the effectiveness of hypnosis seemed less a result of hypnotic suggestibility and more a result of mindfulness. My hypnosis tape made me more aware of my thoughts and actions, and I was able to change them through a sort of mental practice. But that was fine, as long as it worked.

For my next experiment, I decided to try laughter yoga. Founded by an Indian doctor, this combination of yoga and laughter has spread rapidly around the world, and I kept running into references to it as a happiness-inducing activity. Laughter yoga combines clapping, chanting, breathing, and stretching exercises drawn from yoga to calm the mind and the body, and the simulated laughter provoked by the exercises often turns into real laughter.

One joy of living in New York City is that everything is on offer. I easily located a laughter yoga class near my apartment and showed up one Tuesday evening in the basement conference room of a physical therapy office. Twelve of us were led through exercises of yoga breathing and simulated laughter. We did the lion exercise, the ho-ho-ho ha-ha-ha exercise, the cry-laugh exercise, and several others, and I could tell that many other practitioners were really feeling a boost in mood. Two people, in particular, collapsed in fits of real laughter. Not me. The leader was kind and knowledgeable, the other people were pleasant, and the exercises seemed purposeful, but all I felt was a horrible self-consciousness.

As I'd walked into the class, I'd vowed that I'd try it at least three times, but by the time I left, I decided that, as much as folks praised laughter yoga and as valuable as novelty and challenge were to happiness, and even though an exercise in mindful laughter sounded like an excellent idea, laughter yoga wasn't for me.

I moved on to drawing. I hadn't done any drawing or painting since high school, so taking a drawing class would awaken a part of my mind that had long lain dormant. Also, if cultivating mindfulness meant striving to develop nonjudgmental awareness, I suspected that drawing would be a good challenge: it would be hard not to judge my (nonexistent) drawing skill.

I'd read about a "Drawing on the Right Side of the Brain" class that claimed to be able to change the way in which people processed visual information so anyone could learn to draw. Perfect. I figured that, as with laughter yoga, I'd be able to find a "Drawing on the Right Side of the Brain" class in Manhattan, and sure enough, the class was offered by the program's principal New York instructor, right in his own apartment in SoHo. I "indulged in a modest splurge," signed up, and for five days took the subway downtown for a day that started at 9:30 A.M. and ended at 5:30 P.M.

Novelty and challenge bring big boosts in happiness. Unfortunately, novelty and challenge also bring exhaustion and frustration. During the class, I felt intimidated, defensive, and hostile—at times almost panicky

I drew this self-portrait on the first day of class. Later, when I showed it to a friend, she said, "Come on, admit it. Didn't you do a bad job on purpose, to make any progress you made look more dramatic?" Actually, nope. This was my best effort.

I drew this self-portrait on the last day of class. My instructor helped me with all the hard parts, and it doesn't actually resemble me very much, but it does look like a portrait of a person.

with anxiety. I felt drained each night, and my back hurt. I'm not sure why it was so stressful, but trying to follow the instructor's directions, squint, measure against my upheld thumb, and draw a straight line on a diagonal, was physically and even emotionally taxing. One person in our little class had a kind of breakdown and quit after three days. Yet it was also tremendously gratifying to learn something new—to partake of the atmosphere of growth.

Drawing exercised an unaccustomed part of my brain, but apart from that, just the fact that I was taking a class boosted my mindfulness. Being in a different neighborhood at an unusual time of day heightened my awareness of my surroundings; New York City is so beautiful, so endlessly compelling. The rhythm of the day was very different from my typical schedule. I enjoyed meeting new people. Plus—the class worked! I drew my hand, I drew a chair, I drew a self-portrait that, although it didn't look much like *me,* did look like an actual person.

The drawing class was a good illustration of one of my Secrets of Adulthood: "Happiness doesn't always make you *feel* happy." Activities that contribute to long-term happiness don't always make me feel good in the short term; in fact they're sometimes downright unpleasant.

From drawing, I turned to music—another dormant part of my mind. According to research, listening to music is one of the quickest, simplest ways to boost mood and energy and to induce a particular mood. Music stimulates the parts of the brain that trigger happiness, and it can relax the body—in fact, studies show that listening to a patient's choice of music during medical procedures can lower the patient's heart rate, blood pressure, and anxiety level.

Nevertheless, one of the things that I've accepted about myself, as part of "Being Gretchen," is that I don't have much appreciation for music. I *wish* I enjoyed music more, but I don't. Every once in a while, though, I fixate on a song I really love—recently I went through an obsession with the Red Hot Chili Peppers' "Under the Bridge."

The other day, while writing in a coffee shop, I overheard a song that

I love but had forgotten about: Fatboy Slim's "Praise You." I went home, loaded it onto my iPod, and listened to it that night while I was cleaning my office. This song flooded me with tender feelings for Jamie. Yes, we have gone through the hard times and the good! Yes, I have to praise him like I should! This would have been a good activity for February, the month of marriage.

I thought again about Jung playing with blocks to recapture the passionate engagement of his boyhood. When I was little, I used to dance around the room to my favorite music. I was too young to read, so I asked my mother to mark the record of *The Nutcracker Suite* so I'd be able to find it. But I stopped dancing when I got older. Maybe I should try dancing around the room again.

I didn't want anyone walking in on me while I was doing it, and it took a long time before I had an opportunity. I hadn't realized before how rare it was for me to be home alone. Finally, one Sunday afternoon, I told Jamie I was going to stay behind when he took the girls around the corner to visit his parents. After the apartment was empty, I went into our bedroom, turned off the lights, lowered the blinds, and put my iPod into an iPod speaker base. I had to squelch thoughts of self-criticism—that I was a bad dancer or looked goofy.

It was fun. I did feel goofy, but I also felt energized and exhilarated.

I started thinking more about music. I thought I'd accepted the fact that, as part of "Being Gretchen," I didn't really like music, but in fact, the truth was slightly different: I thought I didn't like music, but in fact, I didn't approve of my own taste—I wished I liked sophisticated music, like jazz or classical or esoteric rock. Instead, my taste ran mostly to what might play on a lite FM station. Oh, well. Be Gretchen.

Listening and dancing to music absolutely boosted my feelings of mindfulness. I felt much more aware of music during the day; as I worked in a diner, I really *heard* Abba singing "Take a Chance on Me" over the loudspeaker. This heightened responsiveness to my environment made me feel more present in the moment. Instead of tuning music out, I made music a bigger part of my experience.

KEEP A FOOD DIARY.

I also wanted to apply the principles of mindfulness in a much less elevated context: my eating habits. Studies show that merely being conscious of eating makes people eat more healthfully, and one way to encourage yourself to eat more mindfully, experts agree, is to keep a food diary. Without a record, it's easy to overlook what you eat without noticing it—grabbing three Hershey's Kisses every time you pass a coworker's desk throughout the day or eating leftovers from other people's plates as you clear the kitchen table. In one study, dieters who kept a food diary lost twice as much weight as dieters who didn't bother.

I'd felt guilty for a long time about my mediocre eating habits, and I wanted to eat more healthfully, plus I wanted to lose a few pounds without going on a diet (hardly an original goal—almost seven out of ten Americans say they're trying to eat healthfully to lose weight). Making notes about the food I ate sounded easy enough, and I figured that, of all my various resolutions, this would be one of the easier ones to keep. I bought myself a little notebook.

"I keep a food diary," a friend told me at lunch soon after, when I mentioned my latest resolution. She showed me her calendar, which was crammed with tiny writing detailing her daily intake. "I update it every time I eat."

"They say that keeping a food diary helps you eat better and lose weight," I said, "so I'm giving it a try."

"It's a great thing to do. I've been keeping mine for years."

Her recommendation reassured me that the food diary was a good idea. My friend was thin and fit, plus she was one of the healthiest (if also one of the most eccentric) eaters I knew. I'd just heard her order lunch.

"I'd like the Greek salad, chopped, no dressing, no olives or stuffed grape leaves, plus a side order of grilled chicken and a side order of steamed broccoli." When the food arrived, she heaped the chicken and broccoli onto the salad. It was a *lot* of food, but tasty and very healthy. I ordered the same salad, but without the extra chicken and broccoli. Before we dug in, we sprinkled artificial sweetener over our salads. (She taught me this trick. It sounds awful, but artificial sweetener makes a great substitute for dressing. It's like adding salt; you don't taste it, but it brings out the flavor of the food.)

"I refuse to go on a diet," I told her.

"Oh, me too!" she said. "But try keeping a food diary. It's interesting to see what you eat over the course of a week."

I tried it. My problem: I found it practically impossible to remember to keep a food diary. I've read repeatedly that it takes twenty-one days to form a habit, but in my experience, that just isn't true. Day after day, I tried, but only rarely did I manage to remember to record everything I ate in a day. One problem with not being very mindful, it turns out, is that you have trouble keeping your mindfulness records. Nevertheless, even attempting to keep a food diary was a useful exercise. It made me more attuned to the odds and ends I put into my mouth: a piece of bread, the last few bites of Eleanor's lasagna.

Most important, it forced me to confront the true magnitude of my "fake food" habit. I'd pretended to myself that I indulged only occasionally, but in fact I ate a ton of fake food: pretzels, low-fat cookies or brownies, weird candy in bite-sized portions, and other not-very-healthy snacks. "Food that comes in crinkly packages from corner delis," as one friend described my weakness. I liked eating fake food, because when I got hungry during the day, it was more convenient to grab something fake than to sit down to eat proper food like soup or salad. Plus, fake food was a treat. I'd never buy a real chocolate chip cookie or a candy bar, but I couldn't resist the supposedly low-cal version.

Even though I knew that this kind of food was low in nutrition and high in calories, I kept eating it, and this habit was a daily source of guilt and self-reproach. Each time I thought about buying some fake food, I told myself that I shouldn't—but then I did anyway. I'd tried and failed to give up fake food in the past, but the food diary, incomplete as it was, made me aware of how much fake food I was eating.

I gave up fake food cold turkey—and it felt good to give it up. I'd thought of these snacks as treats and hadn't realized how much "feeling bad" they'd generated—feelings of guilt, self-neglect, and even embarrassment. Now those feelings were gone. Just as I'd seen in July, when I was thinking about money, keeping a resolution to "Give something up" can be surprisingly satisfying. Who would have thought that self-denial could be so agreeable?

I told my sister what I'd done, and she answered, very sensibly, "You basically eat a very healthy diet, so why give up fake food altogether? Limit yourself to a few treats each week."

"Nope, can't do it!" I told her. "I know myself too well to try that." When it comes to fake food, I'm like Samuel Johnson, who remarked, "Abstinence is as easy to me as temperance would be difficult." In other words, I can give something up altogether, but I can't indulge occasionally.

It's true, I have a very particular definition of "fake food." I still drink a huge amount of Diet Coke and Fresca; I still use a ton of artificial sweetener. I also eat a fair amount of candy, which I consider real and not fake. But no more crinkly packages from corner delis, and that's a real step forward. Bananas, almonds, oatmeal, tuna sandwiches, and salsa on pita bread are filling the gap.

My fake-food experience showed me why mindfulness helps you break bad habits. When I became truly aware of what I was eating, I found it much easier to change the automatic choices I'd been making. Two or three times a day, I'd mindlessly been picking up snacks in corner delis—but when I was confronted with what I was doing, I wanted to stop. And it was only after I'd kicked my fake-food habit that I realized what a drain it had been on my happiness. Every day I'd felt uncomfortable twinges of self-reproach, because I knew that kind of food wasn't healthy. Once I stopped that habit, that relentless source of bad feeling vanished.

The mindfulness resolutions for October had been interesting and productive and had boosted my happiness considerably, but more important, my increased awareness had led me to an unrelated yet significant realization: I was at risk of turning into a happiness bully.

I'd become much more sensitive to people being negative, indulging in knee-jerk pessimism, or not having—what seemed to me—the right spirit of cheerfulness and gratitude, and I felt a strong impulse to lecture, which I didn't always manage to resist. Instead of following June's resolution to "Cut people slack," I was becoming more judgmental.

My desire to be a happiness evangelist made me want to meddle. When a guy told me that he hated making small talk and so whiled away the dull hours of a dinner party by doing complex math problems in his head, or when a young woman told me she was going to dental school because she liked the hours that dentists work but that her fantasy was one day to do something involving flowers because flowers were her true passion, I could barely contain myself. "No!" I wanted to tell them. "You're making a mistake, I'll tell you why!" I'd become a happiness boor. In a scene right out of a Woody Allen movie, I practically got into a fistfight with someone about the nature of Zen. "You seem quite *attached* to the theory of nonattachment!" I said snidely. I kept interrupting, I wouldn't shut up, I was such a crusader for the idea of doing a happiness project that I found myself practically shouting people down.

In particular, I kept trying to force clutter clearing onto my friends. My clutter was mostly gone, and I craved the vicarious thrill I got from tackling a truly messy closet. "Listen," Jamie warned me one night. "You mean well, but you're going to offend people if you keep pushing them so hard to clear their clutter."

"But every time I help someone clear their clutter, they're thrilled!" I said.

"It's okay to suggest it, but don't press the issue. You want to be nice, but you might end up rubbing someone the wrong way."

I remembered how recently I'd walked into a friend's apartment and immediately offered clutter-clearing help any time she wanted it. Even at the time, it occurred to me that she might have found my reaction a bit rude. "Okay, you're right," I admitted. "I'll ease up on people."

I called my sister. "Am I annoying you with all my talk about happiness?" I asked.

"Of course not," Elizabeth said.

"Do you think I seem happier?"

"Sure!"

"How can you tell?"

"Well . . . you seem much lighter, more relaxed, and you're not snapping as much. *Not,*" she added quickly, "that you snapped a lot, but you know."

"I've been trying to keep my temper. Probably the fact that you noticed means that I was snapping more than I realized."

"You also seem like you're better about finding the fun in things."

"Like what?"

"Like when we were talking about how to do Eliza's hair for my wedding. That's the kind of thing that might have made you tense before, but now you're just letting her have fun with it without worrying about it too much. Anyway, did I tell you that you've inspired me to try some of your resolutions?"

"Really? That's great! What have you been doing?" I was thrilled to think that my happiness project had influenced someone else.

"For one thing, I'm trying to exercise a lot more—Pilates, hiking, Cardio Barre. I've never had a hobby, so I'm trying to think of exercise as my hobby, you know, 'reframing.' That way it covers fitness and also the atmosphere of growth. Also, my dentist has been after me for years to get my teeth fixed, so I finally 'tackled a nagging task' and got Invisalign put in. I've been eating at home more often; it's healthier and cheaper. And I've been going away more on the weekends—spending money in ways that will make me happy."

"And are these things making you happier?"

"Yes! You're right, it really does work. I was actually kind of surprised."

11

NOVEMBER

Keep a Contented Heart

A T T I T U D E

- Laugh out loud.
- Use good manners.
- Give positive reviews.
- Find an area of refuge.

My happiness project year was almost over, and for November's resolutions, I had to make sure to cram in everything that I hadn't covered. Fortunately, everything I had left to cover fit neatly into one category. Instead of focusing on my *actions*, I focused on my *attitude*. I wanted to cultivate a light-hearted, loving, and kind spirit. If I could put myself into that frame of mind, it would be easier to stick to all my other resolutions.

The British diarist Samuel Pepys reflected from time to time on the nature of happiness. In his entry for February 23, 1662, he wrote, "This day by God's mercy I am 29 years of age, and in very good health, and like to live and get an estate and if I have a heart to be contented, I think I may reckon myself as happy a man as any is in the world, for which God be praised. So to prayers and to bed." (This last phrase, "and so to bed," is Pepys's signature sign-off, much like Walter Cronkite's "And that's the way it is" or Ryan Seacrest's "Seacrest . . . out!").

I was struck by Pepys's inclusion of the qualifying phrase: "and if I have a heart to be contented." It was easy to pass over these words without realizing their tremendous importance. No one is happy who doesn't think himself happy, so without "a heart to be contented," a person can't be happy. That's the Fourth Splendid Truth.

Did *I* have a heart to be contented? Well, no, not particularly. I had a tendency to be discontented: ambitious, dissatisfied, fretful, and tough to please. In some situations, this served me well, because it kept me constantly striving to improve my work and achieve my goals. In most areas of my life, however, this critical streak wasn't helpful. When Jamie surprised me with a gardenia plant (my favorite flower), I fussed because it was too big. I was deeply annoyed when we came back from the hardware store with the wrong-sized lightbulbs—I just couldn't let it go.

It's easier to complain than to laugh, easier to yell than to joke around, easier to be demanding than to be satisfied. Keeping "a heart to be contented," I expected, would help change my actions. I hit on several specific aspects of my attitude that I wanted to change.

First, I wanted to laugh more. Laughing more would make me happier, and it would also make the people around me happier. I'd grown more somber over the last several years. I suspected that I didn't laugh, or even smile, very much. A small child typically laughs more than four hundred times each day, and an adult—seventeen times. I wondered if I hit even that number most days.

Along with a more humorous attitude, I wanted to be kinder. I'd considered kindness a respectable but bland virtue (in the same dull class as reliability and dutifulness), but researching Buddhism, with its emphasis on loving-kindness, had convinced me that I'd overlooked something important. I wanted to practice loving-kindness, but it was such a vague goal—easy to applaud but hard to apply. What strategies would remind me to act with loving-kindness in my ordinary day?

I decided to start with the basic resolution to improve my manners, which weren't as good as they should have been—not just my table manners (though those weren't great either) but my actions to show consideration for others. Perhaps mere politeness wouldn't engender loving-kindness in me, but acting politely would at least give me the appearance of possessing that quality—and perhaps appearance would turn into reality. I wanted to lose my New York City edge. Whenever I go home to visit my parents, I notice that midwesterners really are more friendly. In Kansas City, people seem less hurried (and they are less hurried—a study showed that New York has the country's fastest-walking pedestrians), clerks in stores are more helpful and chatty, drivers give pedestrians a lot of space on the street (in New York, they practically nudge you out of the way with their bumpers). Instead of moving fast and speaking curtly, I wanted to take the time to be pleasant.

Also, I wanted to stop being so critical, so judgmental and finicky. When I was growing up, my parents placed a lot of emphasis on being positive and enthusiastic—to the point that my sister and I sometimes complained that they wanted us to be "fake." Now I'd grown to admire my parents' insistence on banning sarcasm and pointless negativity; it made for a much nicer household atmosphere.

Finally, as a way to help myself stay serene and cheerful, I resolved to discipline myself to direct my thoughts away from subjects that made me angry or irritable.

I wondered whether working on my attitude should occupy an entire month's worth of resolutions, but reading Schopenhauer (oddly enough, given that he's so well known for his pessimism) convinced me of the importance of a cheerful disposition: "Whoever is merry and cheerful has always a good reason for so being, namely the very fact that he is so. Nothing can so completely take the place of every other blessing as can this quality, whilst it itself cannot be replaced by anything. A man may be young, handsome, wealthy, and esteemed; if we wish to judge of his happiness, we ask whether he is cheerful." This month was all about cheerfulness.

LAUGH OUT LOUD.

By now I had no doubt about the power of my Third Commandment: "Act the way I want to feel." If I want to feel happy and lighthearted, I need to act that way—say, by laughing out loud.

Laughter is more than just a pleasurable activity. It can boost immunity and lower blood pressure and cortisol levels. It increases people's tolerance for pain. It's a source of social bonding, and it helps to reduce conflicts and cushion social stress within relationships—at work, in marriage, among strangers. When people laugh together, they tend to talk and touch more and to make eye contact more frequently.

I vowed to find reasons to find things funny, to laugh out loud, and to appreciate other people's humor. No more polite smiling; no more rushing to tell *my* story before the laughter has died after a friend's funny story; no more reluctance to be joshed and teased. One of life's most exquisite pleasures is making people laugh—even Jamie seems more pleased with himself when I laugh out loud at his jokes, and it's almost heartbreaking to see Eliza and Eleanor gaze into my face to watch me laugh.

The other morning, after Eleanor told me the same garbled knock-knock joke for the tenth time, I saw her lower lip start to tremble. "What's wrong, munchkin?" I asked.

"You didn't laugh!" she yowled.

"Tell me again," I said. She did, and the next time, I laughed.

Most of all, though, I wanted to laugh out loud *at myself.* I took myself far too seriously. On the rare occasions that I did manage to laugh at myself, it was very cheering.

This topic was on my mind when I was stuck in a slow-moving line at a soup place (no more fake food for me). Two older women at the head of the line were taking a long time to make their selections.

"Can I try the Spicy Lentil?" asked one woman. She got her miniature cup of soup, tasted it, and said, "Too spicy! Ummm, can I try the Spicy Sausage?"

The clerk behind the counter moved slowly to ladle out another miniature cup and pass it over the counter.

"This one is too spicy too!" the tasting woman exclaimed.

The clerk shrugged without saying a word, but I could read her mind: "Lady, that's why the soups are labeled 'Spicy.' "

I was feeling very proud of myself for not losing my patience at this exchange, but the muttering behind me suggested that others weren't being quite so high-minded.

Just then the tasting woman turned to her friend and said, "Oh, listen to me! I sound like someone from *Curb Your Enthusiasm*. Make me stop!" She burst out laughing, and her friend joined in. I couldn't help laughing, and the people behind me started laughing too. It was astounding to see how this woman's ability to laugh at herself transformed a moment of irritation into a friendly moment shared by strangers.

It was difficult, however, to devise a way to make myself laugh more— at myself or anything else. I couldn't figure out a clever exercise or strategy to get myself yukking it up. I considered watching a funny TV show each night or lining up a series of comedy DVDs to rent, but that seemed forced and time-consuming. I didn't want to get stressed out about my laugh sessions. Was I really so humorless that I had to employ these extreme, unspontaneous measures? In the end, I just reminded myself, "Listen and laugh." I slowed myself down to give people the big reaction that they craved.

Chesterton was right, it *is* hard to be light. Joking around takes discipline. It took willpower to listen to Eliza's endless, convoluted riddles and to laugh at the punch lines. It took patience to give Eleanor the laugh she expected the millionth time she popped her head out from behind a pillow. But they were so tickled to get me laughing that their delight was a great reward. What started out as forced laughter often turned real.

I also made an effort to pay more attention to things I found funny. For example, I'm very amused by the phrase that "X is the new Y." So, for no reason other than I found it fun, I started a list (also keeping my resolution to "Forget about results"):

Sleep is the new sex.

Breakfast is the new lunch.

Halloween is the new Christmas.

May is the new September.

Vulnerability is the new strength.

Monday is the new Thursday (for making plans after work).

Three is the new two (number of children).

Forties are the new thirties, and eleven is the new thirteen (age).

Why did I find these so funny? No idea.

I had the chance to laugh at myself when a book review mentioned the "newly popular genre" of "stunt nonfiction."

"Look at this!" I said to Jamie, rattling the paper in his face. "I'm part of a genre! And not just a genre but a *stunt genre.* 'Method journalism!'"

"What's the stunt?"

"Spending a year doing something."

"What's wrong with that? Thoreau moved to Walden Pond for a year—well, for two years, but same idea."

"It makes my happiness project sound so unoriginal and *dumb,*" I wailed. "Plus I'm not even the only one writing 'stunt nonfiction' about *happiness*! Unoriginal, dumb, and superfluous."

Then I remembered—I knew better; feeling defensive and anxious wasn't the way to happiness. Laugh out loud, make fun of myself, act the way I want to feel, reframe. "Oh well," I said, switching suddenly to a lighthearted tone, "I'm part of a movement without knowing it. I missed the dot-com boom, I barely know how to use an iPod, I don't watch *Project Runway,* but for once I managed to tap right into the zeitgeist." I forced myself to laugh, and I instantly felt better. Jamie started laughing too; he also looked quite relieved that he wasn't going to have to try to jolly me out of a funk.

"Laughing out loud" went beyond mere laughter. Responding with laughter meant that I had to give up my pride, my defensiveness, my self-centeredness. I was reminded of one of the climactic moments in Saint Thérèse's life, a moment when she decided to "Laugh out loud." Typical of the extraordinarily ordinary nature of Thérèse's saintliness, she pointed to a seemingly unremarkable episode as a turning point in her spiritual life. Every Christmas, she delighted in the ritual of opening the presents left in her shoes (the French version of hanging up stockings), but one year, when she was fourteen, she overheard her father complaining, "Well, fortunately, this will be the last year!" Accustomed to being babied and petted by her family, the young Thérèse burst into tears at any cross or critical word, and this sort of unkind comment would ordinarily have caused her to dissolve into sobs. Instead, as she stood on the stairs, she experienced what she described as her "complete conversion." She forced back her tears, and instead of crying at her father's criticism, scorning his gifts, or sulking in her room, she ran down and opened the presents joyfully. Her father laughed along with her. Thérèse realized that the saintly response to her father's exasperation was to "Laugh out loud."

USE GOOD MANNERS.

As part of my research, I'd taken the Newcastle Personality Assessor test which I'd found in Daniel Nettle's book *Personality*, and my results reminded me that I needed to work harder to use good manners. This test is short—just twelve questions—but purportedly provides an accurate as sessment of an individual's personality using the "Big Five" model that has emerged, in recent years, as the most comprehensive, dependable, and useful scientific framework. According to this five-factor model, people's personalities can be characterized by their scores in five major dimensions:

1. Extroversion: response to reward
2. Neuroticism: response to threat
3. Conscientiousness: response to inhibition (self-control, planning)
4. Agreeableness: regard for others
5. Openness to experience: breadth of mental associations

I'd always thought "extroversion" was basically "friendliness," but according to this scheme, a high extroversion score means that people enjoy very strong positive reactions, so that they consistently report more joy, desire, excitement, and enthusiasm. And although I'd often thrown around the word "neurotic," I hadn't quite grasped what it meant. Turns out that people with high neuroticism scores have very strong negative reactions—fear, anxiety, shame, guilt, disgust, sadness—very often directed at themselves.

After answering the twelve questions, I totted up my score:

Extroversion: *low-medium*
Neuroticism: *low-medium*
Conscientiousness: *high*
Agreeableness: *low* (for a woman; if I were a man I'd be *low-medium*)
Openness to experience: *high*

The result struck me as quite accurate. As I'd acknowledged to myself on that subway ride back in April, when I'm in "neutral," I'm neither particularly joyful nor particularly melancholy; I'm low-medium. I'm very conscientious. I was pleased to see that I scored high on openness to experience; I wasn't sure how I'd do there. Most significant, I wasn't surprised by my low agreeableness score. I knew that about myself. When I mentioned to some friends that I'd scored low on agreeableness, like true friends, they all cried as one, "Surely not! You're very agreeable!" I suspect that my friends, as evidenced by their loyal reaction, are more agreeable than I.

"Nothing," wrote Tolstoy, "can make our life, or the lives of other people, more beautiful than perpetual kindness." Kindness, in everyday life, takes the form of good manners, and one way that my low agreeableness showed itself was in my thoughtless habits: I rushed past people on the sidewalk, I didn't often check to see if anyone needed my subway seat, I wasn't careful to say "You first," "No, *you* take it!" or "Can I help?"

In particular, to be more agreeable and kind, I needed to use better manners as a conversationalist. I was a know-it-all: "A really interesting feature of Angela Thirkell's novels is that she sets them in Barsetshire, the imaginary English county described by Trollope." I was a "topper": "You think *you* had a crazy morning, let me tell you about *my* morning." I was a deflater: "You liked that movie? I thought it was kind of boring."

So, to try to cure these tendencies, I looked for opportunities to make comments that showed my interest in other people's viewpoints:

"You're right."

"You have a good memory."

"Tell everyone that story about how you . . ."

"I hadn't thought about that before."

"I see your point."

"What do you think?"

Once I started focusing on my conversational style, I realized I had one particular characteristic that I urgently needed to control: I was too belligerent. The minute someone made a statement, I looked for ways to contradict it. When someone happened to say to me, "Over the next fifty years, it's the relationship with China that will be most important to the

United States," I started searching my mind to think of counterexamples. Why? Why argue just for the sake of disagreeing? I know very little about the subject. Going to law school had intensified this inclination. I was trained to argue, and I prided myself at being good at it—but most people don't enjoy arguing as much as law students do.

In daily life, my argumentativeness wasn't much of a problem, but I'd noticed that drinking alcohol made me far more combative than I usually was, plus it weakened my (not very strong) instinct for good manners. Because I never did drink much and had given up drinking twice while pregnant, and because of my metabolism, I'd developed a very low tolerance for alcohol. Again and again, I lay in my bed after some social event, thinking "Was I as obnoxious as I think?" "Why did I make my point in such a negative way?" And Jamie usually wasn't very reassuring about how I'd behaved.

During this month, I was determined to get control of my combativeness. I might not have thought to accomplish this by quitting drinking, except that when Jamie stopped drinking because of his hepatitis C, I'd cut back even further on my drinking to keep him company in abstinence.

I found it such a relief to be drinking less that I decided to give up drinking practically altogether (a decision that was actually somewhat predictable, because, as I knew from my February research, the fact that Jamie gave up alcohol meant that I was five times as likely to quit drinking). Not drinking made me much happier. I'd never particularly enjoyed the taste of beer or wine—I can't stand real liquor—I'd never enjoyed the "buzz" of alcohol, and I'd much rather spend the calories on eating rather than drinking. I did miss the *idea* of drinking. That's one thing I love about Winston Churchill; I love his zest for champagne and cigars. But as one of my Secrets of Adulthood says, "What's fun for other people may not be fun for you." I had to accept the fact that no matter how much other people enjoyed alcohol, and despite the fact that I wished I enjoyed it, drinking wasn't fun for me. To the contrary—it was a source of bad feeling.

Once I gave it up, mostly, I discovered another reason that drinking had made me rude: it made me sleepy. It was much easier to be polite and agreeable when I wasn't in an agony of exhaustion. As I'd noticed in earlier months, it's easier to feel happier and use good manners when I make the effort to stay physically comfortable: to dress warmly (even when people make fun of my long underwear, double sweaters, or mugs of hot water), to snack more often (I seem to need to eat far more frequently than most adults do), to turn off the light as soon as I feel sleepy, and to take pain medication as soon as I have a headache. The Duke of Wellington advised, "Always make water when you can," and I followed that precept too. It was much easier to behave pleasantly when I wasn't shivering, scouting for a bathroom, or on my second glass of wine.

GIVE POSITIVE REVIEWS.

I wanted to laugh more, I wanted to show more loving-kindness, and I also wanted to be more enthusiastic. I knew that it wasn't nice to criticize—but it was *fun.* Why was it so deliciously satisfying to criticize? Being critical made me feel more sophisticated and intelligent—and in fact, studies show that people who are critical *are* often perceived to be more discerning. In one study, for example, people judged the writers of negative book reviews as more expert and competent than the writers of positive reviews, even when the content of both reviews was deemed to be of high quality. Another study showed that people tend to think that someone who criticizes them is smarter than they are. Also, when a person disrupts a group's unanimity, he or she lessens its social power. I've seen people exploit this phenomenon; when a group is cheerfully unanimous on a topic like "The teacher is doing a great job" or "This restaurant is terrific," such a person takes the opposite position to deflate the group's mood. Being critical has its advantages, and what's more, it's much *easier* to be *hard* to please. Although enthusiasm seems easy and undiscriminating, in fact, it's much harder to embrace something than to disdain it. It's riskier.

When I examined my reactions to other people, I realized that I do often view people who make critical remarks as more perceptive and more discriminating. At the same time, though, it's hard to find pleasure in the company of someone who finds nothing pleasing. I prefer the company of the more enthusiastic types, who seem less judgmental, more vital, more fun.

For example, one evening, as part of a surprise birthday party for a close friend, we went to a Barry Manilow concert, because my friend loves Barry Manilow. Afterward, I reflected that it showed considerable strength of character to be such an avowed Barry Manilow fan. After all, Barry Manilow is . . . well, Barry Manilow. It would be so much safer to mock his music, or to enjoy it in an ironic, campy way, than to admire it whole-heartedly as she did. Enthusiasm is a form of social courage. What's more, people's assessments are very influenced by other people's assessments. So when my friend said, "This is terrific music, this is a great concert," *her* enthusiasm lifted *me* up.

I wanted to embrace this kind of zest. I steeled myself to stop making certain kinds of unnecessarily negative statements: "I really don't feel like going," "The food was too rich," "There's nothing worth reading in the paper." Instead, I tried to look for ways to be sincerely enthusiastic.

For example, one afternoon, at Jamie's suggestion, we left the girls with his parents while we went to a movie. When we came back to pick them up, my mother-in-law asked, "How was the movie?"

Instead of following my inclination to say, "Well, not bad," I answered, "It was such a treat to go see a movie in the afternoon." That's a response that's much more likely to boost happiness—not only in her but also in me.

Giving positive reviews requires humility. I have to admit, I missed the feelings of superiority that I got from using puncturing humor, sarcasm, ironic asides, cynical comments, and cutting remarks. A willingness to be pleased requires modesty and even innocence—easy to deride as mawkish and sentimental.

For the first time, I appreciated the people I knew who were unfailingly ready to be pleased. A prayer attributed to Saint Augustine of Hippo includes the line "shield your joyous ones":

> *Tend your sick ones, O Lord Jesus Christ;*
> *rest your weary ones; bless your dying ones;*
> *soothe your suffering ones; pity your afflicted ones;*
> *shield your joyous ones.*
> *And all for your love's sake.*

At first, it struck me as odd that among prayers for the "dying" and "suffering" is a prayer for the "joyous." Why worry about the joyous ones?

Once I started trying to give positive reviews, though, I began to understand how much happiness I took from the joyous ones in my life—and how much effort it must take for them to be consistently good-tempered and positive. *It is easy to be heavy; hard to be light.* We nonjoyous types suck energy and cheer from the joyous ones; we rely on them to buoy us with their good spirit and to cushion our agitation and anxiety. At the same time, because of a dark element in human nature, we're sometimes provoked to try to shake the enthusiastic, cheery folk out of their fog of illusion—to make them see that the play was stupid, the money was wasted, the meeting was pointless. Instead of shielding their joy, we blast it. Why is this? I have no idea. But that impulse is there.

I wrote about this prayer on my blog, and several readers who identified themselves as "joyous ones" responded.

. . . .

This entry almost made me cry—as one of the joyful ones, I agree wholeheartedly that it can be draining too, and it takes so little to show your appreciation.

I'm one of those people who wakes up happy every day—not because nothing ever goes wrong in my life—because I choose to be happy. Literally. For reasons I don't fully understand, people seem ticked off that I'm in a good mood. But, they want to draw on that energy, too. It is exhausting sometimes.

Gretchen—I am also a joyous one. I choose to be. I choose it every day. I have recently gone through a traumatic breakup because my boyfriend SO couldn't stop blasting my joy. And yet also unrelentingly drawing upon it like a drowning person in a sea. I felt as if I was being pulled under more every day. I had to go or I wouldn't be able to breathe anymore. I didn't know anyone understood.

⠀⠀⠀•⠀⠀⠀•⠀⠀⠀•⠀⠀⠀•⠀⠀⠀•⠀⠀⠀•⠀⠀⠀•⠀⠀⠀•⠀⠀⠀•⠀⠀⠀•⠀⠀⠀•⠀⠀⠀•

These comments reminded me that the joy of the joyous ones wasn't inexhaustible or unconquerable. I started to make a real effort to use my good cheer to support the joyous ones I knew.

To keep my resolution to "Give positive reviews," I resolved to employ the intensive approach I'd used during the Week of Extreme Nice and the Month of Novel Writing. Maybe a week of playing Pollyanna would help accelerate my move toward the positive. In Eleanor Porter's enormously successful 1913 novel, *Pollyanna,* Pollyanna plays the "glad game": whatever happens to her, she finds a reason to be glad about it. My own game, "Pollyanna Week," would be a solid week of *no negative comments.* I knew I should "Act the way I want to feel," and if I wanted to feel enthusiastic, warm, and accepting, I wasn't going to get there by constantly making sniping comments.

I woke up the first morning, deep in thought about Pollyanna Week, and by 7:00 A.M., I'd already broken it. Practically the first thing I said to Jamie was to chide him: "You *never* answer my e-mails, and you didn't answer my e-mail yesterday, so I couldn't get any of those scheduling issues settled. Do we need a babysitter for Thursday night or not?"

The next day, I did the same thing. We were all sitting around before school when Eleanor started pointing to her mouth, in what we thought was a cute way, until she started making gagging noises.

"Quick, get a towel, she's going to throw up!" I yelled.

Eliza darted into the kitchen, but she still hadn't emerged when Eleanor began heaving half-digested milk all over herself, me, and the furniture.

"Jamie, go get a towel!" He'd been sitting, mesmerized by the sight. By the time they both rushed back from the kitchen with dish towels, Eleanor had finished throwing up, and she and I were wallowing in a big, yucky mess.

"Folks, that was *not* the fastest action we could've had," I scolded. "We could've saved a lot of trouble if you'd been faster with those towels." Why did I throw out a negative comment? It added to the general loss of morale without making any useful point.

One lesson that Pollyanna Week taught me was that I could usually make my point, even if it was critical, in a positive way. For example, I broke Pollyanna Week during a game of "Finders, Keepers" with Eliza. The point of Finders, Keepers is to accumulate the most tiles.

"Can I trade my baseball cap tile for your butterfly tile?" Eliza asked after one round.

"Okay."

We played another round.

"Can I trade my globe for your flower?"

"Okay."

We played another round.

"Can I trade my football for your ice cream sundae?"

I'd been getting increasingly annoyed. "Eliza, it's tiresome when you keep trading tiles," I told her. "Just keep what you get, and you can trade them at the end. 'You get what you get, and you don't get upset.'"

"All right," she said cheerfully.

Only later did I realize that I could have phrased my request without criticism: "The game is more fun when we keep it moving fast. Can we trade at the end?"

That night I did a better job, largely because I was so tired that I went to bed at nine. Being asleep is a great way to avoid being critical. But when I said to Jamie, "I'm so exhausted that I'm going to bed now," was that a complaint or a statement of fact? It counted as a complaint. I should've found a positive way to phrase it: "Going to bed sounds so great to me that I think I'm going to turn out the light early."

One big challenge of Pollyanna Week was remembering to keep my goal uppermost in my mind. During the activities of the day, I forgot my resolution. So, borrowing from some of the mindfulness strategies I had tried in October, on the third morning, I started wearing a wide orange bracelet for the rest of Pollyanna Week, as a constant reminder of my goal to make only positive comments. The bracelet worked fairly well—except that once I caught myself complaining to a friend that the bracelet was too heavy and clunky! So much for reminding me to make only positive comments. But I did have moments of triumph. I didn't complain about our loss of Internet service. I didn't grouse when Jamie baked three rich desserts in three nights. When Eliza accidentally ran Eleanor's stroller into the kitchen wall, where it made a dark mark, I let it go without making a fuss. And when Eleanor grabbed my lipstick off the counter, then dropped it into the toilet, I said, "Well, it was an accident."

During Pollyanna Week, I never did manage to go an entire day without a negative comment, but I nevertheless declared it a successful exercise. Though 100 percent compliance was an impossible ambition, making the effort jolted me into an awareness of my usual attitude. The effect of Pollyanna Week lingered long after the week was up.

FIND AN AREA OF REFUGE.

One fact of human nature is that people have a "negativity bias": we react to the *bad* more strongly and persistently than to the comparable *good*. As

I'd learned in February, within a marriage, it takes at least five good acts to repair the damage of one critical or destructive act. With money, the pain of losing a certain sum is greater than the pleasure of gaining that sum. Hitting the best-seller list with *Forty Ways to Look at Winston Churchill* thrilled me less than a bad review upset me.

One consequence of the negativity bias is that when people's minds are unoccupied, they tend to drift to anxious or angry thoughts. And rumination—dwelling on slights, unpleasant encounters, and sad events—leads to bad feelings. In fact, one reason that women are more susceptible to depression than men may be their greater tendency to ruminate; men are more likely to distract themselves with an activity. Studies show that distraction is a powerful mood-altering device, and contrary to what a lot of people believe, persistently focusing on a bad mood aggravates rather than palliates it.

I'd often noticed my own tendency to brood, and to counter this effect, I invented the idea of the "area of refuge." Once when I was back visiting my former law school, I noticed a sign by an elevator that declared that area an "area of refuge." I guess it's where a person in a wheelchair or with some other difficulty should go in case of fire. The phrase stuck in my mind, and I decided that if I found myself dwelling on bad feelings, I'd seek a mental "area of refuge."

As an area of refuge, I often think about Churchill's speeches—in particular, his eulogy for Neville Chamberlain. Or I think about some of the funny things Jamie has done. Years ago, when we were first married, Jamie came into our bedroom in his boxers and announced, "I am LORD of the DANCE!" and hopped around with his arms straight at his sides. I still laugh every time I think about it. A friend told me that she thinks about her children. Another friend—not a writer—makes up short stories in her head. When Arthur Llewelyn Davies, the father of the boys who inspired *Peter Pan,* was recovering from an operation that removed his cheekbone and part of the roof of his mouth, he wrote a note to J. M. Barrie:

Among the things I think about

Michael going to school
Porthgwarra and S's blue dress
Burpham garden
Kirkby view across valley . . .
Jack bathing
Peter answering chaff
Nicholas in the garden
George always

These phrases mean nothing to an outsider, but for him, they were areas of refuge.

By the end of November, I'd realized that one of the most important lessons of the happiness project is that if I keep my resolutions and do the things that make me happier, I end up feeling happier *and* acting more virtuously. Do good, feel good; feel good, do good.

Over the course of the month, I noticed that a frequent subject of my negative comments was Eliza's hair. Jamie and I thought it looked cutest when it hung right above her shoulders, but she begged us to grow it long. "You can grow it long only if you promise to keep it brushed nicely and out of your face," I threatened, repeating the words that untold millions of parents have uttered, to no avail. She promised, but of course, her hair constantly hung in her face.

"Eliza, brush your hair, it's all messy."

"Eliza, you've got the dreaded middle part, part your hair on the side."

"Eliza, get a ponytail holder or a barrette, you need to pull your hair back."

"Eliza, you can't possibly tell me you've already brushed your hair."

This criticism was no fun for her and no fun for me. I wanted to change this pattern. So the next time I wanted to fret about her hair, I said, "Bring me a brush," and I started to brush her hair—not fast and rough, as I sometimes did when I was impatient in the morning, but gently. "I love seeing your hair smooth and shiny," I said. "Your hair looks beautiful."

Eliza looked a little surprised.

The next time I tried the same thing. "Let me brush your hair," I told her. "I love brushing your hair."

She didn't get any better about keeping her hair tidy, but it didn't bother me as much.

12

DECEMBER

Boot Camp Perfect

HAPPINESS

For eleven months, I'd been piling on the resolutions, and for this last month of December, I wanted to try Boot Camp Perfect. I would follow all of my resolutions, all the time. I would aim to see nothing but gold stars glittering on my Resolutions Chart. This goal of perfection was daunting, because following my resolutions took a huge amount of mental discipline and self-control—not to mention, it took a lot of *time*.

So, for the month, I tidied, I cleared, I organized, I turned off the light. I sang in the morning, I laughed out loud, I acknowledged people's feelings, I left things unsaid. I blogged, I asked for help, I pushed myself, I showed up, I went off the path. I wrote in my one-sentence journal. I met with my writers' strategy group and my children's literature reading group. I listened to my hypnosis tape. I didn't eat any fake food. I bought needful things.

Of course, I also failed to do these things. As hard as I tried during Boot Camp Perfect, I still didn't manage to keep all my resolutions. Resolutions! After all these months, I was still astonished at how effectively they worked to make me happy, whenever I did faithfully keep them. I thought often of the 1764 journal entry of Samuel Johnson, who, as an inveterate resolution maker and resolution breaker, is one of the patron saints of the process:

> I have now spent fifty-five years in resolving; having, from the earliest time almost that I can remember, been forming schemes of a better life. I have done nothing. The need of doing, therefore, is pressing, since the time of doing is short. O GOD, grant me to resolve aright, and to keep my resolutions.

Did I have even one single perfect day during December? Nope. But I kept trying. One helpful consequence of my happiness project was that even when I had a bad day, it was a good bad day. If I was feeling blue, I'd run through my mood-boosting strategies: go to the gym, get some work done, keep myself from getting too hungry, cross a nagging task off my to-do list, connect with other people, spend some time having fun with my family. Sometimes nothing really worked, but the nice thing about trying to ameliorate a bad mood by taking those kinds of constructive steps was that even when a day was bad, it had bright spots, and I could look back on a good bad day with satisfaction.

One development had given me a huge shot of encouragement: after I'd posted an offer to send people my Resolutions Chart in case they wanted to see a model as they formulated their own resolutions, I'd started to get e-mails from people describing their happiness projects. Several people had even started their own blogs to track them. I was gratified to think that I'd convinced some readers to try the method and resolutions that had worked for me.

 •   •   •   •   •   •   •   •   •   •   •   •   •   •   •

Thank you very much for sharing your Resolutions Chart. My husband and I are going to create a month of resolutions. I think the exercise will be both fun and a good bonding experience for us after an emotionally rocky few months. We haven't sat down to do it yet (which is yet another symptom of how work keeps us from spending quality time together), just talked about doing it soon, but I've been thinking about simple resolutions—like Date night, Express physical affection, Do something new together, Listen to her/him, Play hookie from work for an afternoon, Go for a drive (we always talk better stuck in a car together). We just realized there are a lot of things we take for granted, having been together for so long, and there are so many little things that we're realizing we have neglected over time that would probably make us happier if we paid attention to them now.

[The introduction to a blog:] I have been inspired recently by The Happiness Project by Gretchen Rubin. I love her idea of studying what makes us happy and then trying to apply it to our own lives. Everyone's happiness project would be unique, but I am sure would have many things in common. She has challenged others to have their own "happiness project" and I am taking her up on this challenge!

I have enlisted a friend to do this with me—I'll call her Jen. And I am trying to see if my husband will join in as well. We will track our journeys together.

Part of my interest in the Happiness Project is learning how some of the principles of happiness might also be applied to children. I will be exploring this as well.

And most important, I know that one of the things that makes me the happiest is to share what I learn with others. So, it will all be posted here. It should be fun!

In the vein of being mindful and showing gratitude to those you appreciate, I've been meaning to share with you the positive effect your blog has had on my life for a while now. You posted a few things on resolutions that inspired me to come up with my own. Knowing that I needed to be specific about things that could be accomplished and that being more social would lead to additional happiness, I wrote out the following three general goals against which I could judge success at the end:

1. Take a Class
2. Volunteer
3. Join a Group

I promptly signed up for two courses to continue learning for my own edification. I also volunteered with the Boy Scout troop that I had been affiliated with while I was in my teens. These two resolutions took up much of my free time for the first half of the year. Recently, I began working toward the third goal and joined a rowing club.

I can tell you, without a doubt, that these three resolutions have led to all of my best experiences this year. I met some important friends in my economics class, have learned how to motivate and lead through my experiences with the Boy Scouts, and am just starting to expand my social circle by joining the rowing club (while getting more exercise). Honestly, when people ask me what I'm "up to," I tell them about the things I'm doing because of those resolutions and really sound interesting. More importantly, I'm feeling fulfilled and definitely happier.

I'm now taking a third course and considering joining a wine club. I also walk five times a week, and keep myself motivated to maintain the habit using many of the suggestions you've shared (the one that sticks with me the most is the one from your dad about just having to put the shoes on and get to the mailbox).

I've learned so much through your research and experience and just want you to know that your work is worth the effort. The impact on my life has been immediate, and I'm certain it will last for many years, if not the rest of my life. Sometimes, people say that if the things they do can influence one person, then it was all worth it. Well, you have!

When I found your blog, a light came on and I thought that the members of our group would love this project as we are all indeed searching for happiness. I was right! When I introduced the idea everyone is so excited to begin. We will meet next Monday and share some of our Commandments and I will then introduce your Resolutions Charts. As you say in your blog, each project will look different, according to the person, but as I continue to read your blog, it has become clear to me that in the end we are all looking for basically the same thing . . . Happiness!

To make your own happiness, to write your own Commandments and check yourself with your own resolutions is simply GENIUS! My group struggles with this search but never had the thought of going and taking happiness for ourselves, we simply try to live better and hope that it comes.

Time will tell but certainly the group is very excited about the prospect and their "homework" which was to begin their own Commandments.

Last week-end my daughter and a friend met me at my mom's house. My daughter is 28 and my mom is 86—I'm somewhere in the middle. My daughter and her friend started talking about the happiness project and some of the precepts they had learned there. My daughter's friend mentioned the idea of really enjoying what you have—such as using the good dishes, not saving the dress for a day that may never come, etc. My mom, who is a VERY frugal woman, began to talk about some demitasse cups that had been passed on to her and how they were boxed up in the closet because she didn't have a display case. I suggested we go to the furniture store and find one she could use, and surprisingly she agreed. We looked at two stores and left with good information about a curio cabinet. On the way out of the second store, Mom noticed a chair that looked very comfortable, and had a heating and vibrating feature that felt good. I ended up paying for half of the chair for her Christmas present and we later ordered the curio as well.

We all know that happiness is not in things. However, at age 86 I was so glad that my mom could have a couple of things that she will really enjoy. Her chair was delivered and she reports that she may never sit anywhere else. When the curio cabinet is delivered we will have a great time putting together the display of her family heirlooms. Thanks for the inspiration!

It made me very happy to think that my blog had helped contribute to the happiness of people I'd never even met. Of course, that was the purpose of the blog—but I was thrilled to discover that it was actually working.

"Your year is almost up," friends kept saying to me. "So, are you happier?"

"Absolutely!" I answered.

"But how do you really know?" one scientist friend asked. "Did you do any kind of systematic measurement over the course of the year?"

"Well, no."

"You didn't have Jamie score you each day or keep a mood chart on yourself or anything like that?"

"Nope."

"So maybe you aren't any happier, you just *think* you are."

"Well," I conceded, "maybe it's my imagination . . . but no. I *know* I'm happier."

"How?"

"I *feel* happier!"

It was really true.

My First Splendid Truth says that if I want to be happier, I need to look at my life and think about *feeling good, feeling bad,* and *feeling right,* in an *atmosphere of growth.* I'd worked on all these elements, and it had made an enormous difference.

For me, it turned out, the most significant prong was the *feeling bad.* My biggest happiness boosts had come from eliminating the bad feelings generated by my snapping, nagging, gossiping, being surrounded by clutter, eating fake food, drinking, and all the rest. In particular, it made me happier to be in better control of my sharp tongue. Nowadays I often managed to pause and change my tone, just a second before I started to rant, or to change my tone in midsentence. I'd even managed to laugh while chiding Jamie about not dealing with the insurance forms or not looking for his missing library book.

At the same time, I was having more *feeling good*—more laughing with my family, talking about children's literature with my book group, listening to music I liked. I'd learned a lot of ways to get more bang for my happiness buck.

Feeling right had been very important to my happiness when I was struggling with the question of whether to switch from law to writing, but it hadn't been the source of many of my resolutions over the past months. At the start of December, however, I was hit by the idea for a goal I wanted to undertake to "feel right" in the coming year: I wanted to get involved in the issue of organ donation. We all hoped that Jamie would never need a liver transplant, of course, but his hepatitis C had made me much more interested in the issue. If I could figure out some small way, myself, to help boost the number of organ donations in the country, I'd feel as though I'd been able to transform an unfortunate personal situation into some larger good. I'd already started gathering a list of names and resources that I wanted to check out. I didn't particularly enjoy this work, but I could see that this project would make me *feel right.*

But what had surprised me most about the First Splendid Truth was the importance of the final prong, the *atmosphere of growth.* I hadn't ascribed much weight to it, even when I'd identified it as the fourth element of happiness. My happiness project had proved to me, however, that the atmosphere of growth was a huge contributor to happiness. Although my instinct was to shy away from novelty and challenge, in fact they are a key source of happiness, even for an unadventurous soul like me. In particular, I'd seen how the atmosphere of growth provided by my blog had become an enormous source of happiness. My successful mastery of that skill had given me feelings of gratification and mastery that in turn had energized me to push myself even harder.

There was another question that people kept asking me: "What about Jamie—has he changed, is *he* happier?" One thing I knew: Jamie wouldn't be very happy if I pestered him to provide a comprehensive analysis of his emotional state. Even so, one night I couldn't resist asking him, "Do you think my happiness project has made you happier? Do you think you've changed at all?"

"Nope," he answered.

But he *had* changed. Without any nagging on my part, he was taking on tasks, such as doing holiday shopping or putting our finances on Quicken, that he'd never done before. He was much better about doing little chores like answering my e-mails and emptying the diaper pail now than he'd been a year ago. Not only did he remember my birthday this month—he wished me "Happy Birthday" the minute we woke up that morning—he organized a family party, got me a present, and took photos (he never takes photos).

He'd absorbed more of my happiness talk than I'd realized, too. One day when we were out doing errands, I overheard him say to Eliza, "When we get to the Container Store, you're going to see something very interesting. Mommy is going to buy something for $5 that's going to make her extremely happy. Very little things can make a person happy, it doesn't matter how expensive something is." The item in question? A sponge holder that fastens to the side of the sink with suction cups. I'd coveted one ever since I spotted this device in my brother- and sister-in-law's apartment. And Jamie was right, I was made extremely happy by that purchase—but he would never have made an observation like that last year. But of all the happiness-boosting things he did, my favorite was the e-mail he sent me after I was angry that he hadn't made a phone call that he'd promised to make:

From: Rubin James
To: Gretchen Rubin
Subject: don't be mad—see below

I confess that when I started the happiness project, I feared that if I stopped nagging and complaining, Jamie would leave all the work to me. That didn't happen. Now, correlation is not causation, so maybe my happiness project had nothing to do with the ways in which he changed—but for whatever reason, the atmosphere in our house was happier. That's not a very scientific standard of measurement. Maybe I was seeing what I wanted to see. Maybe, but who cares?

If I think I'm happier, I *am* happier. That's the Fourth Splendid Truth. The Fourth Splendid Truth may have been the last Splendid Truth I identified, but in fact I'd understood it on some level from that first moment on the bus, when I had the idea for my happiness project. I'm not happy unless I think I'm happy—and by pushing myself to be mindful of my happiness, I can truly experience it.

Although the First Splendid Truth was extremely valuable in showing me how to change my life to be happier, the Second Splendid Truth was more important to my understanding of the nature of happiness.

One of the best ways to make *myself* happy is to make *other people* happy.

One of the best ways to make *other people* happy is to be happy *myself.*

The Second Splendid Truth made clear to me why working to be happy isn't a selfish goal and why, as Robert Louis Stevenson said, "There is no duty we so much underrate as the duty of being happy." When I was feeling unhappy, I felt dispirited, lethargic, defensive, and uninterested in other people; even worse, when I felt angry or resentful, I searched for excuses to feel even more angry and resentful. On the other hand, when I felt happy, I was more likely to be lighthearted, generous, creative, kind, encouraging, and helpful.

December was a crazy time for my sister, Elizabeth. She and her writing partner were writing a pilot for a network TV show (one of the most important work opportunities she'd ever had), she and her fiancé, Adam, had just bought a house, she was planning their wedding, and she was dealing with her recent diagnosis of diabetes. I really wished that I could do something for Elizabeth—then I thought of something I *could* do.

I called her up. "Hey, guess what?"

"What?" she said, sounding harried.

"I've been feeling bad about all the stress you have right now, so I've decided"—I paused for effect—"to do your holiday shopping for you!"

"Gretch, would you really?" she said. "That would be *so great.*" Elizabeth's stress must have been as bad as I'd thought; she didn't even pretend to resist the offer.

"I'm happy to do it!" I told her. And I *was.* Hearing the relief and happiness in her voice made me very happy. Would I have offered to do her shopping, as well as mine, if I'd been feeling unhappy? No. Would it have even occurred to me to try to help her out? Probably not.

The Third Splendid Truth was a different kind of truth. "The days are long, but the years are short" reminded me to stay in the moment, to appreciate the seasons, and to revel in this time of life—December's yuletide atmosphere, the girls' little matching cherry nightgowns, the elaborate bath-time routine.

Most nights, I spent the time before bed racing around, trying to get organized for the morning, or crashed in bed with a book. But Jamie has a lovely habit. We call it "gazing lovingly." Every few weeks, he'll say to me, "Come on, let's gaze lovingly," and we go look at Eliza and Eleanor as they sleep.

The other night he pulled me away from the computer. "No, I've got too much to do," I told him. "I need to finish a few things before tomorrow. You go ahead."

But he wouldn't listen, so finally I went with him to stand in Eleanor's doorway. We "gazed lovingly" at her small figure flung across the huge pile of books that she insisted on keeping in her crib.

I said to him, "Someday we'll look back and it will be hard to remember that we ever had such little kids. We'll say, 'Remember when Eleanor still used her purple sippy cup or when Eliza wore ruby slippers all the time?'"

He squeezed my hand. "We'll say, 'That was such a happy time.'"

The days are long, but the years are short.

During the year, when people had asked me, "So what's the secret to happiness?," at different times I'd answer "Exercise" or "Sleep" or "Do good, feel good" or "Strengthen your connections to other people." But by the end of December, I'd realized that the most helpful aspect of my happiness project hadn't been these resolutions, or the Four Splendid Truths I'd identified, or the science I'd learned, or all the high-minded books I'd read. The single most effective step for me had been to keep my Resolutions Chart.

When I'd started, I'd viewed my chart as just another fun thing to experiment with, like the gratitude notebook. But it had turned out to be tremendously important. Making the resolutions wasn't the hardest part of the happiness project (though it was harder than I expected, in some cases, to identify the appropriate resolution); *following through* was the hardest part. The desire to change was meaningless if I couldn't find a way to make the change happen.

By providing an opportunity for constant review and accountability, the Resolutions Chart kept me plugging away. The phrases "Lighten up," "Give proofs of love," and "Cut people slack" flashed through my consciousness constantly, and I often changed my actions in consequence. When I was annoyed when the woman working next to me at the library kept sighing noisily, I tried to "Imitate a spiritual master"; Saint Thérèse tells the story of how she once broke into a sweat at the effort to conquer her annoyance when a fellow nun made maddening clicking noises during evening prayers. Even if I didn't do a perfect job with my resolutions, I did do *better,* and the more I kept my resolutions, the happier I was.

I'd noticed idly that a lot of people use the term "goal" instead of "resolution," and one day in December, it struck me that this difference was in fact significant. You *hit* a goal, you *keep* a resolution. "Run a marathon" makes a good goal. It's specific, it's easy to measure success, and once you've done it, you've done it. "Sing in the morning" and "Exercise better" are better cast as resolutions. You won't wake up one day and find that you've achieved it. It's something that you have to resolve to do every day, forever. Striving toward a goal provides the atmosphere of growth so important to happiness, but it can be easy to get discouraged if reaching the goal is more difficult than you expected. Also, what happens once you've reached your goal? Say you've run the marathon. What now—do you stop exercising? Do you set a new goal? With resolutions, the expectations are different. Each day I try to live up to my resolutions. Sometimes I succeed, sometimes I fail, but every day is a clean slate and a fresh opportunity. I never expect to be done with my resolutions, so I don't get discouraged when they stay challenging. Which they do.

With each passing month, too, I realized the importance of my First Commandment, "Be Gretchen." As great minds throughout the ages have pointed out, one of our most pressing concerns should be to discover the laws of our own nature. I had to build my happiness on the foundation of my character; I had to acknowledge what really made me happy, not what I *wished* made me happy. One of the biggest surprises of the happiness project was just how hard it was to know myself. I'd always been slightly exasperated by philosophers' constant emphasis on what seemed to me to be a fairly obvious question, but in the end I realized that I would spend my whole life grappling with the question of how to "Be Gretchen."

It's funny; only once it was December and my happiness project was drawing to a close did it occur to me to wonder *why* I'd had the urge to do my happiness project in the first place. Sure, I'd had a bus-ride epiphany about wanting to be happier, and it had been a relief and a thrill to step out of my ordinary life to contemplate transcendent matters—but what had motivated me to stick with it for the whole year?

Jamie told me what he thought. "I think this happiness project is all about you trying to get more control over your life," he said.

Was that true?

Perhaps. The feeling of control is an essential element of happiness—a better predictor of happiness than, say, income. Having a feeling of autonomy, of being able to choose what happens in your life or how you spend your time, is crucial. Identifying and following my resolutions had made me feel far more in control of my time, my body, my actions, my surroundings, and even my thoughts. Getting control of my life was definitely an aspect of my happiness project, and a greater feeling of control gave me a major boost in happiness.

But something deeper was going on as well. I'd begun to understand that, although I hadn't quite recognized it when I started, I was girding myself for some awesome, dreadful challenge, or working to meet some Judgment Day deadline for virtue. My Resolutions Chart is really my conscience. I wonder if one day I'll look back on this year of my happiness project with wonder at my . . . innocence. "How easy it was to be happy, *then*," I might think on some dark, distant morning. How glad I'll be that I did everything within my power to appreciate the life I have now, just as it is.

The year is over, and I really am happier. After all my research, I found out what I knew all along: I could change my life without changing my life. When I made the effort to reach out for them, I found that the ruby slippers had been on my feet all along; the bluebird was singing outside my kitchen window.

ACKNOWLEDGMENTS

Although one of the most important principles I learned during my happiness project is the importance of giving thanks, I can't thank everyone who helped me with my project, because practically every person I know has given me some insight into happiness. I couldn't possibly list them all by name.

Certain people, however, played particularly important roles during the year of my happiness project. Freda Richardson and Ashley Wilson, of course. Lori Jackson and everyone at Inform Fitness. The members of my first children's literature book group: Ana Maria Allessi, Julia Bator, Ann Brashares, Sarah Burnes, Jonathan Burnham, Dan Ehrenhaft, Amanda Foreman, Bob Hughes, Susan Kamil, Pamela Paul, David Saylor, Elizabeth Schwarz, Jenny Smith, Rebecca Todd, Stephanie Wilchfort, Jessica Wollman, Amy Zilliax, and especially Jennifer Joel; and also my second children's literature book group: Chase Bodine, Betsy Bradley, Sophie Gee, Betsy Gleick, Lev Grossman, Caitlin Macy, Suzanne Myers, Jesse Scheidlower, and especially Amy Wilensky. My working writers' strategy groups: Marci Alboher, Jonathan Fields, A. J. Jacobs, Michael Melcher, and Carrie Weber. My book group for adult literature predates the official start of my happiness project but was an unusually helpful source of ideas and happiness: Ann Brashares, Betsy Cohen, Cheryl Effron, Patricia Farman-Farmaian, Sharon Greenberger, Samhita Jayanti, Alisa

Kohn, Bethany Millard, Jennifer Newstead, Claudia Rader, Elizabeth Schwarz, Jennifer Scully, Paula Zakaria, and particularly Julia Bator.

Thanks to the readers who commented on drafts: Delia Boylan, Susan Devenyi, Elizabeth Craft Fierro, Reed Hundt, A. J. Jacobs, Michael Melcher, Kim Malone Scott, Kamy Wicoff, and most of all, Melanie Rehak.

Thanks to all the people who worked with me on various offshoots of the Happiness Project: the far-flung Jayme Stevens; the graphic designer Charlotte Strick; the cartoonist Chari Pere; Tom Romer, Lauren Ribando and the folks at the Chopping Block Web design firm; Melissa Parrish and Tanya Singer at RealSimple.com; Verena Von Pfetten and Anya Strzemien at The Huffington Post; and Michael Newman at *Slate*.

Thanks very much to all my friends from blogland, who have given me so much advice, help, and link love—just to mention a few, people such as Leo Babauta, Therese Borchard, Chris Brogan, Ben Casnocha, Tyler Cowen, Jackie Danicki, Dory Devlin, Erin Doland, Asha Dornfest, Kathy Hawkins, Tony Hsieh, Guy Kawasaki, Danielle LaPorte, Brett McKay, Daniel Pink, J. D. Roth, Glen Stansberry, Bob Sutton, Colleen Wainwright, everyone in the LifeRemix network . . . I could keep going for pages. I only hope I get to meet them all in real life one day.

I can't say enough to thank my blog readers, particularly those whose words I quote. Being able to exchange ideas about happiness with so many thoughtful readers has been extraordinarily helpful—and fun.

A huge thanks to Christy Fletcher, my agent, and to Gail Winston, my editor—working on this book was a very *happy* experience.

Most of all, thanks to my family. You are my weather.

YOUR HAPPINESS PROJECT

Each person's happiness project will be unique, but it's the rare person who can't benefit from starting one. My own happiness project started in January and lasted a year—and, I hope, will last for the rest of my life—but your happiness project can start any time and last as long as you choose. You can start small (putting your keys away in the same place every night) or big (repairing your relationships with your family). It's up to you.

First, to decide what resolutions to make, consider the First Splendid Truth and answer the following questions:

- What makes you *feel good*? What activities do you find fun, satisfying, or energizing?
- What makes you *feel bad*? What are sources of anger, irritation, boredom, frustration, or anxiety in your life?
- Is there any way in which you don't *feel right* about your life? Do you wish you could change your job, city, family situation, or other circumstances? Are you living up to your expectations for yourself? Does your life reflect your values?
- Do you have sources of an *atmosphere of growth*? In what elements of your life do you find progress, learning, teaching, serving, challenge, and increased mastery?

Answering these questions provides a good road map to the kind of changes you might consider. Once you've decided what areas need work, identify specific, measurable resolutions that will allow you to evaluate whether you're making progress. Resolutions work better when they're concrete, not abstract: it's harder to keep a resolution to "Be a more loving parent" than to "Get up fifteen minutes early so I'm dressed before the kids wake up."

Once you've made your resolutions, find a strategy to assess your progress and to hold yourself accountable. I copied Benjamin Franklin's Virtues Chart to devise my Resolutions Chart. Other approaches might be starting a goals group, keeping a one-sentence journal marking your progress, or starting a blog.

Another useful exercise is to identify your personal commandments— the principles that you want to guide your behavior. For example, my most important personal commandment is to "Be Gretchen."

If you'd like to start a group for people doing happiness projects, e-mail me at grubin@gretchenrubin.com for a starter kit. You can also join the conversation about happiness, good habits, and human nature on the free "Better" app. Just search for "Better Gretchen Rubin" in the App Store, or visit betterapp.us; there you can learn more, engage with others, form accountability groups, and join people doing happiness projects together. We can all learn from each other.

THE HAPPINESS PROJECT
MANIFESTO

To be happy, you need to consider feeling good, feeling bad, and feeling right, in an atmosphere of growth.

One of the best ways to make *yourself* happy is to make *other people* happy; one of the best ways to make other people happy is to be happy *yourself.*

The days are long, but the years are short.

You're not happy unless you think you're happy.

Your body matters.

Happiness is other people.

Think about yourself so you can forget yourself.

"It is easy to be heavy: hard to be light." —G. K. Chesterton

What's fun for other people may not be fun for you, and vice versa.

Best is good, better is best.

Outer order contributes to inner calm.

Happiness comes not from having more, not from having less, but from wanting what you have.

You can choose what you *do,* but you can't choose what you *like* to do.

"There is no duty we so much underrate as the duty of being happy." —Robert Louis Stevenson

You manage what you measure.

Loving actions inspire loving feelings.

The opposite of a great truth is also true.

A CONVERSATION WITH GRETCHEN RUBIN

Were you surprised by the success of *The Happiness Project*? It has sold two million copies, it was a #1 *New York Times* bestseller and stayed on the bestseller list for more than two years, and it has been published in more than thirty languages. Did you expect that kind of reception?

Before publication, I knew from the enthusiastic response to the *Happiness Project* blog that my writing on the subject resonated with people, and I worked hard to set the book up for success. But I never expected it would become the phenomenon that it did!

I know what it's like to write a book that doesn't "find its audience" (that's what your editor tells you when your book flops), so it was particularly gratifying to see the book succeed. Many people assume that *The Happiness Project* was my first book, when in fact it was my fourth book. So I'm a classic case of a person working for ten years to become an overnight sensation.

Before the book was published, I had no way to know if my blend of memoir, research, quotation, and experimentation would strike a chord with readers. I'm so happy that it does.

Because of the success of the book, you've had some exciting opportunities. What have been some of the most notable things you've done?

Getting interviewed by Oprah Winfrey was a definite highlight. She recorded the interview at her home in Montecito, so I got to visit "the Promised Land," and I also got to bring my sister, Elizabeth, with me, on a terrific sisterly adventure. Oprah is so . . . *Oprah*. In person, she's exactly the way I'd imagined her to be.

Another highlight was meeting the Dalai Lama. In fact, at the end of our meeting, we needed to walk to the other end of the conference center in the rain, so he grabbed my arm to help him stay steady—yes, I walked arm in arm with the Dalai Lama.

I had dinner with Nobel Prize winner Daniel Kahneman—he's notable for his work on the psychology of judgment, decision making, and behavioral economics, subjects that fascinate me. He's the author of *Thinking, Fast and Slow,* among countless other accomplishments, and a person I was thrilled to meet.

One very fun thing that happened—though I had nothing to do with it—was that *"The Happiness Project"* was an answer on the game show *Jeopardy!*

Less flashy, but very gratifying, was that my personality framework of "Four Tendencies" was written up in a scientific journal.

I've been on the cover of a few magazines. That's surreal.

What has happened in your professional life since *The Happiness Project* was published?

It's hard to believe that a full decade has passed. Since the book came out, I've written four additional books (five, if you count my project *My Color Pilgrimage*, which hasn't yet been published).

In the past decade, one of my favorite undertakings has been to launch the *Happier with Gretchen Rubin* podcast, where I talk about happiness, habits, and human nature with my sister, Elizabeth Craft, who's a TV writer and producer in Los Angeles. To give you a sense of it, some of our segments include "Try This at Home," "Happiness Hack," "Know Yourself Better," "Before & After Story," "Happiness Stumbling Block," "Four Tendencies Tip," and "Listener Question." At the end of each episode we take turns awarding demerits or gold stars related to something that's happened to us. We're sisters, so we don't let each other get away with much.

I've also created several interesting projects: one-sentence journals, habit journals, mugs, page-a-day calendars, 21-day projects. I even designed a coloring book.

My blog (which I now call my "site," because the very word "blog" seems old-fashioned) has been going strong for more than a decade. To celebrate the tenth anniversary, I created an e-book, *The Best of the Happiness Project Blog*. That was a lot of fun to put together.

I started *Ask Gretchen Rubin Live,* a weekly show on Facebook. It's great to get a chance to talk about happiness, habits, and human nature with people in real time.

I launched the free "Better" app to help people make their lives happier, healthier, more productive, and more creative—just search "Better Gretchen Rubin" in your device's app store. I also created my first video course to help more people harness the Four Tendencies.

Plus, as I predicted in the book, I did indeed meet book reviewer David Greenberg at a cocktail party, and we had a nice conversation.

What has happened in your personal life since *The Happiness Project* was published?

By far the most important thing that happened was that my husband Jamie's hepatitis C was cured—a medical miracle.

As I write about in *The Happiness Project* and *Happier at Home,* Jamie got hepatitis C from a blood transfusion during a heart operation when he was eight years old. You really don't want to have hepatitis C; eventually, it destroys your liver. Jamie tried many treatments over the years, but nothing worked. When a new treatment was approved, Jamie went on it right away, and as of January 9, 2015 (a date we celebrate every year), Jamie was cured.

Brief service announcement: if you support organ donation, sign the registry at organdonor.gov, tell your family that you'd want to donate your organs, or post a message with #organdonor. It's a rare privilege to die in a way that permits us to donate our organs, and in a time of sorrow and shock, the people around you might not know what you would've wanted. It's a miracle that my husband gets to keep the liver he was born with. *But things might not have turned out this way.*

Other big news: my family and I got a dog, a delightful cockapoo named Barnaby.

I quit sugar and, really, almost all carbs. (I write about making this change in *Better Than Before.*)

When my children's literature reading group hit twenty members, we had to close the group to newcomers, and I started a second group, and even a third group. Yes, I'm in *three* kid-lit reading groups, and these groups are a giant engine of happiness for me. Plus I'm still in one group where we read books for adults.

The blind date I set up in that long-ago June culminated in a wedding.

I now get up at 6:00 A.M. every morning.

Tell us what the members of your family are doing.

My husband, Jamie, has held several exciting positions over the past decade. He's gone back and forth between private equity and senior roles in New York State government.

Many readers are surprised to realize that Eleanor and Eliza are no longer the little girls, ages one and seven, that they were in *The Happiness Project.*

Now Eliza has gone off to college, which was a major bittersweet family milestone. She's very happy in college—something that has added a lot to my happiness as well. She has a podcast, *Eliza Starting at 16,* in which she explains what's happening in the big wide world of teenagers these days. So if you'd like to hear her views of things, check out her podcast.

Eleanor is enjoying middle school, despite having braces, a lot more homework, and missing her big sister. This is a notoriously challenging stage of life, so I'm happy it's going well for her.

It's such a cliché to say this, but it really is unbelievable how quickly time passes. On the subject of parenting and the passage of time, I did a one-minute video, "The Years Are Short" (you can find it on my website), and of everything I've ever created, I think this short video resonates most with people.

In my sister Elizabeth's life, most important, her son, Jack, was born—he's a big guy now. She's also had a lot of exciting developments in her life as a TV writer and producer: shooting several TV pilots, writing on various TV shows, and launching the podcast *Happier in Hollywood* with her writing partner and friend since childhood, Sarah Fain. She also survived a major house renovation.

What else? In addition to Jamie and my mother-in-law, I've also convinced my father-in-law and numerous friends to join my weight-training gym, Inform Fitness—Elizabeth and her husband, Adam, even joined Inform Fitness in Los Angeles. (If you join this gym because of what you read here, tell them. They get a big kick out of knowing that.)

We still go regularly to Kansas City to visit my parents.

I tried meditation again, and abandoned it again.

We still live in the same apartment in New York City.

You mentioned that since *The Happiness Project* came out, you've published several books about the subject of happiness, broadly conceived. How do your different projects fit together?

My true subject is human nature.

As part of understanding human nature, I'm constantly thinking: How do we know ourselves? How can we change if we want to change?

How can we make our lives happier, healthier, more productive, and more creative—or how can we help other people to do so?

My work is sometimes called "personal development" or "self-help"—the *New York Times Book Review* described me as the "the queen of the self-help memoir"—but I actually describe myself as *self-helpful*. (Really, I'm a moral essayist, but that sounds so dull.)

I'm a kind of street scientist. I do my research by reading voraciously and by observing the people around me; I get a lot of "anecdata" from books, readers, and listeners. Studying undergraduates in a laboratory is one way to learn about human nature, but it's not the only way.

Many people who write about happiness are academics, scientists, historians, or journalists, and I admire and study this work every day. While of course I wouldn't compare myself with figures like Montaigne, Samuel Johnson, La Rochefoucauld, Thoreau, or George Orwell, I write in that tradition.

Each of my books—all the way back to my first book—has tackled an aspect of the overarching subject of human nature.

So after *The Happiness Project,* what led you to write *Happier at Home?*

I was looking for universals in happiness, and there aren't many—but most people do have an idea of *home*. I realized that for me, home had a special role to play in a happy life.

Samuel Johnson wrote, "To be happy at home is the ultimate result of all ambition, the end to which every enterprise and labour tends." Now, perhaps it's debatable whether that's true for everyone, but it's certainly true for me.

So in *Happier at Home,* I dug deeply into the aspects of my life that shape my experience of home, such as possessions, time, body, neighborhood, marriage, and parenthood. Each month has a theme, and I experiment with several concrete, manageable resolutions meant to boost my happiness.

I definitely did some quirky things; for instance, I describe why our apartment features a hidden place, miniature landscapes, and a shrine to children's literature.

I love all my books equally, but my sister says that *Happier at Home* is her favorite book of everything I've written.

From happiness and home, you jumped to the subject of habits, in *Better Than Before*. Why?

After spending many years reading, writing, and talking to people about happiness, I noticed that often when people talk about a significant happiness challenge, or a big boost they've managed to make in their happiness, very often they talk about their *habits*.

Habits are the invisible architecture of everyday life. Studies suggest that we repeat about 40 percent of our behavior almost daily. So if we have habits that work for us, we're far more likely to be happier, healthier, more productive, and more creative.

When we change our habits, we change our lives—but, of course, that just raises the question: Okay, then, how do we change our habits? That's the absolutely fascinating question that I set out to answer in *Better Than Before*.

But as I plunged into the subject of habits, I became increasingly frustrated with what I was reading. Many habit experts argue that there's one *best* way to change our habits. We've all heard this advice. Do it first thing in the morning! Start small! Give yourself a cheat day! Do it for thirty days!

To me, it seemed obvious that there's not one "best" or "right" way. Some people are larks, some people are owls. Some people are moderators, some people are abstainers. Some people like to start small, some people lose interest if they aren't making a bold, sweeping change. Different strategies work for different people.

I wanted to come up with a unified framework that included every single strategy that I saw that worked. I identified *twenty-one*! That's a lot—which is good. Because there are so many strategies, each of us can choose the ones that appeal most to us. One person needs accountability to stick to his habits; another hates to have anyone monitoring what she's doing. One person does better going public with his habit; someone else, by keeping her habit private. And so on.

As one of the twenty-one strategies in *Better Than Before,* you introduce your "Four Tendencies" personality framework that divides people into Upholders, Questioners, Obligers, and Rebels. What is this framework? And why did you end up devoting a whole book to the Four Tendencies?

I have to say, of every intellectual challenge I've ever faced, grasping the Four Tendencies was easily the most difficult. Coming up with this framework just about melted my brain.

As I was researching habit change for *Better Than Before,* I was trying to make sense of patterns that I saw in people's behavior. Why do so many people say, "I can never take time for myself"? Why do many people resist New Year's resolutions with the objection that "January 1 is an arbitrary date"? What about those people who told me, "The minute someone tells me to do something, I don't want to do it"? I could sense that these perspectives were somehow linked in a profound way.

I *knew* there was a deep explanation linking many patterns I observed in the world, but it took me forever to identify the crucial question.

And what *is* that crucial question?

Warning: this sounds like a very dry question, but it's actually enormously significant. *How does a person respond to expectations?* We all face two kinds of expectations: *outer expectations* (a work deadline) and *inner expectations* (keep a New Year's resolution).

Upholders respond readily to both outer expectations and inner expectations. "I do what others expect of me—and what I expect from myself." (I'm an Upholder, by the way.)

Questioners question all expectations. They meet an expectation only if they believe it's reasonable (effectively making it an inner expectation). "I do what I think is best, according to my judgment. I won't do something that doesn't make sense."

Obligers respond readily to outer expectations but struggle to meet inner expectations. "Commitments to others can't be broken, but commitments to myself can be broken."

Rebels resist all expectations, outer and inner alike. "I want to do what I want, in my own way. If you tell me to do it, I'm *less* likely to do it."

Once we know our Tendency, it's much easier to understand ourselves, our strengths and our weaknesses, and the patterns in our behavior. And when we know other people's Tendencies, we understand them much better.

For instance, to meet inner expectations, Obligers *must* have external accountability. They need deadlines, late fees, a friend who'll be disappointed if they don't show up, a teacher who will notice if they skip class, their own sense of duty to be a good role model for someone else. Over and over, people have said to me, "Now that I know I'm an Obliger, for the first time, I'm managing to go to the gym/paint regularly/take my medication."

If you want to know whether you're an Upholder, Questioner, Obliger, or Rebel, you can take the short free quiz at happiercast.com/quiz. More than 1.4 million people have taken it.

After introducing the framework in *Better Than Before*, I was deluged with questions, observations, and requests for more information, which is why I wrote *The Four Tendencies*.

People just keep asking for more, more, more information. For that reason, I created an online video course about the Four Tendencies for those who want to dive deeper into the framework. I also created a free app, the "Better" app, where people can discuss and learn about building happier lives. In particular, there's a lot of discussion about the Four Tendencies, about how to manage yourself, and how to use the framework in romance, at work, as a health-care professional, as a parent. You can find the app by searching "Better Gretchen Rubin" in your device's app store or by visiting betterapp.us from a desktop computer.

I also created a workshop for people who want to lead a group training session about the Four Tendencies. You can license and purchase this material at gretchenrubin.com.

Your most recent project is *Outer Order, Inner Calm*. Why did you write it?

When thinking about myself, or talking to other people, I've been continually surprised by how much clutter matters to happiness. In the context of a happy life, a messy desk or crowded closet is a trivial matter—yet somehow it matters more than it should. For me, and for most people, outer order contributes to inner calm.

I get a crazy burst of energy, cheer, and creativity from clutter clearing, even something as simple as clearing out the medicine cabinet or my in-box. Getting control over the stuff of life makes me feel more in control of my life generally—and if it's an illusion, it's a helpful illusion.

To explore this connection between outer order and inner calm, and to figure out more ways to create outer order in my own life, I started taking notes for what eventually became *Outer Order, Inner Calm*. Really, it began as a lark—it was something I worked on in my free time, for fun, just for myself, and then one day I realized, "Wow, I could turn this into a real project."

One of the biggest things you've done since *The Happiness Project* came out is to start your award-winning podcast, *Happier with Gretchen Rubin*. *The New Yorker* wrote, "Their voices remind you that life is a human project that we're all experimenting with."

Are you having fun with it?

The podcast is an enormous source of happiness for me. It's so fun to get to engage with an audience in a different way. It's a very different kind of creative outlet. I've met many new people and learned many new skills.

Plus, of course, it's a joy to collaborate with my sister, Elizabeth. For years, we'd talked about wanting to do something together, so it was terrific to find this project to do together. We've had so much fun as cohosts, and we've done live shows, gone to conferences, and so on.

One major social change in the ten years since the publication of *The Happiness Project* is that social media plays an increasingly prominent role in our everyday lives. How do you think social media affects our happiness?

This is a subject of tremendous study right now. It's a fascinating question.

Most people tend to emphasize the downsides of social media—for instance, the fact that people feel bad when they compare their lives with the shiny picture presented of other people's lives.

From my own observations, though, I'd say that for most people, the good outweighs the bad. One of the most important elements of a happy life—probably the *most* important element—is strong relationships with other people.

I find, and I think this is true for others, that social media makes it easier to stay in touch with people. I have a broader network; I have deeper connections with people I see rarely; I have an easy way to stay in touch with someone who's close to me.

Does it replace face-to-face interactions? Absolutely not. But I think it can be useful.

Of course, like many things, social media is a good servant but a bad master. If it makes *you* feel bad, or if you find yourself spending hours clicking around when you could be doing other activities that would be more satisfying, then it's not contributing to *your* happiness.

We need to look for ways to stay in control of our use of technology, instead of feeling overmastered by it. Used wisely, it can be a helpful tool in a happy life.

Speaking of social media, you obviously spend a lot of time writing for your site gretchenrubin.com; posting on Twitter, LinkedIn, and Instagram; talking to viewers on your weekly *Ask Gretchen Rubin Live* on Facebook; and all that. You send out a monthly newsletter and the "Moment of Happiness," your daily e-mail with a great quotation. You have your podcast, *Happier with Gretchen Rubin*. Do you worry about spending so much time on these kinds of communications and not having any time to write more books?

That's an important question. Some writers embrace these new tools; some writers consider them a dangerous distraction, or at least a waste of time.

For me, it's a delight to be able to engage with readers on the subject of happiness, habits, and human nature. My audience, who comes to me through a variety of means, has been a huge source of ideas and insight. I don't begrudge the time or effort I spend on social media, on the podcast, and so on, because it's a hugely valuable opportunity.

But I'm careful to make plenty of time in my schedule for reading and writing. Often, when I want to do long stretches of original writing—which is the most challenging kind of work that I do—I'll take my laptop and write at the New York Society Library, a small library a block from my apartment. The library makes me so happy. It has open stacks, a wonderful collection, and lots of writing desks from which to choose. I make it a habit not to use the Internet when I'm there, so I can really focus on thinking and writing.

Over the years, is there a happiness mantra or motto that you've found most helpful?

My First Personal Commandment is to "Be Gretchen." The more my life reflects my true nature, interests, and values, the happier I become.

Of course, to "know yourself" is one of the most ancient precepts of happiness—"Know Thyself" is inscribed on the Temple of Apollo at Delphi—but it's not easy.

Each book I've written since *The Happiness Project* has explored self-knowledge, and in each book, I've tried to help myself and other people to see themselves more clearly. For instance, now I know I'm an Upholder, lark, abstainer, underbuyer, finisher, simplicity lover, counter stripper, and so on.

You've written several books about what you've done to make yourself happier. Do you ever worry that spending so much time working on your personal happiness was, well, selfish and self-centered?

Yes, I sure do. But I've concluded that one of the most pernicious myths of happiness is: "It's selfish and self-centered to try to be happier."

This myth takes a few forms. One holds that "in a world so full of suffering, it's not morally appropriate to seek to be happy." Another is "People who worry about their happiness are wrapped up in their own pleasure and not interested in the world."

But research shows that happier people are more interested in the problems of the world, and in the problems of the people around them. They're more likely to help other people, they're more engaged in social problems, they do more volunteer work, and they contribute more money to charity. They're less preoccupied with their personal issues. They make better leaders and better followers. They're healthier.

By contrast, less happy people are more apt to be defensive, isolated, and preoccupied with their own problems, and unfortunately, their negative moods are catching.

I've certainly noticed this about myself. When I'm feeling happy, I find it easier to notice other people's problems, I feel that I have more energy to try to take action, I have the emotional wherewithal to confront sad or difficult issues, and I'm not as preoccupied with myself. I feel more generous and forgiving.

As I worked on my happiness project, one of my biggest intellectual breakthroughs was the identification of my Second Splendid Truth. There's a circularity to it that confused me for a long time.

One of the best ways to make *yourself* happy is to make *other people* happy.
One of the best ways to make *other people* happy is to be happy *yourself.*

Everyone accepts the first part of the Second Splendid Truth, but the second part is just as important. By making the effort to make yourself happier, you better equip yourself to make other people happier as well. In fact, the epigraph to the book *The Happiness Project* is a quotation from Robert Louis Stevenson: "There is no duty we so much underrate as the duty of being happy." So if it is selfish to want to be happier, we should be selfish—if only for selfless reasons.

Have you added any new happiness resolutions or habits since *The Happiness Project* was published? If so, any favorites?

Oh, I've added so many resolutions and habits!

One of my new favorites is "Cultivate good smells." As I discuss in my book *Happier at Home,* I've become very interested in the sense of smell.

A beautiful fragrance is quick, easy, and delightful—an instant fix of happiness. Unlike many pleasures, it can be enjoyed in an instant, with no cost, no energy, no calories, no time, and no planning. In a flash, I can enjoy the fresh smell of a grapefruit, or the fragrance of clean towels, or the exciting smell of a hardware store (for some reason, no matter where you go, all hardware stores have that same exciting smell).

On the *Happier* podcast, Elizabeth and I talked about how to "Choose a signature color." I'm also preoccupied with color! Such a *beautiful* subject.

With my mother, father, and sister, I've also started the resolution of "update." My mother had observed that when people talk often, they have a lot to say to each other, and when they talk rarely, they have little to say to each other. So now my mother, father, Elizabeth, and I have "update." Every several days, we send out an e-mail with the subject "update," and we recount the most mundane, daily details of our lives. The motto of "update" is "It's okay to be boring." There's no expectation that anyone send a response. What we've found is that knowing these dull little details of one another's lives makes us feel far more connected to one another, and when we do talk, we have a lot more to say. This idea of "update" has really resonated with other people.

Do you feel pressure to be happy all the time?

No, I don't. Part of happiness is acknowledging when and why we're not feeling happy.

In your pursuit of happiness, what have you discovered about work/life balance?

I don't really think about work/life balance. My mantras are "I have plenty of time for the things that are important to me" and "I want to cram my life with the things I love." I've realized that I just don't have time for the things that don't reflect my interests, values, and temperament, so they have to fall away.

If something's important to me, I make room for it on my calendar—I actually write it as an entry. I can't wait until I have some free time to do it. I never have any free time.

I love to work, so it's sometimes hard for me to put down my book or step away from my laptop to spend time with my family and friends. So I schedule "quitting time" and "read for fun" just the way I'd schedule a dentist's appointment.

Now, this approach wouldn't work for everyone—for instance, Rebels tend to dislike putting items on their calendars. But for an Upholder like me, my calendar is a great way to get clarity on my values.

After all that you've written . . . are you happier?

I've always been a pretty happy person. Over the last several years, I've managed to make myself happier, and more consistently happy, because I've learned so many strategies. I have fewer feelings of guilt, boredom, anger, and resentment, and more feelings of enthusiasm, tenderness, and growth. So while my inner nature remains unchanged, my experience of my life is much happier.

Just for fun, let's do some lightning round–style questions:

Nervous habit: Hair twisting.

Habit that would surprise other people: How much coffee, tea, and diet soda I drink every day.

Least favorite job ever: Waitressing. Boy, I was a terrible waitress.

Favorite places in New York City: Bethesda Fountain in Central Park, New York Society Library, the Metropolitan Museum, and my in-laws' apartment (which is right around the corner from where we live).

Number of unpublished books locked in a desk drawer: Three novels.

Nickname: My sister, Elizabeth, calls me "the happiness bully."

Superpower: I try to see what everyone sees and notice things that no one has noticed. I aim to make observations that make people think, "Yes, *of course,* I've seen this myself, but somehow I never quite put it into words."

I'm also a very fast typist.

The failure that taught you the most: My book *Forty Ways to Look at JFK* sold very few copies and didn't get much attention, and my disappointment convinced me that I wanted to forge a direct connection with readers so that I could engage with people directly about my subjects.

Vows to yourself that you've broken: As a four-year-old, I vowed I would grow up to live in a purple house. I don't live in a purple house, but it's true that my apartment does have two purple rooms. Also, when my family was debating whether to get a dog, I vowed that if we did get a dog, he would be very well trained. Barnaby is *not* well trained (and no, I don't hold him responsible for that).

Most dramatic habit change: After reading Gary Taubes's book *Why We Get Fat* during a spring-break vacation in 2012, I started eating a very low-carb diet. Overnight, I quit sugar, flour, rice, pasta, starchy vegetables, and most fruit. The power of the Strategy of the Lightning Bolt! How I love being free from my sweet tooth. (I write about this habit change in my book *Better Than Before*.)

Inexplicable aversion: I can't stand to read a book or watch a movie, play, or TV show that includes the plotline of unjust accusation.

Most precious possessions: My friends and family, of course. After that—my laptop, my backpack, my running shoes, my three desktop monitors, my MetroCard, my family photo albums, my fingertip-less gloves, and my hard-boiled egg cooker.

Something that would surprise other people about you: I never read reviews or profiles of me or my books.

Chief complaint of my daughters: That I eat yogurt in a weird way.

Favorite TV show: *The Office* (American version) and *The Wire*. And every show that Elizabeth creates.

Books that blew your mind: Christopher Alexander, Sara

Ishikawa, and Murray Silverstein's *A Pattern Language*, Elias Canetti's *Crowds and Power*, *The Autobiography of Benjamin Franklin*, Wayne Koestenbaum's *Jackie Under My Skin*, Flannery O'Connor's *The Habit of Being*, James Boswell's *The Life of Samuel Johnson*, Virginia Woolf's *A Writer's Diary*, and *Complete Essays of George Orwell*.

Distill everything you've learned in one sentence: "There's no magic, one-size-fits-all solution to creating a happier, healthier, more productive, and more creative life; we can build a better life only on the foundation of our own nature, our own interests, and our own values." Is it cheating to use a semicolon?

Future plans: To live happier ever after.

SECRETS OF ADULTHOOD

We're *more* like other people, and *less* like other people, than we suppose.

Things often get harder before they get easier.

It's easier to keep up than to catch up.

The things that go wrong often make the best memories.

We can't make people change, but when we change, others change, and a relationship changes.

Most decisions don't require extensive research.

Working is one of the most dangerous forms of procrastination.

Every room should include something purple.

Don't let the perfect be the enemy of the good.

Nothing stays in Vegas.

When the student is ready, the teacher appears.

Starting *again* is harder than starting.

Go slow to go fast.

Don't expect to be motivated by motivation.

Sometimes we can minister to the spirit through the body.

Everything looks better arranged on a tray.

Something that can be done at *any* time is often done at *no* time.

It's easier to change your surroundings than yourself.

The days are long, but the years are short.

PARADOXES OF HAPPINESS

Accomplish more by working less.

Keep an empty shelf, and keep a junk drawer.

Strive to be emotionally self-sufficient so you can draw closer to other people.

Everything matters. Nothing matters.

Trying to be more virtuous can undermine your sense of virtue.

Hell is other people. Heaven is other people.

Silence is sometimes the best reply.

Flawed can be more perfect than perfection.

Make people happier by acknowledging that they're not feeling happy.

Spend out, to become rich.

Succeed by failing.

Think about yourself so you can forget yourself.

Happiness doesn't always make you *feel* happy.

Be selfless, if only for selfish reasons.

Being very accessible sometimes makes it hard to connect with people.

Sometimes material desires have a spiritual aspect.

Wait. Now.

You can be generous by taking.

Accept yourself, and expect more of yourself.

EXCERPT FROM
THE FOUR TENDENCIES

After *The Happiness Project* was published, many people asked me, "How did you get yourself to follow all those resolutions?" And I'd answer, "Well, I thought those resolutions would make me happier, so I decided to give them a try, and if they did make me happier, I've kept doing them." And then I'd inevitably get the follow-up question, "But how did you get yourself to *do* them?"

This exchange always puzzled me. I wanted to do them, so I did them. What was the big deal?

Now I know. Now that I've identified the Four Tendencies—my personality framework that sorts people into Upholders, Questioners, Obligers, and Rebels, I know that I'm an Upholder.

1

The Four Tendencies

THE ORIGIN OF THE FOUR TENDENCIES
•
HOW THE TENDENCIES WEAVE
THROUGHOUT OUR CHARACTERS
•
WHY IT'S HELPFUL TO
IDENTIFY OUR OWN TENDENCY
•
WHY IT'S HELPFUL TO IDENTIFY
OTHERS' TENDENCIES

I didn't realize it at the time, but when I walked through the door of the Atlantic Grill restaurant one blustery winter afternoon, I was heading to one of the most significant conversations of my life.

As I bit into my cheeseburger and my friend picked at her salad, she made a comment that would occupy my mind for years. In an offhand way, she mentioned, "I want to get myself in the habit of running, but I can't, and it really bothers me." Then she added, in a crucial observation, "When I was on the high school track team, I never missed track practice, so why can't I go running now?"

"Why?" I echoed.

"Well, you know, it's so hard to make time for ourselves."

"Hmmm," I said.

We started talking about other things, but even after we'd said good-bye, I couldn't stop thinking about our exchange. She was the same person she'd been in high school, and she was aiming to do the same activity. She'd been able to go running in the past, but not now. Why? Was it her age, her motivation, her family situation, the location, team spirit, or something else?

She assumed that we all have trouble "making time for ourselves." But actually I *don't* have any trouble making time for myself. How were she and I different from each other?

I would spend the next few years trying to answer these questions.

THE ORIGIN OF THE FOUR TENDENCIES

They say there are two kinds of people in the world: those who divide the world into two kinds of people, and those who don't.

I'm definitely the first kind. My great interest is human nature, and I constantly search for patterns to identify what we do and why we do it.

I've spent years studying happiness and habits, and it has become obvious to me that there's no magic, one-size-fits-all answer for building a happier, healthier, more productive life. Different strategies work for different people—in fact, what works for one person may be the *very opposite* of what works for someone else. Some people are morning people; some are night people. Some do better when they abstain from a strong temptation; others, when they indulge in moderation. Some people love simplicity; some thrive in abundance.

And not only that. As I pondered my friend's observation about her running habit, I sensed that deep below the "night people vs. morning people" sorts of differences, there existed some kind of bedrock distinction that shaped people's natures—something profound, but also bold and obvious—that nevertheless eluded my vision.

To help figure out what I was missing, I posed a number of questions to readers of my website, including: "How do you feel about New Year's resolutions?" "Do you observe traffic regulations—why or why not?" "Would you ever sign up to take a class for fun?" As readers' responses poured in, I saw that distinct patterns were threaded through the various answers. It was almost *weird*—as though groups of people had agreed to answer from the same script.

For instance, about New Year's resolutions, a subset of people gave virtually identical answers: "I'll keep a resolution if it's useful, but I won't start on New Year's Day, because January 1 is an arbitrary date." They all used that word: "arbitrary." I was intrigued by this specific word choice, because the *arbitrariness* of the January 1 date had never bothered me. Yet these people were all giving the same answer—what did they have in common?

And many people answered, "I don't make New Year's resolutions anymore because I never manage to keep them—I never make time for myself."

Another group said, "I never make resolutions because I don't like to bind myself."

There was some meaningful design here, I knew it, but I just couldn't quite see it.

Then finally, after months of reflection, I had my eureka moment. As I sat at my desk in my home office, I happened to glance at my messy handwritten to-do list—and suddenly it hit me. The simple, decisive question was: *"How do you respond to expectations?"* I'd found it!

I'd discovered the key. I felt the same excitement that Archimedes must have felt when he stepped out of his bath.

I was sitting still, but my mind was racing forward with thoughts about *expectations*. I grasped at that moment that we all face two kinds of expectations:

- outer expectations—expectations others place on us, like meeting a work deadline
- inner expectations—expectations we place on ourselves, like

keeping a New Year's resolution

And here was my crucial insight: Depending on a person's response to outer and inner expectations, that person falls into one of four distinct types:

Upholders respond readily to both outer expectations and inner expectations

Questioners question all expectations; they meet an expectation only if they believe it's justified, so in effect they respond only to inner expectations

Obligers respond readily to outer expectations but struggle to meet inner expectations

Rebels resist all expectations, outer and inner alike

It was that simple. With just one single, straightforward question, all of humanity sorted itself into these categories.

Now I understood why my friend had trouble forming the habit of running: She was an Obliger. When she'd had a team and a coach expecting her, she had no trouble showing up; when she faced her own inner expectations, she struggled. I understood those repetitious comments about New Year's resolutions. And I understood much, much more.

The Four Tendencies framework clarified the striking patterns of behavior I'd perceived, and I was able to make sense of what everyone else had seen—but no one else had noticed.

When I mapped the complete system on a sheet of paper, in four symmetrical overlapping circles, my framework showed the elegance of a fern frond or a nautilus shell. I truly felt that I'd uncovered a law of nature: human nature.

Or maybe I'd created something more like a Muggle Sorting Hat.

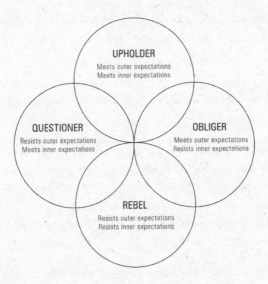

Once I'd identified the framework, I worked to deepen my under-standing. "The Strategy of the Four Tendencies" became the first chapter in *Better Than Before,* my book about habit change; I wrote about the Four Tendencies on my website, gretchenrubin.com; my cohost and sister, Elizabeth Craft, and I talked about the Four Tendencies on our weekly podcast, *Happier with Gretchen Rubin.* Every time I discussed the frame-work, readers and listeners responded.

Most people can identify their Tendency from a brief description, but for people who aren't sure or who want their answers to be analyzed, I designed a quiz. Hundreds of thousands of people have taken the Four Tendencies Quiz, which appears in chapter 2 or at happiercast.com/quiz. People's answers to the quiz, as well as their open-ended responses, gave me an additional trove of insights. (For one thing, I've noticed that people's Tendencies influence their willingness to take the quiz. Questioners some-times ask, "Why should I spend my time and effort taking this quiz?" and Rebels sometimes think, "You're telling me to take this quiz? Well,

I won't do it.")

To test my observations about the Four Tendencies, I decided to run a study of the framework among a nationally representative sample, to examine a geographically dispersed group of U.S. adults with a mix of gender, age, and household income.

The most important thing I discovered? The distribution of the Four Tendencies. At 41%, Obliger was the largest Tendency. Next came Questioner, at 24%. The Rebel Tendency had the fewest members, at 17%—I'm surprised that the survey put the number that high—and my own Tendency, the Upholder Tendency, was just slightly larger at 19%. The study also confirmed many of my observations about the Four Tendencies; for instance, when considering New Year's resolutions, Upholders are most likely to make them; Rebels dislike them; Questioners make resolutions when the time seems right rather than waiting for an arbitrary date; and often Obligers give up making resolutions altogether because they've struggled in the past.

As I refined the framework, I even assigned a color to each Tendency, by using the model of a traffic light. Yellow represents Questioners, because just as a yellow light cautions us to "wait" to decide whether to proceed, Questioners always ask "Wait, why?" before meeting an expectation. Green represents Obligers, who readily "go ahead." Red represents Rebels, who are most likely to "stop" or say no. Because there's no fourth traffic-light color, I chose blue for Upholders—which seems fitting.

The more I've studied the Tendencies, the more I've come to see their tremendous influence.

When we consider the Four Tendencies, we're better able to understand ourselves. This self-knowledge is crucial because we can build a happy life only on the foundation of our own nature, our own interests, and our own values.

Just as important, when we consider the Four Tendencies, we're better able to understand other people. We can live and work more effectively with others when we identify their Tendencies—as coworkers and bosses, teachers and coaches, husbands and wives, parents and children, health-care providers and patients.

Understanding the Four Tendencies gives us a richer understanding of the world.

HOW THE TENDENCIES WEAVE
THROUGHOUT OUR CHARACTERS

Our Tendencies are hardwired: they're not the result of birth order, parenting style, religious upbringing, gender. They're not tied to extroversion or introversion. They don't change depending on whether we're at home, at work, with friends. And they don't change as we age. We bring these Tendencies into the world with us.

To a degree that surprises me, most people do indeed fall squarely into one of the four camps. While it can sometimes be difficult to identify a child's Tendency (I still can't figure out the Tendency of one of my daughters), by adulthood we clearly fit into a particular Tendency that shapes our perceptions and behavior in fundamental ways. Unless we go through some catastrophic, character-reshaping experience—such as a near-death experience, a grave illness, or a serious bout with addiction—our Tendencies don't change.

Depending on history and circumstance, though, our Tendency might be more or less helpful as we make our way in the world. In North Korea, a Questioner's questions might get him thrown in jail, while in Silicon Valley a Questioner's questions might win her a promotion.

Also, there's an enormous range of personalities, even among people who share the same Tendency. Regardless of Tendency, some people are more or less thoughtful than others, or ambitious, intellectual, controlling, charismatic, kind, anxious, energetic, or adventurous. These qualities dramatically influence how they express their Tendencies. An ambitious Rebel who wants to be a well-respected business leader will behave differently from one who doesn't care much about having a successful career.

People often argue that they're a mix of Tendencies. They tell me, "I'm an Obliger and an Upholder," or "My Tendency changes depending on where I am or who I'm with." This may sound sensible, but I must say that when I ask a few more questions, the person falls easily within a single Tendency, almost without exception.

To be sure, as discussed in the sections on "Variations Within the Tendency," people often "tip" in the direction of a Tendency that overlaps with their own, but nevertheless they still remain firmly located within a core Tendency.

And, of course, it's also true that no matter what our fundamental Tendency, a small part of each of us is Upholder, Questioner, Obliger, and Rebel.

All of us meet an expectation when we don't want to bear the consequences of ignoring it. The Rebel wears his seat belt after he pays a few big fines.

All of us may question why we should have to meet an expectation, or become annoyed by inefficiency, or refuse to do something that seems arbitrary.

We all meet some expectations because they're important to someone else. The most determined Upholder will sacrifice her regular Monday-morning meeting if her child is recovering from surgery.

And whatever our Tendency, we share a desire for autonomy. We prefer to be asked rather than ordered to do something, and if our feeling of being controlled by others becomes too strong, it can trigger "reactance," a resistance to something that's experienced as a threat to our freedom or our ability to choose.

After I'd described the Four Tendencies at a conference, a guy walked up to me and said, "I think everyone should be able to drive at whatever speed they think is safe, so I must be a Questioner!"

I smiled, but the fact is, it's not a simple matter of "I ignore the speed limit, so I'm a Questioner," or "I refuse to wash dishes, therefore

I'm a Rebel," or "I love to-do lists, so I'm an Upholder." To identify our Tendency, we must consider many examples of our behavior and our reasons for our behaviors. For example, a Questioner and a Rebel might both reject an expectation, but the Questioner thinks, "I won't do it because it doesn't make sense," while the Rebel thinks, "I won't do it because you can't tell me what to do."

I've learned that while each of the Four Tendencies poses its difficulties, people find the Obliger and the Rebel Tendencies the most challenging—whether as a member of that Tendency themselves or dealing with that Tendency in others. (Which is why the Obliger and Rebel sections in this book are longer than the Upholder and Questioner sections.)

Many people try to map the Four Tendencies against other personality frameworks, such as the Big Five personality traits, StrengthsFinder, the Enneagram, Myers-Briggs, VIA—even onto the four houses of Hogwarts.

I'm fascinated by any scheme that helps me to understand human nature, but I think it's a mistake to try to say that "this" equals "that." Each framework captures a certain insight, and that insight would be lost if all of the systems were dumped together. No single system can capture human nature in all of its depth and variety.

Also, I think that many personality frameworks cram too many elements into their categories. By contrast, the Four Tendencies describe only one narrow aspect of a person's character—a vitally important aspect, but still just one of the multitude of qualities that form an individual. The Four Tendencies explain *why we act and why we don't act.*

WHY IT'S HELPFUL TO IDENTIFY OUR OWN TENDENCY

When I describe the Four Tendencies, I sometimes get the impression that people try to figure out the "best" Tendency and shoehorn themselves into it. But there's no best or worst Tendency. The happiest, healthiest, most productive people aren't those from a particular Tendency, but rather they're the people who have figured out how to harness the strengths of their Tendency, counteract the weaknesses, and build the lives that work for them.

With wisdom, experience, and self-knowledge from the Four Tendencies, we can use our time more productively, make better decisions, suffer less stress, get healthier, and engage more effectively with other people.

If we don't understand our place in the Four Tendencies, however, we may fail to pinpoint the aspects of a particular situation that's causing us to succeed or fail. For instance, a literary agent told me, "I represent a journalist who did excellent work at a newspaper. No trouble with deadlines, great work ethic. But now he's on leave from the paper to write a book, and he's got writer's block."

"I bet it's not writer's block. He's probably an Obliger," I said. "He had no trouble working when he had to meet frequent deadlines. But with a distant deadline and little supervision, he can't work. He should ask his editor to check in with him every week, or join a writers' group, or you could ask him to submit pages to you every month. Just some system of external accountability."

Also, if we don't understand the Four Tendencies, we may have unrealistic assumptions of how people may change. One woman wrote, "My husband is a Rebel. I feel frustrated thinking that this is actually his character and that he'll never change. Is it possible that a Rebel is just someone who hasn't 'grown up' and realized that the world doesn't run on doing only what you 'feel like' doing at the moment? And that he will eventually change his attitude?" I didn't want to say it bluntly in my response, but gosh, no, at this point I *don't* think he'll change.

People often ask me, "Should your Tendency determine your choice of career?" Every Tendency could find a fit with just about every job, but it's interesting to think about how career and Tendency might interact. For instance, I know a professional dog trainer who is an Upholder, and he brings an Upholder spirit to it. But I can imagine how Questioners,

Obligers, and Rebels could also do that work.

Even if people from each Tendency *could* pursue any career, that doesn't mean they *should*. The Four Tendencies can help us identify why we might enjoy certain kinds of work more—or less. One reader wrote, "Now I see why I hate my job. I am 100% Questioner, and also a tax accountant. I don't care about keeping up with the details of what's ultimately a large set of arbitrary rules that make no sense, and this has been a major hurdle in my success and happiness at work."

Knowing our own Tendency can allow us to show ourselves more compassion by realizing, "Hey, I'm this type of person, and there's nothing wrong with me. I can make the best of it." As one Upholder wrote, "My parents always told me to loosen up, my late husband always told me to loosen up, now my daughter tells me to loosen up. But now I know I'm much happier when I follow the rules that I've set for myself."

One Rebel explained:

Realizing that I'm a Rebel revealed why years of therapy failed. We'd analyzed my dearth of discipline, tried and rejected techniques that backfired (accountability? ha). It's not just that some techniques don't work for Rebels. It's that we're told (and often believe) that something is deeply wrong with us. An otherwise high-functioning, highly successful grown-up who still struggles to pay bills, complete projects, and follow through on, well, anything? Who struggles to meet everyone's expectations—even our own? That's not merely unusual; in today's world, it sounds downright pathological. But your framework assures us it's not. It's been freeing to focus on what works for me rather than what's wrong with me.

An Obliger wrote:

As a TV writer, I've struggled miserably with my inability to stick to any kind of personal deadline, yet I've always been a dutiful employee who submits scripts on time to my boss. I've given this tendency many names: laziness, being irresponsible, being a child in grown-up clothes, and many terms that wouldn't get past your spam filter. By giving me a new name—Obliger—you've given me a way to accept myself. I can put the self-loathing aside and concentrate on devising clever ways to trick myself into doing stuff. It's already made me more productive, but more importantly, it's made me much happier.

When we recognize our Tendency, we can tweak situations to boost our chances of success. It's practically impossible to change our own nature, but it's fairly easy to change our circumstances in a way that suits our Tendency—whether by striving for more clarity, justification, accountability, or freedom. Insight about our Tendency allows us to create the situations in which we'll thrive.

WHY IT'S HELPFUL TO IDENTIFY OTHERS' TENDENCIES

On the flip side, when we understand others' Tendencies, we're more tolerant of them. For one thing, we see that a person's behavior isn't aimed at us personally. That Questioner isn't asking questions to undermine the boss or challenge the professor's authority; the Questioner always has questions. A reader wrote, "I've lived with a Rebel for the past seven years. It's comforting to know that his way of being is as natural for *him* as being an Obliger is for *me*."

Knowing other people's Tendencies also makes it much easier to persuade them, to encourage them, and to avoid conflict. If we don't consider a person's Tendency, our words may be ineffective or even counterproductive. The fact is, if we want to communicate, we must speak the right language—not the message that would work most effectively with *us,* but the message that will persuade the *listener.* When we take into account the

Four Tendencies, we can tailor our arguments to appeal to different values.

On the other hand, when we ignore the Tendencies, we lower our chances of success. The more an Upholder lectures a Rebel, the more the Rebel will want to resist. A Questioner may provide an Obliger with several sound reasons for taking an action, but those logical arguments don't matter much to an Obliger; external accountability is the key for an Obliger.

A reader sent me this hilarious list of lightbulb jokes that captures the distinctions among the Tendencies:

How do you get an Upholder to change a lightbulb?
Answer: He's already changed it.

How do you get a Questioner to change a lightbulb?
Answer: Why do we need that lightbulb anyway?

How do you get an Obliger to change a lightbulb?
Answer: Ask him to change it.

How do you get a Rebel to change a lightbulb?
Answer: Do it yourself.

A Questioner nutritionist told me, "My goal is to improve the way people eat in this country. I'm writing a book to explain how cultural and economic systems shape the way people eat." She firmly believed that if her book presented the arguments in a sufficiently logical way, people across the country would change their eating habits. Questioner!

But to communicate effectively, we must reach people through *their* Tendency, not our own. That's true for doctors, professors, coaches, bosses, spouses, parents, coworkers, teachers, neighbors, or people in any walk of life who want to persuade others to do what they want—in other words, it's true for all of us.

Even for messages meant for a wide audience, it's possible to convey information to strike a chord with every Tendency. I heard a creative example one afternoon when I spoke about the Four Tendencies at a business conference. Before introducing me, the group's head had explained, at considerable length, why it was important that participants show up on time, in the right place, for the rest of the weekend's conference activities.

After I gave my talk, I was delighted to hear him aim his reminders at each of the Four Tendencies. He said, "To you Upholders, thanks in advance for cooperating with my request for promptness. Questioners, I gave you a bunch of reasons for why you need to show up on time at all the meetings. To you Obligers, I'm watching you, and I'm counting on you to be there promptly. Rebels, save it for the bar later." *Exactly!* Even the vocabulary we choose may resonate differently among the different Tendencies. A Rebel child might respond better if asked, "Do you feel like playing the piano now?" while an Upholder child would be happy to be reminded, "Time to practice the piano."

Just in the area of health, people's failure to listen to their doctors carries a huge cost. Poor diet, inactivity, alcohol and prescription drug abuse, and smoking are among the leading causes of illness and death in the United States—all behaviors that are within our conscious control. When we take people's Tendencies into account, we're more likely successfully to persuade them to cut back on sugar, go for a twenty-minute walk, do their rehab exercises, give up booze, or take their medications.

But it's important to remember that the Four Tendencies framework is meant to help us understand ourselves more deeply, not to limit our sense of identity or possibility. Some people say, "When you define yourself, you confine yourself." I think systems of self-definition are very helpful—because they serve as a starting point for self-knowledge. The Four Tendencies framework isn't meant to be a box that cramps our growth or a label that determines everything about us, but rather a spotlight that can illuminate hidden aspects of our nature.

When we understand ourselves and how our Tendency shapes our perspective on the world, we can adapt our circumstances to suit our own nature—and when we understand how other people's Tendencies shape *their* perspectives, we can engage with them more effectively.

With the Four Tendencies, we see how a subtle shift in vocabulary, or a quick conversation, or a minor change in procedure can be enough to change a person's entire course of action. And that matters. If this patient takes his blood-pressure medication regularly, he'll live longer. If this student completes her professor's assignments, she won't fail the course. If this husband and wife can speak to each other calmly, their marriage will last. And if I stop sending out work emails over the weekend, I won't annoy the people with whom I work.

One of the big daily challenges of life is: "How do I get people—including myself—to do what I want?" The Four Tendencies makes this task much, much easier.

Published in the United States by Crown Publishers, an imprint of the Crown Publishing Group, a division of Random House LLC, a Penguin Random House Company, New York. Reprinted by permission.

READING GROUP GUIDE

1. Gretchen argues throughout *The Happiness Project* that striving to be happy is a worthy, not selfish, goal. Do you agree? Do you think that Gretchen was right to devote so much time and attention to her own happiness? Why or why not? Do you spend much time thinking about your happiness?

2. *The Happiness Project* is packed with quotations. Which quotation resonated most with you? Do you have a quotation that has been particularly meaningful in your own life, one that you've included in your e-mail signature or taped to your desk, for example?

3. One of Gretchen's resolutions is to "Imitate a spiritual master." Do you have a spiritual master? Who is it? Gretchen was surprised to realize that Saint Thérèse of Lisieux was her master. Do you know why you identify with your spiritual master?

4. Gretchen observes that outer order contributes to inner calm, and many of her resolutions are aimed at clutter clearing. Do you find that clutter affects your happiness?

5. One of Gretchen's main arguments is "You're not happy unless you think you're happy," and she spends a lot of time thinking about her happiness. However, many important figures have argued just the opposite. For example, John Stuart Mill wrote, "Ask yourself whether you are happy, and you cease to be so." What do you think? Does striving for happiness make you happier, or does it make happiness more elusive?

6. Did reading this book make you want to try any of the resolutions? If so, which ones?

7. A criticism of *The Happiness Project* might be that writing a "year of . . ." book is gimmicky. Did you like the "experiment for a year" approach, or did it strike you as a cliché? Why do you think so many authors are drawn to this structure?

8. Many memoirs recount the author's struggle to be happy in the face of a major challenge like cancer, divorce, an unhappy childhood, and the like. In the book's opening, Gretchen notes that she has always been pretty happy. Nevertheless, did you find her reflections on happiness helpful? Or do you think it's more valuable to read an account by someone facing more difficulties?

9. Gretchen writes, "Everyone's happiness project will be different." How would your happiness project be different from Gretchen's? How might it be the same?

10. What was the one most valuable thing you learned from *The Happiness Project* about happiness—for yourself?

If you're reading *The Happiness Project* with your church group, your spirituality book group, or the like, e-mail me at grubin@gretchenrubin. com if you'd like the one-page discussion guide that focuses on the spiritual aspect of the book.

RESOURCES

I've created dozens of free resources to help people make their lives happier, healthier, more productive, and more creative. I hope you find this material useful as you create your own happiness project.

The "Better" App

To get the free "Better" app—all about happiness, good habits, human nature, and the Four Tendencies—search for "Better Gretchen Rubin" in your device's app store or visit betterapp.us. There you can learn more, engage with others, form accountability groups, and join with other people doing happiness projects together.

To download any of the resources listed below, go to gretchenrubin.com/resources.

The Happiness Project

Start a Happiness Project Group: This guide will help you start a group for people doing happiness projects together. From a group, we get ideas, energy, and accountability.

Daily Time Log: This chart will help you track how you spend your time each day.

Resolution Chart: You can see the resolution chart I used for my own happiness project, for inspiration, and the last page is blank so you can use it as a template for yourself.

Happiness Paradoxes: This one-pager highlights some of the most powerful paradoxes of happiness.

Happiness Project Manifesto: This one-pager sums up my key conclusions about how to make our lives happier.

***The Happiness Project* Coloring Book Sample Page:** The activity of coloring helps to focus the mind and rest the body in a constructive, creative way. This sample page comes from my book *The Happiness Project Mini Posters: A Coloring Book: 20 Hand-Lettered Quotes to Pull Out and Frame.*

Comic: "My Quest for a Passion": With cartoonist Chari Pere, I created a comic to document my "quest for a passion."

Top Tips for Happiness: This collection gathers some of the most popular tips lists related to happiness.

Patron Saints: In this one-pager, I briefly describe my patron saints.

***The Happiness Project* Discussion Guide:** A one-page discussion guide for book groups, work groups, accountability groups, and the like.

***The Happiness Project* Spiritual Discussion Guide:** A one-page discussion guide for spirituality book groups, Bible study groups, retreats, and the like.

Happier at Home

9 Tips for Being Happier at Home: Top tips for being happier at home.

Happier at Home **Discussion Guide:** A one-page discussion guide for book groups, work groups, accountability groups, and the like.

Happier at Home—**Behind the Scenes:** An amusing insider's look at some material that didn't make it into *Happier at Home.*

Better Than Before

Start a Habits Accountability Group: This starter kit will help you launch a group for people who want to work on their habits together. We get energy, ideas, and accountability from being part of a group.

Discussion Guides for *Better Than Before:* These discussion guides will help guide conversation for book groups, work groups, faith- and spirituality-based groups, and the like.

Checklist for Habit Change: This one-page chart will help you deploy the many strategies for habit change as you work on a crucial habit that you want to master.

***Better Than Before* Habits Manifesto:** This one-pager sums up my key conclusions about how we most effectively master our habits.

Tips for Exercising Better Than Before: Learn tips for building the crucial habit of exercise.

Tips for Working Better Than Before: Learn tips for building the work habits that will allow you to be more productive and creative.

Tips for Eating Better Than Before: Learn tips for improving your eating habits.

Tips for Reading Better Than Before: Learn tips for strengthening your habit of reading.

Daily Time Log: This log is useful to use as you apply the Strategy of Monitoring.

The Four Tendencies

Four Tendencies Quiz: Want to find out whether you're an Upholder, Questioner, Obliger, or Rebel? Take the quick, free quiz at happiercast.com/quiz. More than 1.4 million people have taken it.

The "Better" App: My free app, "Better," will help you harness the Four Tendencies framework to create a better life. Join the lively conversation, ask questions, and join accountability groups. Search "Better Gretchen Rubin" in your device's app store or go to betterapp.us.

Discussion Guide for *The Four Tendencies*: This discussion guide will help guide conversation for book groups, work groups, faith- and spirituality-based groups, accountability groups, and the like.

Flash Evaluation for the Four Tendencies: The flash evaluation is a quick, informal way to determine someone's Tendency.

Nutshell Guide to the Four Tendencies: This short resource sums up the main aspects of each of the Four Tendencies.

Starter Kit for an Accountability Group: If you want to launch an accountability group (Obligers, you know you need this!), this guide will help you get started.

Tips for Using the Four Tendencies at Work: This one-pager gives a quick guide to using the Four Tendencies when dealing with a boss, a colleague, an employee, a client, or a customer.

Tips for Using the Four Tendencies with Children and Students: This one-pager gives a quick guide to using the Four Tendencies for parents, teachers, professors, and coaches.

Tips for Using the Four Tendencies in Health Care: This one-pager gives a quick guide to using the Four Tendencies when dealing with a patient or health-care client.

Tips for Using the Four Tendencies with Spouses and Sweethearts: This one-pager gives a quick guide to using the Four Tendencies when dealing with a spouse or sweetheart.

Video Courses

I've created video courses for people who like to learn by video: courses.gretchenrubin.com.

Happier with Gretchen Rubin Podcast

Wedding Readings: I've put together a collection of wedding readings suggested by readers, listeners, and viewers.

Funeral Readings: I've put together a collection of funeral and memorial-service readings suggested by readers, listeners, and viewers.

My 81 Favorite Works of Children's and Young-Adult Literature: I'm a huge fan of kid lit, and I made a list of my very favorite books.

Interview with Gary Taubes: Gary Taubes inspired the Strategy of the Lightning Bolt for me, and in this interview, I talk further with him about his research into sugar.

Podcast Manifesto: This one-pager sums up my aims for how to make the best possible podcast.

Subscribe for Free

Each month, in the Gretchen Rubin e-mail, I'll send a newsletter with interesting links, updates, bonuses, and anything I think would be engaging for readers: gretchenrubin.com/#newsletter.

Every day, in the "Moment of Happiness" e-mail, I'll send you a quotation about happiness or human nature every morning: gretchenrubin .com/#newsletter.

SUGGESTIONS FOR FURTHER READING

Many extraordinary books have been written about happiness. This list doesn't attempt to cover all the most important works, but instead highlights some of my personal favorites.

SOME WORKS IN THE HISTORY OF HAPPINESS

Aristotle. *The Ethics of Aristotle: The Nicomachean Ethics,* ed. Hugh Tredennick, J. A. K. Thomson, and Jonathan Barnes. New York: Penguin, 1976.

Bacon, Francis. *The Essays.* New York: Penguin, 1986.

Boethius, Anicius Manlius Severinus. *The Consolation of Philosophy.* Translated by Victor Watts. New York: Penguin, 2000.

Cicero, Marcus Tullius. *On the Good Life.* Translated by Michael Grant. New York: Penguin, 1971.

Dalai Lama and Howard C. Cutler. *The Art of Happiness: A Handbook for Living.* New York: Riverhead, 1998.

Delacroix, Eugène. *The Journal of Eugène Delacroix*, 3rd ed. Translated by Hubert Wellington. London: Phaidon Press, 1951.

Epicurus. *The Essential Epicurus.* Translated by Eugene Michael O'Connor. New York: Prometheus Books, 1993.

Hazlitt, William. *Essays.* London: Coward-McCann, 1950.

James, William. *The Varieties of Religious Experience: A Study in Human Nature.* New York: New American Library, 1958.

La Rochefoucauld, François de. *Maxims of La Rochefoucauld.* Translated by Stuart Warner. South Bend, Ind.: St. Augustine's Press, 2001.

Montaigne, Michel Eyquem de. *The Complete Essays of Montaigne.* Translated by Donald Frame. Palo Alto, Calif.: Stanford University Press, 1958.

Plutarch. *Selected Lives and Essays.* Translated by Louise Ropes Loomis. New York: Walter J. Black, 1951.

Russell, Bertrand. *The Conquest of Happiness.* New York: Liveright, 1930.

Schopenhauer, Arthur. *Parerga and Paralipomena,* vols. 1 and 2. Translated by E. F. J. Payne. Oxford, England: Clarendon Press, 1974

Seneca. *Letters from a Stoic.* Translated by Robin Campbell. New York: Penguin, 1969.

Smith, Adam. *The Theory of Moral Sentiments.* Washington, D.C.: Gateway Editions, 2000.

SOME INTERESTING BOOKS ON THE SCIENCE AND
PRACTICE OF HAPPINESS

Argyle, Michael. *The Psychology of Happiness,* 2nd ed. New York: Taylor & Francis, 2001.

Cowen, Tyler. *Discover Your Inner Economist: Use Incentives to Fall in Love, Survive Your Next Meeting, and Motivate Your Dentist.* New York: Dutton, 2007.

Diener, Ed, and Robert Biswas-Diener. *Happiness: Unlocking the Mysteries of Psychological Wealth.* Malden, Mass.: Blackwell, 2008.

Easterbrook, Gregg. *The Progress Paradox: How Life Gets Better While People Feel Worse.* New York: Random House, 2003.

Eid, Michael, and Randy J. Larsen, eds. *The Science of Subjective Well-Being.* New York: Guilford Press, 2008.

Frey, Bruno, and Alois Stutzer. *Happiness and Economics: How the Economy and Institutions Affect Human Well-Being.* Princeton, N.J.: Princeton University Press, 2002.

Gilbert, Daniel. *Stumbling on Happiness.* New York: Knopf, 2006.

Gladwell, Malcolm. *Blink: The Power of Thinking Without Thinking.* New York: Little, Brown, 2005.

Haidt, Jonathan. *The Happiness Hypothesis: Finding Modern Truth in Ancient Wisdom.* New York: Basic Books, 2006.

Lyubomirsky, Sonja. *The How of Happiness.* New York: Penguin Press, 2008.

Nettle, Daniel. *Happiness: The Science Behind Your Smile.* New York: Oxford University Press, 2005.

———. *Personality: What Makes You the Way You Are.* New York: Oxford University Press, 2006.

Pink, Daniel. *A Whole New Mind: Why Right-Brainers Will Rule the Future.* New York: Riverhead, 2005.

Schwartz, Barry. *The Paradox of Choice: Why More Is Less.* New York: HarperPerennial, 2004.

Seligman, Martin. *Authentic Happiness: Using the New Positive Psychology to Realize*

Your Potential for Lasting Fulfillment. New York: Free Press, 2002.

———. *What You Can Change and What You Can't: The Complete Guide to Successful Self-Improvement.* New York: Knopf, 1993.

Thich Nhat Hanh. *The Miracle of Mindfulness.* Translated by Mobi Ho. Boston: Beacon Press, 1975.

Wilson, Timothy. *Strangers to Ourselves: Discovering the Adaptive Unconscious.* Cambridge, Mass.: Harvard University Press, 2002.

EXAMPLES OF OTHER PEOPLE'S HAPPINESS PROJECTS

Botton, Alain de. *How Proust Can Change Your Life.* New York: Vintage International, 1997.

Frankl, Victor E. *Man's Search for Meaning.* Boston: Beacon Press, 1992.

Gilbert, Elizabeth. *Eat, Pray, Love: One Woman's Search for Everything Across Italy, India and Indonesia.* New York: Penguin, 2007.

Jacobs, A. J. *The Year of Living Biblically: One Man's Humble Quest to Follow the Bible as Literally as Possible.* New York: Simon & Schuster, 2007.

Jung, C. G. *Memories, Dreams, Reflections.* New York, Vintage Books, 1963.

Krakauer, Jon. *Into the Wild.* New York: Villard, 1996.

Kreamer, Anne. *Going Gray: What I Learned About Sex, Work, Motherhood, Authenticity, and Everything Else That Really Matters.* New York: Little, Brown, 2007.

Lamott, Anne. *Operating Instructions.* New York: Random House, 1997.

———. *Traveling Mercies: Some Thoughts on Faith.* New York: Pantheon Books, 2005.

Maugham, W. Somerset. *The Summing Up.* New York: Doubleday, 1938.

O'Halloran, Maura. *Pure Heart, Enlightened Mind.* New York: Riverhead, 1994.

Shapiro, Susan. *Lighting Up: How I Stopped Smoking, Drinking, and Everything Else I Loved in Life Except Sex.* New York: Delacorte Press, 2004.

Thoreau, Henry David. *Walden: Or, Life in the Woods.* Boston: Shambhala Publications, 2004.

A FEW HELPFUL BOOKS ABOUT RELATIONSHIPS

Demaris, Ann, and Valerie White. *First Impressions: What You Don't Know About How Others See You.* New York: Bantam Books, 2005.

Faber, Adele, and Elaine Mazlish. *How to Talk So Kids Will Listen and Listen So Kids Will Talk.* New York: Avon Books, 1980.

Fisher, Helen. *Why We Love: The Nature and Chemistry of Romantic Love.* New York: Henry Holt, 2004.

Gottman, John. *The Seven Principles for Making Marriage Work.* London: Orion, 2004.

Sutton, Robert I. *The No Asshole Rule: Building a Civilized Workplace and Surviving One That Isn't.* New York: Warner Business, 2007.

SOME OF MY FAVORITE MEMOIRS OF CATASTROPHE

Beck, Martha. *Expecting Adam.* New York: Penguin, 2000.

Broyard, Anatole. *Intoxicated by My Illness.* New York: Clarkson Potter, 1992.

Didion, Joan. *The Year of Magical Thinking.* New York: Knopf, 2005.

Mack, Stan. *Janet and Me: An Illustrated Story of Love and Loss.* New York: Simon & Schuster, 2004.

O'Kelly, Gene. *Chasing Daylight: How My Forthcoming Death Transformed My Life.* New York: McGraw-Hill, 2005.

Shulman, Alix Kates. *To Love What Is.* New York: Farrar, Straus, 2008.

Weingarten, Violet. *Intimations of Mortality.* New York: Knopf, 1978.

SOME OF MY FAVORITE NOVELS ABOUT HAPPINESS

Colwin, Laurie. *Happy All the Time.* New York: HarperPerennial, 1978.

Frayn, Michael. *A Landing on the Sun.* New York: Viking, 1991.

Grunwald, Lisa. *Whatever Makes You Happy.* New York: Random House, 2005.

Hornby, Nick. *How to Be Good.* New York: Riverhead Trade, 2002.

McEwan, Ian. *Saturday.* New York: Doubleday, 2005.

Patchett, Ann. *Bel Canto.* New York: HarperCollins, 2001.

Robinson, Marilynne. *Gilead.* New York: Farrar, Straus, 2004.

Stegner, Wallace. *Crossing to Safety.* New York: Random House, 1987.

Tolstoy, Leo. *Anna Karenina.* Translated by A. Maude. Oxford, England: Oxford University Press, 1939.

———. "The Death of Ivan Ilyich," in *The Death of Ivan Ilyich and Other Stories.* Translated by T. C. B. Cook. London: Wordsworth Editions, 2004.

———. *Resurrection.* New York: Oxford World Classics, 1994.

———. *War and Peace.* Translated by Rosemary Edmonds. New York: Penguin, 1957.

Von Arnim, Elizabeth. *Elizabeth and Her German Garden.* Chicago: W. B. Conkey Co., 1901.

THE BOOKS THAT MOST INFLUENCED
MY OWN HAPPINESS PROJECT

Franklin, Benjamin. *The Autobiography of Benjamin Franklin*. New Haven, Conn.: Yale University Press, 1964.

Thérèse of Lisieux. *Story of a Soul,* 3rd ed. John Clarke, O.C.D. Washington, D.C.: ICS Publications, 1996.

Everything written by Samuel Johnson.